personality in politics

ALAN C. ELMS
University of California, Davis

Under the Series Editorship of
IRVING L. JANIS
Yale University

HARCOURT BRACE JOVANOVICH, INC.

NEW YORK   CHICAGO   SAN FRANCISCO   ATLANTA

For Roz

Copyrights and Acknowledgments

BASIC BOOKS, INC. for the table "Personality and Role: A Typology" from *Political Woman* by Jeane J. Kirkpatrick, © 1974 by Center for the American Woman and Politics, Basic Books, Inc., Publishers, New York.

CALIFORNIA AGGIE for the article "Cannikan Can Be Stopped." Reprinted by permission.

HOUGHTON MIFFLIN COMPANY for the table "Classification of Moral Judgment into Levels and Stages of Development" from Sizer, Theodore R., *Religion and Public Education*, "Moral and Religious Education and the Public Schools" by Lawrence Kohlberg. Copyright © 1967 by Houghton Mifflin Co. Used by permission of the publisher.

NATIONAL CONFERENCE OF CHRISTIANS AND JEWS for the table "Classification of Moral Judgment into Levels and Stages of Development" from Sizer, Theodore R., *Religion and Public Education*, "Moral and Religious Education and the Public Schools" by Lawrence Kohlberg. Copyright © 1967 by Houghton Mifflin Co.

THE VIKING PRESS for the excerpt from *Facing the Lions* by Tom Wicker. Copyright © 1973 by Tom Wicker. Reprinted by permission of Viking Penguin, Inc.

YALE UNIVERSITY PRESS for the tables from James David Barber, *The Lawmakers*. Reprinted by permission of the publisher, Yale University Press.

Page 200 constitutes a continuation of the copyright page.

preface

He placed higher value on knowing what men did than on having the power to cause them to do it. It seemed to Morgan that the largest questions to be explored, the greatest gambles to be taken, were within oneself, not in the arenas of society. Yet, professionally, he was fascinated by the politician and his subtle art, his not inconsiderable risks of self and material, the visions and urgings that drove him. *

TOM WICKER

When I was a child in rural Arkansas, everyone I knew was a Democrat. Franklin Delano Roosevelt was our great President, leading us to victory in war as he had led us out of the Depression. When Harry Truman took over the job, he was assumed to be a good man too. With everyone agreed on the political essentials, there were few if any serious political arguments among my people and no cause to wonder whether a person's political views had anything to do with his personality.

Then we moved into town and began subscribing to the Arkansas *Gazette,* a statewide newspaper. For several years my newspaper reading had been limited mainly to the comic strips; but at the age of nine, I suddenly discovered the Letters to the Editor. In that column people were arguing fiercely—in large part about flying saucers, which first attracted my attention, but also about President Truman and Senator Fulbright. I had never known before that politics could be so interesting or that people could get so angry about issues so remote from their daily lives.

I have long since given up on flying saucers, but politics still fascinates me. Although I have gradually developed certain concerns about political issues and some interest in the structure of the political system, I am still most interested in the people of politics—both the people who fill important political roles and the people who get angry or happy or bored or cynical about what the politicians do in those roles.

iii

* Tom Wicker, *Facing the lions.* New York: Viking Press, 1973.

The expression of personality characteristics in political behavior is often entertaining, but it is also important. During the Vietnam War and later during the Watergate-related scandals, "the system" was frequently blamed for our national troubles. The political system is tremendously significant in giving people opportunities to express certain kinds of behavior and in restraining them from other kinds. But people eager to take advantage of the system, people driven by their private needs to use the system in unanticipated ways, were necessary before the American entrapment in Vietnam and the Nixon Administration's involvement in Watergate could happen. Understanding the system is only a part of understanding politics; understanding the role of personality and the interactions of personality and system is also vital.

I do not argue in this book whether personality is more, less, or just as important as the system in determining political behavior. Both are essential, so both must be studied. Instead, I devote most of the book to a discussion of what has actually been discovered about the role of personality in politics.

A great deal of evidence on that role *has* been discovered. "Personality and politics" is now one of the most popular research areas in political science, and it is drawing increasing attention from psychologists and sociologists. My selective introduction to this research may be somewhat different in emphasis from what a political scientist would have written, but I have avoided any attempts to draw disciplinary boundaries. Political scientists trained in psychology, psychologists who study the political-science literature, other social scientists with various odd professional backgrounds—all have made important contributions to the field.

In part because of its diverse origins, the field includes a wide range of theoretical orientations as well as of content areas. At this relatively early stage in the development of the field, I see little point in trying to impose a single theoretical structure on all the available data. The approach I find most helpful is a broad functional analysis, stressing what political involvement *does* for the people involved, in terms of satisfying both conscious and unconscious needs. I therefore use a functional approach to organize the material in several chapters, and I occasionally refer to it in others. However, I do not try to fit every piece of research discussed into a neat functional framework. One great advantage of the functional approach is that it is *not* neat. It acknowledges that the motives influencing human behavior overlap substantially, that the same behaviors may serve different motives in different people, and that similar motives can generate widely different patterns of behavior. We cannot yet rank the overall importance of various motives and personality characteristics in determining political behavior; but we can say with some assurance that the number of important motives is more than one or two, and that the paths of personality development that lead to political involvement are many and complex.

Personality and *politics* are two of the most ambiguous words in the social sciences. I interpret *personality* as including any individual psychological variations that influence behavior. Some psychological reactions are found in equal intensity in virtually all individuals, given the right stimulus; these I say little about. Personality enters the picture when a psychological characteristic common to all people is found to vary in intensity or expression among different individuals (for example, sexual desires), or when a characteristic is found in some people and not in others (for example, achievement motivation).

For brevity's sake, *politics* in this book refers mainly to elective politics in the United States or to attempts to influence elected American officials. I am aware that political behavior occurs in other nations and that important political processes exist that do not focus on elected officials. But rather than trying to say a little about everything political, I prefer to deal in somewhat more detail with a restricted range of topics. Recent and contemporary political behavior is stressed, here as in the "personality-and-politics" field itself. Other emphases reflect my greater familiarity with certain research areas. **v** For this reason, minority and women's political movements receive less specific attention than some readers might wish. However, substantial portions of the book are at least indirectly relevant to these topics, and certain types of political participation by women are directly considered.

My debts in writing this book are many. Irving L. Janis of Yale University first asked me to write it and kept reminding me over the next several years that I had said "yes." Judith Greissman has been an unusually encouraging and industrious editor. Irene Pavitt's careful line-by-line editing of the manuscript sharpened my language and my thinking. John B. McConahay of Duke University and Irving L. Janis also read the manuscript in detail and made many constructive suggestions. The book is much improved as a result; they should not be held responsible for its remaining deficiencies. William Potter, Edmond

Costantini, and James McEvoy, all of the University of California at Davis, as well as other political scientists, psychologists, sociologists, and psychiatrists gave me helpful advice and inspiration. Joan Randall, Vivienne Chaumont, and Jo Potter were generous with their time in typing early drafts of the manuscript; Joan Randall went far beyond the call of duty in typing the final draft and in offering thoughtful comments along the way. My wife, Roslyn, and my daughters, Heather and Laurel, allowed me to work on the book during many evenings and weekends that should have been spent with them. My greatest debt is to Roz, whose love, understanding, and political acumen have over the years greatly improved the relationship between personality and politics in my own life.

ALAN C. ELMS

contents

1

plain, people

the political personality
of the
average American citizen

Politics starts with the people. Not just "people," but *the* people, as in "We, the people of the United States": the ordinary men and women whose votes give political leaders whatever power they enjoy and whose postelectoral assent or dissent has historically determined how far that power extends. The focus of political discussion is often on the leaders; but politics in the United States cannot be fully understood without carefully considering the behavior of its "common" citizens as well.

People have personalities. The role of personality in politics is often discussed largely in terms of politicians' personalities; but the personal qualities of the "common" citizens also help to shape the political course of the nation. Much of the research on ordinary people's political behavior has, curiously, ignored personality. Our consideration of that research will therefore be selective, mainly noting the points at which definite personality influences have been established. This chapter begins at the logical beginning, with the political development of children, and then examines adult political motives. Because many ordinary people are no longer interested in ordinary politics, the chapter concludes with a discussion of political alienation. The extraordinary politics of extremism and activism will be dealt with in Chapter 2.

political socialization

Young children rarely play the game of "Voter." They do not read comic books about the lives of famous Senators. They do not collect gubernatorial bubble-gum cards. When a Presidential speech is broadcast on television, they usually turn away or complain that they are missing "The Wonderful World of Disney" or "Superfriends."

Children are not born political animals. They must learn that government exists. They must learn its scope, its functions, its processes. They must learn to identify those who are a part of government, as well as the government figures' appropriate behaviors. In addition to acquiring this knowledge, children develop emotional reactions to it, and acquire political behaviors appropriate to their own interests and capabilities. All this political development (or *political socialization*, as social scientists call it) takes place as children simultaneously form their basic personalities and acquire a mass of nonpolitical knowledge, attitudes, and behaviors.

Indirect political learning begins long before children know anything about politics as such. In their first year they may learn that parents, and by extension other adults on whom they must depend, can generally be trusted or should be viewed with distrust. As parents begin to impose behavioral limits, children may acquire feelings of comfort or discomfort in connection with such external regulation, which, in turn, may develop into tentative attitudes toward what adults call "law and order." As they learn to walk, talk, and engage in social activities, children may also acquire different degrees of confidence in their ability to interact with the world beyond the family (Erikson, 1951). Clear relationships between these early patterns of personality development and adult political behavior are hard to demonstrate. Further, any such relationships can be changed substantially by a great variety of later experiences. Nevertheless, political behavior plainly involves more than the learning of specific political acts. It emerges from the context of the child's total experience of life.

PRESIDENTIAL BENEVOLENCE

The first result of direct political learning will likely be a vague patriotic image of America as the child's country and of the President as that country's leader. Young children understand little about the President's real political functions. Instead, according to the classic

President Gerald Ford at a bicentennial celebration.

studies of political socialization, they see him as a kind of superfriend. The President is much wiser and more powerful than the child's own father, and works much harder (Hess and Torney, 1967). He can "stop bad things before they start," and he "makes people be safe" (Greenstein, 1965). A majority of the children questioned in these and other studies conducted in the late 1950s and early 1960s agreed with such grandiose statements as "The President knows more than anyone" and "The President is about the best person in the world."

Why have children's views of the President been so benevolent? Probably, in the first place, because their parents and teachers described him benevolently. Few reliable data exist on the political information young children actually receive. But there has been sufficient adult veneration of the Presidency, and sufficient tradition of protecting children from the "harsh realities," to assure that most of the information most children get about most Presidents is positive. This is particularly likely during children's early formal education, when teachers are expected to avoid expressing personal political views, to support the general political system, and to idolize Washington, Lincoln, and any other past Presidents they mention.

Furthermore, young children have yet to develop complex reasoning abilities (Flavell, 1970). They therefore tend to translate whatever they learn about politics into simple, personalized terms. (For instance, they often refer to government in general as "he," apparently seeing it as one child described it: "It's more or less a great leader and it makes our decisions and things of that sort" [Adelson, 1971].) Even adult criticism of the President is unlikely to survive in children's simple conceptual structures unless such criticism constitutes a large part of their fund of knowledge on the Presidency. Information may be most easily processed if it resembles concepts with which children are already familiar, such as parental qualities or television heroics.

Fathers were particularly important in early hypotheses about children's benevolent views of the President. The President might be seen as a better man than the child's father, but not as a different sort of man; he was the father "writ large." Some writers have gone further in this psychoanalytic vein, suggesting that children come to like the President for the same reason that they come to identify with their father: both are powerful and sometimes frightening people, and children's anxiety is reduced by regarding them as mighty friends rather than as enemies (Easton and Dennis, 1969).

Watergate might lead us to consider children's uncritical assessments of the President—*any* President—with some anxiety of our own. The early researchers chose instead to see such childhood attitudes as contributing to political stability in the United States. If children began their political life by viewing the President so enthusiastically, then they might be less likely to feel cynical and alienated toward the government later in life. Or so the argument went until a few years ago.

It now appears that children have no inherent need to view the President benevolently (although their tendency to do so may be fairly hard to overcome), and that the Republic is in no immediate danger of collapse even when they become troubled by Presidential misbehavior. Perhaps if John Kennedy had lived to serve another term and had been succeeded by one of his brothers or by another Eisenhower, we would never have learned that children are capable of anti-Presidential thoughts. But within the span of one childhood, we experienced the assassinations of two Kennedys and of Martin Luther King, the fighting and the losing of the war in Southeast Asia, and the forced retirement or resignation of two unpopular Presidents. Through it all, the nation's children watched and listened.

The first defections from the benevolent image of the Presidency were found among children whose backgrounds differed substantially from those of the white, middle-class youngsters initially studied. Black children, particularly after the "long hot summer" of 1967 and particularly as they got older, were found to view the President less than idealistically (Abramson, 1972; Liebschutz and Niemi, 1974). Recently Mexican-American children also have tended to be more critical of the President than urban, white schoolchildren, except in the earliest grades (Garcia, 1973; Lamare, 1974). Children in the poverty culture of the East Kentucky hills, where the federal government and its representatives have never been particularly popular, appear downright antagonistic toward the President (Jaros, Hirsch, and Fleron, 1968). Forty-one percent of the East Kentucky fifth-through eighth-graders tested in March 1967 said the President worked less hard than most men, as compared with a similar response by only 3 percent of a large sample of Chicago schoolchildren in 1958 (Hess and Easton, 1960). Further, 27 percent of the Kentuckians said the President was less honest than most men (23 percent said he was more honest), whereas only 1 percent of the Chicago sample said the President was less honest.

These comparisons are complicated not only by cultural differences but by actual changes in the person of the President and in his behavior. As the Vietnam War reached its height in 1967, Lyndon Johnson was widely accused of a "lack of credibility" or worse. Even if parents and teachers had continued to avoid criticizing Johnson in the interests of the country, both the war itself and the antiwar, anti-Johnson protests were revealed to children daily on television. Representative data on the attitudes of American children toward Johnson are not available; but in 1971, attitudes toward Richard Nixon and the war were measured among a broad sample of East Coast children, the majority of whom were middle- and upper-class whites (Tolley, 1973). Forty percent disagreed with the statement "President Nixon is doing the right thing in Vietnam" (31 percent agreed). Forty-five percent disagreed with "The President always tells the truth about the war" (29 percent agreed). A rash of post-Watergate surveys has shown further erosions in children's beliefs about the President's morality and goodness, or at least a change in emphasis from Presidential goodness to Presidential power (Greenstein, 1974; Lupfer and Kenny, 1974; Arterton, 1974).

The development of these critical responses toward the President raises questions about whether earlier, largely benevolent views indeed came from children's attempts to reduce anxiety by emphasizing a powerful figure's positive features. As Christopher Arterton (1974) observes, "a president exercising his capability of doing great harm should produce ever increasing anxiety." According to the anxiety-

5

reduction hypothesis, therefore, Nixon should have become more popular among children after Watergate rather than less. Perhaps he might have, had the anxiety-reduction process been working alone. But other influences were no doubt operating at the same time, including a huge increase in televised criticisms of the President and parents' and teachers' greater willingness to voice criticisms directly to children. Perhaps children themselves took advantage of the situation to project disliked characteristics of their imperfect fathers onto the convenient target of the President. (It should also be noted that many children continued to idealize the President even at the height of the Watergate revelations. Out of several Watergate-period studies of predominantly white populations, only one [Arterton, 1974] found generally anti-Presidential attitudes among children, and that was in the anti-Nixon bastion of Boston.)

Furthermore, American children, including those belonging to racial minorities, tended to maintain a generally positive evaluation of the government as a whole even when their evaluation of the President declined (Sears, 1975). Indeed, the events leading up to and following Richard Nixon's resignation may have helped children to differentiate more clearly between the person of the President and the government in general. Nixon's early rejection of efforts to investigate his Watergate involvement apparently led many children to assume, at least temporarily, that the President is above the law (Green-

6

The Nixons greet two future voters.

stein, in press). Gerald Ford's pardon of Nixon may have strengthened such a belief among some children; but Nixon's fall from power to disgrace should have provided a clearer lesson about Presidential limits.

What should we teach our children about the President? In the early 1960s, it seemed that if you wanted a stable democracy, you should teach them that the President is kind and good and strong. But many of the children who were taught those lessons must eventually have participated in the anti-Presidential demonstrations of the middle and late 1960s. Their behavior suggests a rephrasing of the question: Is it better for children to be taught distrust of the President at an early age and perhaps to learn a little trust later, or for them to be trusting at first only to be disillusioned later? Some degree of eventual disillusionment is almost inevitable, unless the child either is very dense or begins with an East-Kentucky-style rock-ribbed cynicism about the entire national government. Even in the research conducted during the Eisenhower and Kennedy years, children had substantially moderated their idealistic political views by the time they reached junior high school; and cynicism is a way of life for many older adolescents. Studies in areas other than politics (for example, Janis, 1959) suggest that exaggerated trust followed by disillusionment is a reliable recipe for irrational rage. However, early cynicism followed by later strengthening of that cynicism through observations of Watergate-style politics could produce an equally undesirable apathy. A middle way in teaching, with some indication of our leaders' human fallibility but without hammering away at it, seems the optimal choice. 7

LATER CHILDHOOD AND ADOLESCENCE

Children's attitudes toward the President do not entirely determine their later political behavior. As they grow older, they also begin to understand the role of Congress, the Supreme Court, and various state and local governing bodies. At times children may develop more faith in these institutions than in the Presidency. They begin to conceive of themselves as political actors in some fashion, and develop ideas as to how effective or ineffective their influence may be (Knutson, 1974a). They are also likely to acquire a party identification—usually before they have any clear ideas as to what the party stands for, and more often than not because it is the party of one or both parents. (Lately, increasing numbers of children have begun calling themselves Independents, apparently with no better idea of that term's meaning than of Democrat or Republican.) This party identification may then begin to bias their further political socialization—influencing children's interpretation of political news; making them initially more sympathetic toward one candidate and therefore more likely to give that candidate's views a close hearing; perhaps leading them ultimately to associate more often with people who share the same party label (Niemi, 1974).

Party identification can also play an important role in children's continuing personality development. They may have first asked their parents, "What are we?" when they found that their friends seemed to have a political identity while they did not. "I'm a Democrat" or "I'm a Republican" can be a comfortingly quick response when someone else later asks them what they are. "I'm an Independent" can make them feel ahead of the game.

For a time, children may gain an added sense of strength from the realization that they share the political views of their fathers (or, increasingly, of their mothers; Beck and Jennings, 1975). But as they enter adolescence, party label may become as useful a means to differentiate themselves from their parents as it earlier was to identify themselves with the parents. Ordinarily, this adolescent flirting with new political identities is unlikely to result in a permanent shift any further from the parents' traditional party label than to the status of Independent. But under the impact of a major social trauma, such as the Depression—or perhaps the Vietnam War or Watergate—a tentative political identity may harden into permanence, influencing not only the youth's own later political behavior but also that of his or her children (Beck, 1974). Millions of such conversions in a decade are the stuff of democratic revolution.

The study of adolescent political development has lagged well behind research on the political socialization of elementary-school children. For a time it seemed that with their party label already announced and with their basic fund of political knowledge amassed by the end of the eighth grade if not sooner, adolescents were hardly worth studying. One massive survey of high-school students, parents, and teachers (Langton and Jennings, 1968) even concluded that high-school civics courses have no significant effect on the political attitudes, knowledge, or interest of white students. (Black students did show significant increases in political knowledge and other criteria, perhaps because they were less exposed than whites to politics prior

8

to high school. Unfortunately, the civics courses also increased black students' tendency toward passive loyalty rather than toward active political participation.)

However, more recent research (Adelson, 1971; Jennings and Niemi, 1974) has revealed sharp changes in many young people's political thinking from the beginning of adolescence to its midpoint or later. For one thing, political thought tends to become much more abstract during those few years. When Adelson asked twelve- and thirteen-year-olds to tell him the purpose of laws, typical answers were "So that people don't get hurt" or "So people don't steal and kill." Fifteen- and sixteen-year-olds responded instead: "To ensure safety and enforce government" or "They are basically guidelines for people. I mean, like this is wrong and this is right and to help them understand." The typical twelve-year-old still personalizes the government in the form of judges and criminals; the typical fifteen-year-old is able to talk about government as a means for society to function.

Younger adolescents also tend to be highly authoritarian (even "bloodthirsty," according to Adelson), seeing criminals as deserving of cruel treatment and seeing the government as inherently good—the latter view continuing the childhood concept of governmental benevolence. But if development continues normally, within a few years adolescents begin to think seriously about general principles of fair treatment, about the criminal's motives other than sheer evilness, about the long-term as well as the short-term effects of government policies. With these new ideas, based on the increasing ability to think in terms of complex abstractions (and perhaps also on the personal exploration of several potential identities), adolescents' authoritarianism diminishes or disappears. 9

Finally, younger adolescents tend to take one political question at a time, dealing with it as best they can; older adolescents—at least those who have become interested enough in politics to think about it a good deal—may develop an entire ideology within which to fit each political issue. A thoroughly developed ideological structure is rare in adolescents of any age; but in those who have it, it is one more indication that political growth need not stop in the eighth grade.

From a personality standpoint, adolescent political development is perhaps most interesting for its diversity. We sometimes get a hint of individuality in the political comments even of small children (Coles, 1975); but they are usually secondhand remarks, dependent upon someone else's personality. Middle adolescents are fully capable of doing their own thinking and developing their own beliefs, based as much on their unique personalities as on the political "reality" around them. Ideologies right and left, simple and complex; elaborate utopias and angry revolutionary impulses; junior-prom-queen electioneering and door-to-door precinct work—all and more can be found in adolescents, intermingled with personal motives, defensive maneuvers, tentative identities in astonishing profusion. Few case studies have been conducted of adolescent political development, but its complexity and variability demand such research. Survey studies reveal much about what adolescents know and feel about politics, but they let too much slip through the cracks in terms of how adolescents got that way. And the importance of understanding adolescent political development is hard to deny: the sixteen-year-old is, after all, no more than two years away from becoming a legally qualified voter.

political needs

In 1950 my father took me to my first political rally. Helen Gahagan Douglas was a candidate for one of California's U.S. Senate seats, and the rally was on her behalf; but its main theme was "Nix on Nixon." I knew hardly anything about either candidate; in fact, I don't remember ever having heard Richard Nixon's name before. But I did know whose side we were on, and I enjoyed singing anti-Nixon parodies of popular songs in between eating free hot dogs and drinking free soda pop. I especially liked the hot dogs. Maybe the only way San Diego Democrats could guarantee a good crowd in those days was to promise food and drink; but I was too naive to think of that. It just seemed to me that any political party willing to hand out free hot dogs for a few songs and a round of applause deserved my support. The newspaper letters-to-the-editor columns had earlier aroused my interest in electoral battles; the rally confirmed it. I was hooked on politics then and there.

How do other children get hooked on politics? Researchers have so far not told us. They have been so busy discovering *when* children learn about various components of politics, and *what* they learn, and *how* they feel about it, that they have directed little attention to *why* children become interested in politics at all. The prevailing assumption is that if parents and teachers say politics is important, children will see it as important. That may be so, to a moderate degree. Parents and other adults do focus children's attention on certain aspects of the world, and parental approval or disapproval often serves as an important motivator for children's interest. But surely other motives also strengthen political interest or involvement—including a desire for hot dogs.

A good deal more theorizing and research has focused on adults' reasons for political involvement. *Involvement* is used very loosely here, since much of the work in this area has been concerned simply with reasons for holding political attitudes rather than with motives for overt political activity. Few adults are politically active, but most hold some sort of political attitudes, which, if nothing else, may influence their vote.

Attitudes are predispositions to feel or act positively or negatively toward certain sets of objects. Political attitudes differ from other kinds of attitudes only in the nature of their objects: political figures, political goals and processes. Therefore, general theories about why people develop and hold attitudes have been readily applied to political attitudes, and vice versa. Psychologists have seldom concluded that attitudes are acquired at random or are inherited genetically; instead, a widely held assumption is that attitudes are *functional*. That is, they are acquired because they satisfy an individual's needs; they are retained because they continue to serve those or other needs effectively; they are changed when the original attitudes are no longer as useful for need satisfaction as new attitudes.

Attitude functions have been categorized in several ways. One of the first, and still one of the most useful, categorizations was developed by Smith, Bruner, and White (1956). In 1947 they interviewed ten men for nearly thirty hours each to determine what role their attitudes toward Russia played in their personalities. Out of masses of data, the researchers identified three main functions of these attitudes: *social adjustment, object appraisal,* and *externalization.* These categories not only describe the major uses to which individuals are likely to put their political attitudes; they also parallel the three major theoretical emphases in attempts to explain the motives for adult political behavior.

SOCIAL ADJUSTMENT

Social adjustment reflects the role of attitudes in "maintaining relationships with other people." This is a particularly important function for the individual whose need for social support or social contact is strong. In Smith, Bruner, and White's study, for instance, a subject named Grafton Upjohn struggled hard to come up with definite opinions about Russia, even though he knew little about the country and cared less, apparently in order to maintain friendships with the prestigious researchers whose approval he desired. Upjohn was somewhat unusual in the strength of his social needs, having dropped sharply in social class since childhood; but some need for affection or approval from others is widespread. The possibility that children adopt early political attitudes at least in part to win affection from or to placate their parents has already been mentioned. Children's development of a patriotic identification with their country, or minority members' identification with their ethnic group, may not only promote friendship with others sharing similar views but also may raise the individual's own self-esteem.

In recent years, to emphasize that this functional category involves, more than just going along with the views of other people, M. Brewster Smith (1973) has relabeled it "mediation of self–other relationships." People may feel a need to differentiate themselves from others as well as to align themselves with others. I pointed out in the previous section that adolescents often espouse different political views from their parents to strengthen their sense of possessing a distinct identity. Among Smith, Bruner, and White's subjects, a man named Hilary Sullivan voiced strongly pro-Russian views, in part to shock people to whom he could therefore feel superior. This more broadly labeled category might also be taken to include what Daniel Katz (1960) has labeled the "value-expressive function" of attitudes, "the function of giving positive expression to [one's] central values and to the type of person he conceives himself to be." Katz sees such value expression as a basic human need.

In the narrow sense of satisfying the need to get along with others, the social-adjustment function encompasses the most popular social-scientific explanations of political attitude development during the past several decades: Children acquire their political attitudes mainly from their parents, who got them from their parents, not only because that is the easiest thing to do but because there are strong social reinforcements within the family for going along. And adults show political attitudes similar to those of their geographic, ethnic, religious, and social-class fellows because they might otherwise be ostracized.

Recently, however, such demographic predictors of political views

12

as social class and geographic region have been growing less accurate (Pomper, 1975). When voters in at least some parts of the country are interviewed in detail about the reasons why they hold specific political views, social-adjustment concerns like Grafton Upjohn's seem hard to find. For instance, when Karl Lamb (1974) interviewed twenty-three Orange County, California, suburbanites in great detail about their lives and their politics, only one indicated that he felt any social pressure to modify his political views (away from the John Birch Society line to something milder), and he refused to do so. The rest indicated that they were "not aware of subtle or unsubtle pressures toward political conformity on the job, in the neighborhood, or within their circle of friends," although in several instances they mentioned friends with whom they had "agreed to disagree" or to keep silent about political issues. If Orange County, reputed to be one of the most staunchly conservative and conformist voting areas in the country, is so tolerant of at least moderate political diversity, "getting along with others" may by now be well down in the ranks of motives for adopting political attitudes nationwide.

OBJECT APPRAISAL

Object appraisal, the next category in Smith, Bruner, and White's list of attitude functions, better describes Orange Countians' political motives. Object appraisal is a person's use of attitudes in "trying to size up the world around him and to place it in relation to his major interests, ongoing concerns, and cherished aspirations." People seem to need to give structure to their environment, and attitudes can help them do this by providing convenient categories in which to pigeonhole new information, as well as convenient responses toward whatever falls into a particular pigeonhole. Purely random responses toward new stimuli would be both inefficient and often unrewarding. But if you have developed a positive attitude toward a class of rewarding objects in the past, and therefore respond positively to a new object falling into that class, you can save time otherwise spent in choosing a response, and you should also increase your rewards.

13

The Orange County residents interviewed by Lamb generally reserve their strongest political feelings for issues that hit close to home —both figuratively and literally. They are concerned about air pollution, property taxes, public access to beaches; and their positions on these issues are not much constrained by traditional political affiliations. A Republican neurologist who works in a state psychiatric hospital is bitterly angry at Ronald Reagan because Reagan cut the state mental-health budget. A Republican engineer favors welfare payments for unemployed engineers, despite his general conservatism. The most liberal people in the group strongly oppose the building of a public housing project in their neighborhood because they feel it would lower the value of their houses. All these people could be accused of hypocrisy, but in truth they are less concerned with consistency than with what they perceive as their immediate material interests.

So far, object appraisal resembles the motivational model of classic economic theory, in which individuals are assumed always to act rationally to minimize their costs and to maximize their benefits in economic transactions. But Smith, Bruner, and White have more in mind than appraising the economic benefits of one's attitudes. They cite as an example of object appraisal the views of Ernest Daniel, an unskilled worker, who likes Russia because there "an unskilled workingman would be given the chance to develop to the top of his capacity, and would in any event be protected from financial insecurity." But they also cite the views of a very religious subject, Albert Rock, who condemns Russia for its rejection of "moral values and of faith in an ultimate [religious] reward." People seek to defend not only economic interests but also "intellectual and artistic interests," "ethical ideals," and the well-being of other people with whom they empathize. These are all conscious goals whose attainment may be furthered by developing good feelings about objects that appear positively related to the goals and bad feelings toward objects negatively related to the goals. Several Orange County suburbanites in Lamb's study held negative attitudes toward "hippy-looking" youth, whom they felt were challenging their cherished "work ethic"; they became equally hostile toward the men of the Nixon Administration, whom they saw as undermining the same ethical system while pretending to venerate it.

The belief in "voter rationality" was undermined in the earliest days of quantitative political science research. Voters were found to be pitifully misinformed about the leading issues of the day, and to vote largely on the basis of political party affiliation or demographic category. But recently, "voter rationality" has attained new respectability, as studies such as Lamb's have shown voters to devote considerable thought to the issues that interest them personally, and as mass surveys show greater voter attentiveness to candidates' individual qualities and to important political issues, with correspondingly

14

less inclination toward party-line voting (Verba and Nie, 1972; Pomper, 1975; Nie and Verba, 1975). The political drowsiness of the Eisenhower years, from which the largest amount of evidence for voter conformity and lack of interest in issues was drawn, is now beginning to be recognized as unrepresentative of American voters' characteristic political behavior. The electrified alertness to which many of them were awakened by crisis after crisis during the past decades may also be unrepresentative. But in response to the crises still to come in the next decades, an acute state of object appraisal may become both characteristic and essential.

EXTERNALIZATION

Some researchers regard neither social adjustment nor object appraisal as genuinely involving personality. They therefore include in discussions of "personality and politics" only the final category in Smith, Bruner, and White's list of functions—externalization. In so doing, they ignore both the scope of contemporary personality theories and the evidence for wide variations in reliance on other attitude functions, politically and otherwise. As Smith, Bruner, and White have shown in their case studies, some people stress object appraisal in their political views, while others stress social adjustment; and the stress can often be traced to a particular pattern of personality development or of current personality needs. Modern ego psychology, the successor to classic Freudian psychoanalytic theory, emphasizes individuals' realistic coping with the objective world and their mutually influential interaction with other individuals, as do most other current personality theories. Nonetheless, externalization apparently continues to be the most intriguing function of political attitudes for many students of the field.

15

Externalization refers to coping with one's inner psychological problems by treating outside objects and events as if they were the inner difficulties. The examples typically given for this function are of neurotic or psychotic behaviors—shooting at a President, for instance, because you have long bottled up your rage against your father. But externalization much more often involves rather mild tendencies—as when Smith, Bruner, and White's subject Albert Rock, silently annoyed with his hypochondriacal wife, strongly criticizes "the Russian attempt to weaken the home and family," thereby nicely reinforcing the suppression or repression of his own impulse to weaken his family by leaving it. Robert Lane (1962), in a detailed case study of fifteen working-class men, presents an even more interesting example: Rapuano, son of a poor Italian immigrant, intelligent, resourceful, relatively free of prejudice, generally open-minded. His personality is complex, and on the whole he seems psychologically healthy. But the cultural conflict he experienced during his childhood, between the traditions of his immigrant family and the behavior patterns acceptable at school, has left him somewhat confused about his own identity and often more angry than the occasion warrants. His anger tends to be directed against certain groups (Communists, gangsters) who violate the ordinary behavioral codes of the society in which he now lives. Rapuano would probably not feel motivated to see a psychotherapist, and the family doctor would not see any problems serious enough to refer him to one. But Rapuano's internal difficulties with identity and with controlling his aggressive impulses have led him to an externalization-based political position, in which he advocates the necessity for the government to control the nation tightly and to suppress deviant political behaviors.

All of these examples involve desires that the person has not been able to fulfill because of anxiety. Smith, Bruner, and White also identified another kind of externalization, involving desires that have not been fulfilled because of outer circumstances. In these cases, rather than externalizing the desire and then giving it "a properly energetic belaboring" as in the above examples, the individual may display considerable enthusiasm toward the desire as it is expressed in the behavior of others. Research subject John Chatwell, for instance, was distressed that his job in a patent law office did not allow him to produce usable goods for society. His strong praise for Russian industrial productivity appeared to be a way of expressing, rather than of controlling, his desires through externalization.

The influence of externalization on specific political views is hard to demonstrate, except in intensive case studies like those of Lane or of Smith, Bruner, and White. These studies suggest that externalization is widespread in its relatively mild forms, particularly in shaping attitudes toward foreign policy and other political issues that have little immediate impact on a person's life (see also Christiansen, 1965). Its contribution to personally significant domestic political attitudes, however, is likely to be subordinate to social adjustment and particularly to object appraisal, at least in clinically "normal" individuals. More powerful externalization effects will be explored later in this

16

chapter with regard to alienation and in Chapter 2 in connection with political extremism.

RELATIVE IMPORTANCE OF POLITICAL NEEDS

Smith, Bruner, and White's categorization of attitude functions is convenient and can easily be applied to attitudes toward a variety of political objects. But it is by no means the only way to analyze politically related needs. Robert Lane (1969), for instance, felt that the three categories lump too much together, are "too undifferentiated." He therefore proposed his own list of ten categories of human needs particularly applicable to political thinking. The ten include several categories resembling Smith, Bruner, and White's, such as "social needs: affiliation, approval, being liked." But they also include more specific categories, such as consistency needs, needs for the expression of aggression, and needs for autonomy, which are not clearly included in the previous categorization. In addition to his earlier case studies of workingmen, Lane has done his own thorough examination of the political ideas of twenty-four college students and has found considerable evidence for the political relevance of these ten needs. I wonder, though, whether Lane himself may be lumping too many needs together in his ten categories, and whether it might not be useful to discriminate twenty, or forty, or a hundred needs. I wonder where to stop.

It would be useful at this point to know which needs are *most* influential in determining the degree and direction of a person's involvement with politics. We might then decide to study closely the first three, or ten, or however many we have the time and energy for, and not worry about the less important ones. Smith, Bruner, and White point out that such rankings of importance are likely to vary widely for different groups and individuals. But even if we had averages merely for a random sample of American voters, it would be a useful start.

No one has yet provided such a ranking. However, Stanley Renshon (1974) has statistically compared two possible motives for political involvement in a group of college students: *civic obligation* and the *need for personal control*. Civic obligation is the individual's feeling (presumably inculcated by parents and schools) that in order to be a good citizen, he or she should show some degree of political interest and activity. This sort of concern would probably fall into

17

Smith, Bruner, and White's social-adjustment category. The need for personal control, as defined by Renshon, is "a basic need to gain control over [one's] physical and psychological life-space," which, applied to politics, means a need to have some influence on the political systems that bear on one's own life. Such a need would probably fall mainly within the scope of object appraisal in Smith, Bruner, and White's system, although its satisfaction might serve social-adjustment and externalization functions as well. (A single kind of political act or attitude will often satisfy more than one need and serve more than one personality function.)

Renshon studied these two motives, as well as feelings of political alienation, political interest, and other variables, in three hundred undergraduates at the University of Pennsylvania during 1970–71. At the time of the study, anti–Vietnam-War political activity continued at a high level. Renshon found that feelings of civic obligation contributed rather little to the students' decision either to campaign for antiwar Congressional candidates or to join the April 24, 1971, March on Washington. The desire for personal control made the strongest contribution of all the variables Renshon studied.

Renshon has by no means proved that a need for personal control is the single most powerful motive underlying political behavior, nor did he set out to do so. His correlations do suggest that people who feel that they have little influence on their environment, and that government policies bear heavily on their lives, are more likely to participate in certain political activities than people who don't feel so. But he did not investigate whether these people who feel that politics is important but that they have litle personal control of it also share other needs, such as for identity or for peer approval, which might be even stronger than the personal-control need. Further, Renshon studied a group of subjects in whom that particular combination of feelings of little personal control, perceptions of strong government influence, and high political participation, might be unusually common: college students at the height of the Vietnam War, when the military draft was still in effect and represented for many the major intrusion of government into their lives. Under other circumstances, the need for personal control might be rather less important in influencing the level of political activity, compared with such concerns as civic responsibility. The reverse of the Renshon results can also occur, as in numerous studies showing that people who feel they already have high personal control (*political efficacy* is the more usual term)

18

are more likely to be politically active than those low in perceived personal control. The high–political-efficacy people in these studies were probably so active not because they desired still more personal control but because they had found they could reliably expect a solid payoff for their efforts (see Campbell, Gurin, and Miller, 1954; Prewitt, 1968; Verba and Nie, 1972).

Future research should tell us not only what the relative political importance of various psychological needs is for the general population, but how the need rankings vary among different segments of the populace and at different time periods, both in the individual's life and in the life of the nation. The needs that most often motivated Americans to act politically in the 1930s were not necessarily the important political needs in the 1960s—although they may be regaining strength in the late 1970s. Under certain circumstances, free hot dogs may motivate more votes than a sense of civic responsibility.

the uninterested and the alienated

The most popular choice in the 1972 Presidential election was not Richard Nixon. It was Nobody.

There are always plenty of votes for Nobody. The high-water mark of voter involvement in the last half-century, reached in the Kennedy–Nixon Presidential election, included less than two-thirds of eligible voters. In 1972 almost one-half of the electorate stayed home on Election Day. Elections for lesser offices, held at other times, typically show even poorer turnouts. Some failures to vote are unavoidable or unintentional: illness, economic necessity, bad weather, changes of residence, all may place obstacles in the potential voter's path. But a substantial proportion of the "votes" for Nobody are cast deliberately. Either the nonvoters have grown up with little interest in politics and little sense of its relevance to their own lives, or they have decided that, although political issues are important, casting a vote for a candidate is useless, because the candidates are equally bad or because the governmental system is itself bad or unresponsive. The first kind of "No"-voter might be called "uninterested"; the second kind is usually identified as "alienated."

The *uninterested* apparently strike most social scientists as uninteresting. Some demographic data have been collected on them: they are more likely than people who vote regularly to be young, black,

19

female, Southern, poorly educated, just plain poor, or more than one of the above (Flanigan, 1972). They tend to know little about politics —presumably more a result than a cause of their lack of interest, although Paul Sniderman (1975) suggests that shortcomings in political learning can make politics seem too complicated to be worth following. Fortunately, the percentage of uninterested citizens has decreased steadily over the past two decades, at least in that major bastion of uninterest, the South. Educational levels have increased; the federal government has made itself visibly important during the racial and political upheavals of the period; and, at the same time, television may have made the political drama a very personal matter to many more people. Perhaps other factors in the decline of the uninterested, including changes in personality patterns, will become visible through further research.

POLITICAL ALIENATION

The *alienated* have been studied much more intensely. They supply their own drama: they have been interested enough in politics to feel angered or disappointed by it and to reject it. They may vote, but if they do, their vote is likely to be a vote of dissent rather than of agreement. They may be even more active politically than the average voter, but their aim is to change the whole system or a substantial part of it, not to further the *status quo*.

20   Alienation has been one of the staples of research on political behavior for many years. As in most studies of political behavior, the bulk of the research has been directed toward such demographic variables as social class and educational level, both because such information is relatively easy to obtain through large-scale survey techniques and because those variables often seem to explain a good deal about the behaviors involved. Typical demographic findings are similar to those for the uninterested (Schwartz, 1973), perhaps because the questionnaires most often used to measure alienation do not discriminate clearly between the uninterested and the genuinely alienated. When you ask people whether they agree with such statements as "These days a person doesn't know whom he can count on" or "There's little use writing to public officials because often they aren't really interested in the problems of the average man" (Srole, 1956), they are likely to say "yes" whether they have simply never cared about politics at all or whether they are actively opposed to the system.

An even greater problem with these demographic studies of aliena-tion has recently become evident. When most people were satisfied with the political system in this country, it was possible to look at the few who were not and to identify rather quickly their most obvious differences from the majority—usually, differences associated with low socioeconomic status. But in the post-Kennedy era, dissatisfaction began to spread. More and more people grew unhappy with the gov-ernment's role in the Vietnam War, regardless of how they thought the war should be handled. More and more became dissatisfied with the government's policies on the economy, on energy and environment, on minority rights—again, regardless of which side they were on. By 1970, according to David C. Schwartz's extensive studies (1973), the old reliable negative relationship between alienation and socioeco-nomic status—the lower the status, the higher the alienation—had virtually disappeared. So many people had become alienated to a sub-stantial degree, regardless of social class, age, education, race, sex, or whatever, that research on demographic variables had lost much of its usefulness, either in predicting what groups of people would most likely become alienated or in explaining how they got that way. Other researchers have continued to find relationships between demographic variables and certain measures of alienation, most notably in terms of race: alienation has recently increased much more sharply among blacks than among whites. But almost every recent study of alienation shows substantial increases across all major demographic categories in the past decade (for example, Boyd, 1974; Miller, 1974a; Citrin, McClosky, Shanks, and Sniderman, 1975).

21

Even though alienation has become widespread, however, it is not all-pervasive. Some people are more alienated than others; some show alienation mainly toward national or local or party politics, but not toward other aspects of the political scene; some remain insistently unalienated. Demographic variables alone appear unable to explain satisfactorily these variations in the quantity and quality of alienation. Personality variables have been less studied in relation to political alienation than they should be, but some suggestive findings are available. They can be conveniently organized in terms of Smith, Bruner, and White's (1956) categories of political-attitude functions.

SOCIAL ADJUSTMENT

This function has received the least attention as a foundation for alienated attitudes. Jack Citrin (1974) has suggested that since a good deal of the alienation recently detected through public-opinion surveys has not been translated into political activism, it may in many cases be merely a mouthing of "fashionable clichés." Such alienated clichés appear particularly fashionable among the Berkeley, California, residents whom Citrin mainly studies. Among people between the ages of eighteen and thirty, Berkeleyites were more than twice as likely as a national sample to report feeling strong alienation (Citrin, McClosky, Shanks, and Sniderman, 1975). Berkeley's countercultural reputation no doubt attracts the already alienated; but the general atmosphere of alienation among the young there probably induces others who are not particularly alienated to say they are.

Alienation can also be a useful position to take for purposes of identity formation. It is more popular among the young than among the old throughout the country, no doubt in part because the young often perceive the old as part of the established political system and therefore find rejection of that political system an effective way of differentiating themselves from the older generation. Also, although blacks in general are more alienated than whites, alienation is highest among blacks who identify with the black movement (Miller, 1974b). In part this increased alienation surely comes from their greater awareness of political and economic inequities; but again, it is likely to be strengthened by the usefulness of alienated attitudes in giving them an identity distinct from the dominant culture.

22 OBJECT APPRAISAL

Black perception of government maltreatment is one example of how an effort to evaluate one's world as accurately as possible, and to organize one's observations into a meaningful model of reality, can lead to alienation. The political system does *not* operate to treat everyone equally, and political leaders are *not* all uniformly trustworthy. People whose personalities allow them or compel them to look closely and clearheadedly at politics in this country are therefore likely to become at least somewhat alienated. The evidence that alienation has increased along with the increasing clarity and personal relevance of political issues (for example, Miller, 1974a) can therefore be counted as evidence for the role of object appraisal. So can the evidence that among at least some demographic categories—such as, again, blacks—the more educated people are, the more they are likely to distrust government figures (Finifter, 1970).

Object appraisal does not operate on alienation only in one direction, however. A person who understands the current political scene very well may find good reason to feel alienated; but a person who cannot understand the political scene at all may feel equally alienated. In an important study done before the recent spread of alienated attitudes (McClosky and Scharr, 1965), high alienation was found to be associated with low intellectual orientation, high psychological inflexibility, high anxiety, low ego strength, high hostility level, and similar characteristics. These relationships held firm even among persons of equal socioeconomic level. According to McClosky and Scharr, the direction of causation leads largely from personality to alienation rather than vice versa: inflexible, unintellectual, anxious, hostile people will probably fail to learn how to use the political system effectively for their own purposes, or to understand its operations sufficiently to feel comfortable with it. Paul Sniderman (1975) has recently provided a similar argument for the relationship between low self-esteem and alienation. People who feel strong doubts about their own worth tend to withdraw their interest from "the main channels of social communication, and in any event, are less attentive and receptive to information which passes along these channels. In addition to being more poorly exposed to information circulating through the society, persons with low self-esteem are also less likely to understand correctly the information which they do receive." As a result, "democratic politics can easily appear a disorderly and unintelligible process, serving no apparent purpose, producing only conflict or confusion." So ineffective as well as effective object appraisal can become a pathway to alienation.

23

EXTERNALIZATION

McClosky and Scharr's (1965) unintellectual, inflexible, anxious, and hostile individuals had more reason than poor political learning to become alienated. They also appeared likely to cope with their psychological problems by externalizing them into the political arena—particularly by seeing the political system rather than themselves as rigid, stupid, and hostile. When people respond in this way, the political system may in turn begin to act really hostile and rigid toward them, thus confirming their suspicions and strengthening their alienation. (Of course, such people need not direct their concern toward politics at all. Many people with personality patterns such as those described by McClosky and Scharr will be so absorbed in their own psyches and difficult interpersonal relationships that they may register on surveys as politically uninterested rather than as politically alienated. Those who do become politically alienated through externalization are likely to be passive alienates rather than activists; they don't like the political scene, but they don't know what to do about it.)

Several case studies of alienation through externalization are available (Lane, 1962, 1969; Keniston, 1965). The process described by Keniston is especially intriguing. His subjects were male Harvard students who as children had seen their fathers as weak and their mothers as talented, frustrated, and seductive. They failed to identify with the father but became intensely involved on an emotional level with the mother—so intensely that in later reaction to this "devouring" relationship, they came to reject any kind of strong emotional commitment, including political commitments. Keniston's Harvard men were culturally and philosophically as well as politically alienated, on a much broader scale than most of the people counted as "alienated" in mass surveys. Their peculiar maternal relationship is also probably rather rare in the population as a whole. But they do indicate that externalization can be an important source of alienation in the sensitive and the well-informed, as well as in the poorly educated fringes of society.

REQUIRING THE ALIENATED TO VOTE

Ralph Nader and others have recently proposed that all American citizens of voting age be required to vote. They are dismayed at the low voter turnouts in this country, particularly during the 1972 Presidential election, and they feel that required voting would boost other kinds of citizen participation in politics as well as increasing the vote itself. Other countries have been able to impose at least a minimal level of participation through such a law; why not the United States?

The idea is tempting, but it does not seem to me to acknowledge fully the diverse reasons people have for not voting. As I have indicated, many of our alienated citizens are as well informed about politics as the unalienated—perhaps in some ways even better informed. But these well-informed alienates often vote already, and participate politically in other ways, even though (or because) they feel distressed at the direction in which the nation is moving. Insisting that they vote is unlikely to raise the level of political participation very much; such a requirement might even add to their alienation. Instead, the obligatory ballot box is most likely to bring out the unin-

24

terested and the passively alienated—the people who know the least both about candidates and about issues, and who understand little about the rules of the political "game." They tend to make their voting decisions (if any) on trivial or irrational grounds (Flanigan, 1972). Dan Nimmo (1970), an expert on political campaigning, argues that it is precisely such individuals who are most susceptible to modern mass-media campaigns, where personal style rather than political substance is emphasized, where millions of dollars are spent on developing a synthetic image of the candidate, and where television—preferably via the quickie commercial—is the principal means of campaigning. One sometimes hears the argument that if alienated citizens were really aroused, they would vote for major reforms in the political system, and maybe that is what Ralph Nader hopes will happen if they are required to vote. But the passive alienated often turn out to be mere "aginners," voting for the candidate who can most arouse their hatred and envy against other segments of society. With so little information and interest concerning the substantive issues of the campaign, the passive alienates may be forced to rely on those emotions almost exclusively in developing their vision of politics; and they may therefore find it easier to vote for destructive candidates than for political rebuilders.

The passive alienated and the uninterested should not be completely ignored, on the assumption that they won't bother anyone if they're left alone. An intelligent and wealthy demagogue may eventually be able to marshal their support, even if they aren't required to vote. But insisting that they vote will not lessen their hostility and ignorance, and by the time other efforts to improve the quality of their participation begin to take effect, our government may have suffered major wounds from these reluctant balloters. Ralph Nader and other advocates of increased political participation should perhaps instead direct their attention toward reforming the early political socialization of our children—if not in the home, then at least in the schools and on television. Politics may not interest young children quite as much as sex, but we should be at least as concerned with what they hear in the streets about politics as about sex, and as concerned with making politics a constructive and meaningful part of their lives. If we remain passive on such matters ourselves, we may within another ten or fifteen years discover in our maturing youth the most politically alienated—and therefore the most dangerous—generation in American history.

25

2

farther out

extremists and activists

American politics is mostly played out in the mainstream. Of those citizens willing to identify themselves with a political group, the vast majority opt for a standard Republican or Democratic affiliation. Few even of the alienated or the independent identify themselves as radicals, either of left or of right. One recent estimate of support for the positions of several far-rightist organizations, based on public opinion polls, arrives at a figure of around 5 percent of the adult population, although many fewer people participate in such groups (McEvoy, 1971). Support for far-leftist groups and causes is similarly low. Even among college youth during the most activist period of the 1960s and on the most activist campuses, 15 percent of the student body seems to have been a maximum level of serious participation in activist causes (Horn and Knott, 1971); and again, a much smaller percentage of participation was evident nationwide.

If I allotted pages relative to the number of people showing a particular variety of political behavior, this chapter on extremism would be extremely short. But extremists have influenced American political history far out of proportion to their number. Several of our Founding Fathers were extremists in their day, and the extreme leftists of the early 1900s have been memorialized by the social-welfare programs central to our current system of government. Right-wing extremism has enjoyed its own surges of popularity during the nation's development (Hofstadter, 1965; Lipset and Raab, 1970), and

26

The People's Army Jamboree receives a hostile response from citizens of Portland, Oregon.

the rightist American Independent party has been the most successful third party in recent years.

Psychologists look closely at extremists for another reason. "Normal" people are sometimes dismayingly unuseful in the search for a psychological understanding of political behavior. If you look at 200 million people whose political views are not much different from each other and most of whose personal backgrounds included hearing the same political banalities from their parents, experiencing the same fairly comfortable American upbringing, you may not be able to sort out very well the unremarkable influences that produced their unremarkable views. But if you look at a few hundred thousand people who share rather remarkable views, and if you can find several remarkable characteristics in their personal backgrounds or current patterns of psychological functioning that they do not share with the 200 million, you may begin to detect direct relationships between psychological processes and political views.

The subtitle of the chapter, "Extremists and Activists," reflects the linguistic problems in this research area. *Extremist* is a relative rather than an absolute judgment; it depends on where the mainstream is currently located and often on who is making the judgment. Ten years ago I thought of myself as fairly far left, mainly because of my positions on Vietnam and on civil rights. But without much shifting my own position, I soon became hardly more than a moderate liberal, as several hundred thousand younger people and a few older ones caught up with me and kept on moving left. Most social scientists who conduct research on the political extremes are themselves liberal-to-left in political orientation, so they tend to call politically active rightists "extremists" and politically active leftists "activists." I must confess to doing the same at times; it comes easy. "Radical rightist" and "radical leftist" sound more even-handed, but by no means all antiwar demonstrators or civil-rights activists are very far left in their general political views. That is where some of the confusion has come from in analyses of the personality characteristics of *the* radical left. (Other sources of confusion are evident in analyses of the radical right.)

Most of this chapter is concerned with the *moderately* radical right or left. Currently active American Nazis, Communists, and Weathermen are truly minuscule in number and seldom available for study. However, one possible foundation for violent extremist movements is examined in the final section.

rightists

Is Archie Bunker human?

28   If he is, a good many people think he shouldn't be. Archie Bunker is, of course, the "hero" of "All in the Family," one of the most popular comedy programs in television history. Archie is a working-class white Anglo-Saxon Protestant, and he's proud of it. He is also a super-patriotic, prudish, anti-intellectual, racial and religious bigot, who calls his wife a dingbat and his son-in-law a Polack meathead. Much of the time he is shown as boorish, arrogant, and ignorant—if not downright stupid.

Hardly anyone has ever complained to CBS about Archie's negative characteristics. We all know Archie Bunkers, and the one on television doesn't seem a gross misrepresentation of the type. It's the good things about Archie Bunker that some people don't like—the little signs that show him to be human after all, rather than a fascist beast. Archie occasionally betrays feelings of love toward his wife, of sympathy toward his daughter, of kindness toward his fellow man. Although he usually mangles the English language and often insults people with a Bronx cheer, he sometimes manages to deflate a fellow windbag with a riposte that we wish we'd thought of.

The early complaints were mostly that regardless of whether Archie Bunker was depicted sympathetically, he was giving racial slurs a national audience they had seldom enjoyed and was thereby promoting prejudice. There is a little evidence that the show appeals more to the already prejudiced than to the unprejudiced (Vidmar and Rokeach, 1974), but none as far as I know that it increases prejudice. When that type of complaint began to wear thin, it was followed by still more complaints dealing specifically with Archie's good qualities. These said, in various ways, that there's no such thing as a lovable bigot. If Archie is a bigot, if he goes around denouncing the "coloreds" and the "dagos" and the "chosen people," then it is simply inaccurate to show him as loving or lovable. Bigots are not human.

This view of Archie Bunker as an inaccurate portrayal of the bigot was given its most publicized presentation by Laura Z. Hobson (1971), herself the author of the well-known anti–anti-Semitic novel *Gentleman's Agreement*. "I don't think you can be a black-baiter and lovable, nor an anti-Semite and lovable," she protested. Archie was too nice; he used racial slurs but not the worst ones. CBS should show "the real thing for a while," should "lay it on the line about bigots" if they wanted to depict bigots, instead of presenting this dishonest picture of Archie Bunker as both bigoted and (sometimes) likable.

The *New York Times* (1971) got a lot of mail in response to Laura Hobson's article, and most letter-writers agreed with her. Some repeated the earlier criticism that the show makes bigotry more acceptable just by depicting it openly. But several writers concentrated on the theme that Archie was too nice to be believed. A college professor argued that the real Archie Bunkers would be heard praising Hitler and his "unfinished genocidal policies. . . . This is the language one hears around those oil-cloth kitchen tables." A woman cheered the article: "A bigot may be tolerated, ignored, rejected or laughed at, but loved? Never!" A man asserted that "surely Archie Bunker and Lieut. William Calley are kin."

Bunker may share certain characteristics with Lieutenant Calley, convicted of multiple murders in connection with the My Lai massacre, but the implication of that last remark seems to be that neither of them is related to the rest of the human race. This strikes me as an alarming assumption to make about anyone, in the absence of hard

The Bunker family.

evidence. The letter-writers (and Miss Hobson) may have thought they had the hard evidence, in terms of their own observations of prominent racists or rightists or other people who seemed to resemble Archie Bunker. More than likely, though, they had simply been listening to the social scientists.

AUTHORITARIANISM AND EXTERNALIZATION

The idea of the totally unlovable bigot probably did not begin with social scientists. But it received a massive boost from them in *The Authoritarian Personality,* one of the most influential social psychological works of the twentieth century (Adorno et al., 1950). The main argument most readers extracted from this book's ·thousand pages was that people who are notably prejudiced against Jews show a unitary personality syndrome, a set of beliefs and symptoms organized into a general authoritarian personality pattern that is basically different from the personalities of nonauthoritarians. These authoritarians are likely to be politically and economically conservative, extremely conventional in their values, hostile toward minorities and social deviants of any kind. Most important, they respond toward social relationships hierarchically, showing great deference to those higher in status than themselves and trying to domineer those lower in status.

In a thousand pages it is possible to present a good deal of evidence for one's hypotheses, and it is also possible to introduce many qualifications of one's basic assertions. The authors of *The Authoritarian Personality* presented both. But most readers apparently were so fascinated by the concept of the unitary personality syndrome, in which anti-Semitism is somehow intimately related to concerns about other people's sexual deviance and one's own toughness, that they ignored the qualifications and complications. The image of the inhuman rightist bigot was born—or, if not born, at least prodigally nurtured.

Other social scientists were intrigued with the authoritarian syndrome too, but not so much as to make them overlook the data. A multitude of controversies soon arose, and have continued ever since, about just how good the data supporting the authoritarian personality concept really are—particularly the data from the California F Scale (F for "fascism"), the basic questionnaire designed to measure authoritarianism. The F Scale has been criticized for being poorly phrased, for being contaminated by agreement response set (the tendency to agree with questionnaire items regardless of their authoritarian or nonauthoritarian content—itself perhaps an authoritarian characteristic), for measuring several specific sets of attitudes and values rather than a general syndrome, for confusing authoritarianism with rightist ideology. (Adorno et al. noted the existence of left-wing as well as right-wing authoritarians, but the F Scale shows a fairly strong correlation with measures of political conservatism.) Many offshoots of the original F Scale are now available, some of them intended to correct its deficiencies and some of them intended to replace it completely (for example, Rokeach, 1960). But the F Scale itself has proved to be surprisingly robust, and in spite of its shortcomings, it has received many kinds of validation through correlations with behavior (for example, Elms and Milgram, 1966) as well as with other kinds of questionnaires (for example, Kish and Donnenwerth, 1972).

Although the California F Scale has remained controversial among social scientists, a more basic aspect of the "authoritarian personality" research appeared for a time to have approached the status of a scientific principle, at least among "knowledgeable" laymen: the con-

31

clusion that the authoritarian personality pattern, and therefore both racism and rightist extremism, develop mainly through externalization. Criticisms of Archie Bunker as too nice a guy probably derive in large part from widespread public acceptance of that conclusion. Everybody knows that right-wing racist superpatriots get that way because they're crazy; how can Archie be normal?

The tracing of the externalization path in the original research on authoritarianism is very persuasive, at first glance. One of the beauties of authoritarianism, from a psychological standpoint, was that a multitude of apparently diverse characteristics seemed to be consistently related in a somehow unitary whole. The original researchers explained this anomalous package of symptoms with a hypothesis about the syndrome's childhood origins, involving influences that presumably continue to operate in adulthood. Preauthoritarian children, according to Adorno et al. (1950), experience problems with impulse control, as do all children. But their problems are particularly acute because their burgeoning sexual and aggressive impulses are handled harshly by authoritarian parents, who are insensitive to their children's needs and who wish to preserve their own rigid ways of living. Therefore these children cannot learn effective ways to express their basic urges and instead develop unconscious psychological defenses to block or divert such expression. By the time they reach adulthood, they will have elaborated these early defenses into the full array of authoritarian symptoms: overidealization of parents and similar authority figures; redirected hostility toward those they see as different from and hierarchically inferior to themselves, such as blacks and Jews; strong hostility toward explicit sexual expression by others, as too likely to arouse their own repressed sexual impulses; and so on.

Clinical interviews with a sample of the most extreme scorers on the California F Scale appeared to support this psychoanalytically flavored account of authoritarian externalization. However, the interview procedures were criticized for, among other things, failing to control the influence of interviewer bias (Hyman and Sheatsley, 1954); and of course the F Scale was already suspect. These criticisms do not totally invalidate the interview findings, and they appear not to have dampened public enthusiasm for the externalization account of rightist and racist views. But they do leave considerable doubt about the general applicability of the externalization explanation either to the subjects of the initial authoritarianism research or to the right-wing extremists of today.

32

Later research specifically directed at the psychological bases of extreme conservatism, rather than at authoritarianism in general, has provided additional evidence for the importance of externalization among at least some samples of rightists. Herbert McClosky (1958), in a large-scale survey of Minnesota residents, found rightist views

> to be far more characteristic of social isolates, of people who think poorly of themselves, who suffer personal disgruntlement and frustration, who are submissive, timid, and wanting in confidence, who lack a clear sense of direction and purpose, who are uncertain about their values, and who are generally bewildered by the alarming task of having to thread their way through a society which seems to them too complex to fathom.

McClosky feels that such individuals "are unusually defensive and armored in the protection of their own ego needs," and that their conscrvative views are based to a considerable degree on their projection of their impulses (particularly aggressive ones) onto politics. McClosky's interpretation of rightist motives is supported by data from his personality questionnaires, but it appears also to owe a good deal to the clinical interviews conducted by Adorno et al.

A more recent series of studies is more remote in time and place from Adorno et al.'s work but ends up at very nearly the same place. Glenn Wilson (1973) and his colleagues began their research, two decades after the Adorno study and a continent or more away, in an attempt to develop a clearer measure of psychological conservatism than the California F Scale. Through extensive experimentation (mainly in England, New Zealand, and Australia), they developed a Conservatism Scale, consisting of fifty words and phrases for which people were asked merely to indicate general approval or disapproval: "death penalty," "school uniforms," "chastity," "coloured immigration," and so on. Statistical analysis of patterns of approval and disapproval indicated the existence of a basic dimension of conservatism–liberalism on which individuals could be fairly readily located. Furthermore, this dimension revealed high correlations between the same sorts of diverse attitudes as in the authoritarian personality syndrome. Wilson et al. found it hard to hypothesize that people who approve of the death penalty should also consistently approve of chastity and disapprove of "coloured" immigration, merely through chance association of these attitudes in the childhood and adolescent learning process. Nor did they think it likely, as Hans J. Eysenck (1954) has argued, that

33

these relationships would occur merely as the result of a particular pattern of values having been developed and passed down through a specific social class; in fact, they found these same relationships occurring in all social classes. Wilson therefore concludes, in rather similar manner to Adorno et al., that a few underlying personality processes work to produce these diverse visible signs of conservatism.

Wilson regards psychological conservatism primarily as a defensive response to "anxiety in the face of uncertainty." This fear of uncertainty is in turn hypothesized to come from "feelings of insecurity and inferiority," which may in turn arise both from "genetic factors such as . . . low intelligence, lack of physical attractiveness, . . . and female sex," and from "environmental factors such as parental coldness, punitiveness, rigidity and inconsistency." The genetic factors of course depend on environmental responses for their effect: being a woman, even being an ugly woman, does not naturally lead to feelings of insecurity. The environmental factors Wilson lists are pretty much a description of the typical authoritarian parent, as identified by Adorno et al.

Wilson and his colleagues have so far failed to report any direct observations of what authoritarian parents do to their ugly, slow-witted, and/or female children in order to make them insecure and therefore defensive. Furthermore, serious questions have already been raised about the validity of the Conservatism Scale and the methodology of the Wilson group (Ray, 1972; Boshier, 1972; Ashmore, 1975; McEvoy, in press). Wilson's evidence that authoritarian parents produce psychologically conservative children by generating inferiority feelings in them appears, at least so far, to be considerably less conclusive than Adorno et al.'s evidence that authoritarian parents produce authoritarian children by forcing them to bottle up their frustrations. What is striking is that from rather different theoretical orientations and using rather different procedures and subject samples, the Adorno group and the Wilson group both arrived at the same conclusion: that the externalization onto political objects of private psychological problems, and not simply children's learning what their parents and others teach them, must be hypothesized to account for the particular sets of beliefs most characteristic of the modern political right.

ARE RIGHTISTS NATURALLY STUPID?

Although externalization has been the most popular explanation for extreme rightist views, it is by no means the only one. Deficiencies in the externalization data are matched by evidence that many rightists are *not* notable externalizers (Chesler and Schmuck, 1969; Elms, 1969); therefore, alternate or additional explanations for their extremism are necessary. An early alternative falls roughly into the object-appraisal category, more specifically into the *defective*–object-appraisal category. Whereas Glenn Wilson suggests that the slow child comes to feel inferior, therefore defensive, therefore conservative, this alternative proposal in its simplest form is that rightists are innately more slow-witted than leftists and therefore have more difficulty reaching intelligent judgments about politics.

One of the first empirical studies of this proposition was published in 1925, when a psychologist named Henry T. Moore presented sketchy evidence showing that politically conservative college students scored noticeably poorer than liberals on measures of reaction time, "ease of breaking habits," quickness of judgments under pressure, and particularly "independence in the face of majority influence." Moore argued that these differences were probably based on "innate differences in type of neuro-muscular machinery." He warned that "government of the hyperkinetic by the phlegmatic and for the phlegmatic" was likely to "develop periods of stress and strain." Coolidge and Hoover were to serve for seven long years after Moore's paper was published.

Moore's highly restricted data (all from Ivy League students) indicated no *general* intellectual superiority of leftists over rightists, but a flurry of papers on radicals and conservatives in the 1920s and 1930s did. By 1954 a somewhat more complex view of the relationship between inherited abilities and political position had been developed by British psychologist Hans J. Eysenck. According to Eysenck, a general conservative or liberal political position is learned through exposure to the political teachings popular among members of one's social class; the position is therefore acquired rather than inherited. But the conservative position is transformed into an authoritarian or fascist position by one's inherited lack of ability to learn to control one's impulses. If you have failed to learn impulse control very well, you may be particularly receptive to conservative positions that allow you to express your aggressive and other impulses readily. You may also assume other people have a hard time controlling their impulses, so you are likely to favor blunt methods of social control.

Adopting the term from William James, Eysenck identifies this trait of difficulty in learning impulse control as "tough-mindedness." Tough-mindedness, according to Eysenck, is not always characteristic

35

of conservatism; there are also "tender-minded," easily conditioned and therefore tightly self-controlled conservatives (mainly religious rather than political in orientation). Figure 1 shows the tender-minded–tough-minded dimension of political beliefs in combination with the radical–conservative dimension, along with the location of various political attitudes on these dimensions in a factor analysis using British subjects. It is the "tough-minded" conservatives of the upper–right-hand quadrant, with their emphasis on harsh external control of other people's impulses, who are embodied in Archie Bunker and memorialized psychologically in the California F Scale.

Unfortunately, Eysenck's evidence for these provocative hypotheses was weak from the beginning (see, for instance, Christie, 1956), and his more recent work (Eysenck, 1971) has added little to the case for innate authoritarian pigheadedness. Other researchers have found Eysenck's dimensions (particularly the tough/tender one) hard to locate in their own factor analyses; and as far as I know, no one has convincingly demonstrated any differences in the learning of impulse control between leftists and rightists. Extreme rightists may voluntarily constrict their processes of object appraisal, by limiting their information sources only to trusted right-wing authorities (see, for instance, the discussion of Frank and Mary McGee, members of the John Birch Society, in Lamb, 1974, p. 266). But regardless of how tempting it may be for liberals to believe in the natural stupidity of the right, the evidence is lacking.

Another object-appraisal basis for rightist extremism is more convincing, at least in some instances. As previously noted, Eysenck argued that people are taught their general left or right orientation. Other researchers (for example, Hyman and Sheatsley, 1954) have argued that the entire constellation of rightist views and the apparently associated sexual and aggressive concerns of the authoritarian personality are learned, particularly in a working-class environment. At least one empirical study (Mosher and Mosher, 1965) has indicated that children may acquire authoritarian beliefs directly from parental statements rather than indirectly from authoritarian child-raising techniques. In light of this and similar evidence, combined with the evidence for externalization-based authoritarianism, several researchers have suggested the existence of two distinct kinds of authoritarianism: *cognitive* (learned, or object-appraisal–based) and *ego-defensive* (Sanford, 1973; Greenstein, 1973). The distinction seems to me a reasonable one to apply to analyses of rightist psychological foundations as well—except that it omits our third functional category.

36

Figure 1
Distribution of attitudes with respect to tough-mindedness and radicalism

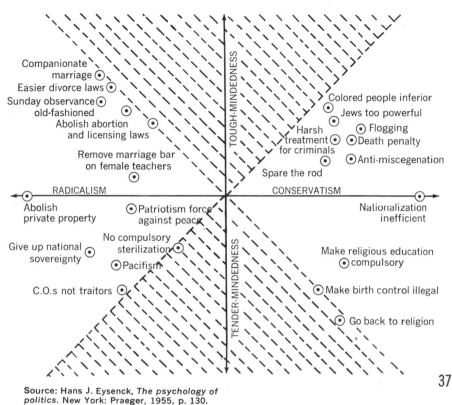

Source: Hans J. Eysenck, *The psychology of politics.* New York: Praeger, 1955, p. 130.

37

THE SOCIAL CONCERNS OF THE RIGHT

The authors of *The Authoritarian Personality* themselves felt that more than externalization is involved in the expression of full-fledged authoritarian views. High scorers on the California F Scale were thought of not as fascists but as *potential* fascists, likely to be sympathetic to a true fascist movement if one became available in this country, but also likely to control their fascist predispositions if the social climate was discouraging. In other words, Adorno et al. saw authoritarian trends as influenced by, if not originating in, the social-adjustment function.

In hindsight, they would have done well to place considerably more emphasis on that function as a basis for extremist political views. Most subsequent research on authoritarianism ignored it completely. However, within a few years several social scientists (for example, Pettigrew, 1961; Bettelheim and Janowitz, 1964) were providing evidence for the role of social pressures in the expression of racial prejudice, and social concerns also became an important element in discussions of the origins of right-wing extremism.

Initially, the proposition was made (by several writers in Bell, 1963) that people become radical rightists in response to status anxiety. That is, they see themselves as rapidly gaining or losing social status, and in order to ensure the social status they desire, they voice super-patriotic political views and denounce as un-American anyone they consider a potential competitor for status. Some evidence exists that members of certain rightist groups are indeed less "status-stable" than average (for example, Rohter, 1965), but as much or more evidence is available that rightists are at least as stable in social status as anyone else (for example, Wolfinger et al., 1964; Elms, 1969; McEvoy, 1971; Hikel, 1973).

However, *social* status—in terms of social class, income, occupational level—may not be the real issue. *Value* status seems to be the major worry among the rightists to whom I have talked; and a similar concern is often visible in other studies. Among the Dallas rightists I interviewed ten years ago, few were seriously worried about their economic situation, but many mentioned their distress that their long-held values were being ignored or rejected by other social groups. James McEvoy has similarly identified perceptions of value threat as basic to George Wallace's appeal in the North, and to some extent in the South, during the 1968 Presidential campaign. Long-established racial prejudices are also often significant in support for Wallace; but even those who show no strong racial prejudice may be attracted to Wallace's denunciations of welfare programs and other "privileges" for minorities, which they can interpret as support for recently challenged values of achievement and individual effort.

Such feelings of threatened value status are not primarily externalizations of repressed urges, although in some cases externalization may make an additional contribution to extremist behavior. The values usually summarized as the "Protestant Ethic" *have* come under seri-

38

Rally in support of the Vietnam War.

ous attack in recent years, through the several subdivisions of the youth movement, through various minority-oriented programs (including compulsory school-busing and Affirmative Action hiring programs), and through political opposition to Barry Goldwater and Richard Nixon, who supposedly epitomized the Protestant Ethic. When people see these values as central to their own self-concept and to their personal reputations (if not their socioeconomic status), they may not need any repressed hostilities left over from childhood to motivate them to join superpatriotic organizations that promise to combat the value attacks.

Not all social-adjustment uses of rightist politics are that serious, at least to the rightists themselves. The rightist view of national and world politics, once developed and elaborated by the classic authoritarian or paranoid personality, is a transforming lens whose operation can be fascinating even to the nonparanoid. Some of my Dallas subjects treated politics as a puzzle, neatly fitting this or that little bit of innocuous "evidence" into a grand picture of worldwide conspiracy—not because they felt any strong paranoid hatred, but because puzzles are fun and because in Dallas that kind of puzzle is popular and readily available. Others played out their rightism as a social role, a role well rewarded by the approval of important people in the Dallas social structure. And one man told me he didn't really believe much of the rightist propaganda, but he had plenty of spare time at work to write letters to newspaper editors, and the newspapers were much more likely to print denunciations of Communist sympathizers than discussions of flower gardens.

40

If Archie Bunker's politics and prejudices satisfied only his powerful unconscious sexual and aggressive urges, repressed since childhood, perhaps he would be as thoroughly unlovable as Laura Hobson demands. Indeed, the most extreme and most emotionally disturbed person in my sample of Dallas rightists complained that even his own children hated him, and I could easily believe him. But Archie seems to rest his beliefs only partly on those repressed urges, which are not enough of a problem in themselves to make him the offensive superpatriotic bigot he often is. He comes from a working-class New York background where such views are common conversational gambits, attempts at social adjustment rather than externalizations. He lives in a small world where the blacks and the Puerto Ricans and the long-haired white youths may at times be genuine competitors for scarce jobs and at other times may at least seem a threat to the values he learned to venerate as a child. Such origins in reality appraisal or social adjustment don't make Archie's beliefs any more palatable, any more intelligent, than if they were entirely externalizations. But if we recognize them for what they are, they may make Archie and his non-fictional rightist brethren more understandable, more like real people than bigotry-based caricatures.

leftists

No single book has done for the American left what *The Authoritarian Personality* did for the right. Perhaps none was necessary. Most Americans seem always to have known that radical leftists are crazy and that their craziness is intimately bound up with their feelings toward their parents. But despite the absence of a commanding book in the field, research on leftists has closely followed the sequence of events already illustrated by research on the right. The sequence, with parenthetical examples from the rightist research, goes this way: (1) a large portion of the public holds certain ingrained assumptions (Army generals are worthy of adulation; minorities are the scum of the earth; a good father is an authoritarian father); (2) social scientists collect data that are interpreted as contradicting those assumptions (in simplified form, the data seem to show that authoritarians are bad people through and through); (3) the public—or at least the educated public—begins to accept the social scientific judgment (which may in some cases fit better with their own biases than the old stereotypes did); (4) finally, other social scientists collect new data that are used to discredit the old hypotheses (most rightists are shown to be relatively normal in all regards except their political views).

The most popular public assumptions about leftists, through most of this century, seem to have been that they are intentionally wreckers rather than builders, are personally immoral, and are psychologically tainted—at the least, shallow rebels against their justly stern parents; at most, uncontrollably impulsive wildmen. Until recently, psychologists could hardly refute these assumptions, since little research had been done on American leftists other than on lapsed Communists, who tended to fit the public stereotypes in some regards (Almond, 1954). Then came the rising of the student left.

Probably no single group in the history of political psychology has been studied so thoroughly as leftist student activists. The scientific

41

Antiwar demonstration at the Capitol.

concentration on them is understandable: they were available; they were mostly willing to be studied; and they were important. Rightists, in general, had been hard to find, were reluctant to talk with psychologists, and only potentially posed a serious problem for society. The student leftists were already at the barricades.

ARE LEFTISTS NATURALLY INTELLIGENT?

The early findings about the student left were highly gratifying to most of the social scientists involved, both because the data flatly contradicted popular assumptions about leftists (confirmations of common sense can be rather boring) and because they supported many researchers' own personal and political biases. Leftist activists were found to be more intelligent than randomly sampled students, more creative, more independent, more emotionally sound. They also came from better-educated families, more often majored in the liberal arts than in utilitarian fields like engineering, and displayed higher moral development (Sampson, 1967; Haan, Smith, and Block, 1968; Keniston, 1969). The general public could not have been more wrong.

No social scientist, as far as I know, has ever seriously argued that leftists are naturally stupid, but some began to argue on the basis of the early data that leftists are naturally smart. The argument is similar to the effective–object-appraisal hypothesis we previously encountered as an explanation of some forms of alienation (and, indeed, those forms of alienation may lead to leftist activism; Schwartz, 1973): if people are intelligent enough to realize what is happening in this country and psychologically healthy enough to act on their awareness of the facts, they will inevitably choose leftist answers to the country's problems. Leftist activists are not only the cream of the nation's crop of young people, the argument goes, they are leftist activists *because* they are the cream of the crop.

This argument is no doubt partly right. I have interviewed a number of leftist students who were outstanding in both intelligence and character and whose motives for political activism were as worthy as those of our noblest national heroes. Detailed case studies (notably by Keniston, 1968) show similarly praiseworthy qualities among other leftist activists.

Unfortunately for liberal biases, young activists of other political persuasions appear just as praiseworthy. The early research tended to compare leftist activists with the mass of the student body, who were not active at much of anything beyond weekly beer blasts or pot parties. But when Larry Kerpelman (1972) and other researchers compared leftist activists with rightist activists, they found many more similarities than differences. Yes, activists are likely to be more creative, independent, psychologically healthy, and so on than nonactivists; but if you are an activist, the direction you're active in doesn't seem to make much difference in these criteria. As an old song puts it, "You gets there just the same." 43

What does make enough difference to produce a left-wing activist rather than a right-wing one? Parents' political views, for one thing. Long before most leftists observe enough of the real political world to form their own views, their leftist parents will have given them a leftist framework for looking at the world. Rarely does a leftist activist come from a rightist family, or a rightist from leftist parents. Even political moderation seems infrequent among parents of genuine leftists (Wood, 1974). Parents seldom indoctrinate their children with detailed political teachings (Jennings and Niemi, 1974), but they may teach certain general values that help their children to judge new political information in ways that lead in a particular political direction (Kraut and Lewis, 1975). The parents' own political activities and interests may also become a basis for identity formation in their children, although young leftists often try to establish a separate identity by exaggerating the distance between their views and those of their parents or by insisting that they are more activist than their parents ever were (Keniston, 1968; Donovan and Shaevitz, 1973).

LEFTWARD SOCIAL ADJUSTMENT

We have already moved, with our discussion of identity formation, into Smith, Bruner, and White's social-adjustment category of political-attitude functions. The social-adjustment function has received considerably less attention for leftists than for rightists, although rightist critics often accuse leftist students of being "sheep," hoodwinked by the Communists or another evil group into abandoning patriotism and decency. One of the early classics of attitude research, a study of Bennington College students during the New Deal era (Newcomb, 1952), did, in fact, find the influence of liberal classmates and faculty to be an important factor in shifting young women leftward. Later studies (Keniston, 1973; Wood, 1974) suggest a fairly modest role for leftist peer influence unless the individual is already primed by family background and personal experience.

During the early days of the Berkeley Free Speech Movement and during the latter days of the anti–Vietnam-War movement, unusually large proportions of college students supported or participated in what were generally described as "leftist" political activities (Lipset, 1972). It is reasonable to assume that many of those students were not strongly committed to a leftist political position, but were responding to social-conformity motives at a time when leftist activism was the most popular political position on campus. Even some thoroughly alienated "hippies," who usually scorned political activity, appear to have occasionally been turned on by the superheated Berkeley political scene of the 1960s (Block, 1968). The leftist involvement of those students, whose psychological health is in some doubt, leads us to a quick look at leftist externalization.

LEFTISTS AS "CRAZIES"

That means we are also back to the old American view of leftists as crazy people who don't even have sense enough to respect their parents, and who—reversing the usual authoritarian pattern of submission to the high and the mighty—take out their hatred of Dad on whatever authority figure is available. This externalization explanation of leftist activism has been defended at length by at least one prominent social scientist (Feuer, 1969). In one form or another, it turns out to be largely true of a limited number of left-wing activists and true to a limited degree of a large number of leftists.

The limited number have been called different names by different researchers: "discontinuity activists" (Block, 1968), "dissenters" (Smith, Haan, and Block, 1970), "nihilists" (Liebert, 1971), "ideologues" (Donovan and Shaevitz, 1973). The names do not completely overlap, but they all describe truly extreme leftists who have serious psychological problems and whose childhood relationships with their parents were seriously impaired. They typically display high hostility levels, relative lack of impulse control, strong concern with satisfaction of their own needs rather than with the highly principled stands more common to leftist activists. They report unusual difficulties with parents who were notably inconsistent in their own behavior, either being privately indulgent while demanding public displays of propriety and achievement (Block, 1968), or displaying wide fluctuations of warmth and coldness toward the child (Liebert, 1971). They rebel against parental values as teen-agers, but they often remain concerned that they have let their parents down by engaging in this rebellious behavior.

Even the much larger number of leftist students who identify to some extent with parental values, and whose psychological health is generally good, tend to report a higher level of family conflict than is typically reported by other students (Wood, 1974; Kraut and Lewis, 1975). As Wood puts it, "the worse relations a student had with his or her parents, the more likely he or she was to be an activist." Do these students too, then, turn left as a way of externalizing antiparental hostility onto the broad political scene?

If they do, the externalization process must be considerably more complex than its early (and some current) advocates assumed. Keep in mind that these same students tend to go farther left the farther left their parents are; so they are not simply rebelling against parental political values. They often describe their main political disagreement with parents as dealing with tactics rather than with issues; they see themselves as putting into practice what their parents only talk about (Keniston, 1968). They also tend to disagree with parents on issues of life style (marijuana use, premarital sex) but not on traditional political topics. Perhaps rather than externalizing antiparental hostility through

45

political activism, these young leftists are merely carrying the openly critical, think-for-yourself give-and-take of their family life out into the big political world. (Rightist students' home life appears to include considerably fewer open conflicts, and their later life styles and political activities reflect similar constraint [Donovan and Shaevitz, 1973].) Or perhaps family conflict places greater emphasis on social-adjustment processes outside the family, as Kraut and Lewis (1975) suggest:

> A student's conflict with and detachment from his family may lead him to be influenced more by other aspects of his social environment, including a peer group more liberal than the general population, . . . a liberalizing college education, and a specific set of social issues—the draft, the war in Vietnam, drug laws—conducive to youthful disaffection.

Although researchers continue to disagree on the relative importance of various factors influencing leftist political development, they do seem to have begun agreeing that the left—even the student left—cannot be regarded as a homogeneous group for purposes of psychological analysis. As with rightists, similar political behaviors may satisfy diverse psychological functions, and the origins of the behavior patterns cannot be understood until the underlying functions are differentiated. Likewise, different kinds of political behavior may satisfy the same set of functions in one individual on different occasions. Robert Liebert (1971) has pointed out in defining two categories of leftist activists at Columbia, the "idealists" and the "nihilists," that most leftists there fall between these "polar extremes . . . and, further, continuously shift in position, depending on both external events and inner readjustment."

46

CAUTIONS AND FORECASTS

That last caution is worth underlining. It is easy to assume, when you are focusing on personality determinants of political behavior, that a particular personality syndrome will always lead to a particular behavior. But, at best, personality only *predisposes* to certain behaviors, given the appropriate external circumstances—and the circumstances are seldom appropriate. Changes in child-raising procedures after the Second World War may have supplied an unusually large number of students in the 1960s who were predisposed to activism when their own high ideals or low impulses clashed with societal controls; but an obviously unjust war and several other supportive circumstances were apparently necessary to channel these students into antigovernment political activism (Wood, 1974). Perhaps even more important was a military draft of college-age males who were to be sent to fight in that unpopular war (Levine and Denisoff, 1972). The availability of students with the right kind of family background for leftist activism is unlikely to have changed much in the last few years; the status of various social ills, racial and environmental, has not changed much; but American draftees are no longer fighting in Vietnam, and as of this writing the campuses of America are reasonably quiet.

What circumstances might reactivate the pool of activist-predisposed youth in this country? Social scientists have had such a poor track record in predicting either late-1960s activism or early-1970s quietism that the reader would be foolish to accept any predictions even if I were foolish enough to make them. But it is at least suggestive that the only real pockets of activism remaining on most campuses are of women fighting for the women's movement, of homosexual students fighting for "gay" liberation, and of minority–ethnic-group members fighting for minority–ethnic-group rights. An occasional student is active in other causes; an occasional student is even active in one of the above causes without being a member of the appropriate minority. But as with the potential draftees, the most powerful motivation is

March for women's rights.

47

apparently to see oneself deprived of satisfactions for one's own needs. Few mass movements have been sustained for long on pure idealism.

This is not to say that mass movements should be condemned for their selfishness, or even that every person involved in movements to gain rewards for his or her own social category is primarily operating for selfish ends. The college students who constitute the largest and most active segments of the black power, feminist, and other such movements are often among the least objectively deprived members of their class. But if a person is *not* strongly deprived of pressing need satisfactions, it does seem to help a lot to have a clear basis for identifying with those who are deprived, at least if we are talking about political behavior that lasts longer than a few rallies and a march or two.

Nor do I want to leave the impression that political action based mainly on altruistic ideals is always more desirable than action based on self-interest or empathic identification with those similar to but less fortunate than oneself. Principled political action has its own psychological and practical problems, as we shall see in the last section of this chapter.

superego-tripping

The advertisement on the opposite page appeared in the *California Aggie,* student newspaper of the University of California's Davis campus, on November 5, 1971. It was part of one of the last nationwide efforts at mobilizing the student left. The protest combined peace and ecology appeals, because the nuclear bomb test in question was seen both as contributing to the arms race and as harming Alaskan wildlife. The ad was apparently sincere; indeed, its wistful tone reminds me of Charlie Brown's famous rhetorical question in a *Peanuts* cartoon: "How can we lose when we're so sincere?" But the bomb went off as scheduled, so the students lost, and they have hardly been heard from since.

The Cannikin protest was an unusually straightforward display of a psychological process that appeared widespread among the leftist activists of the 1960s. Robert Jay Lifton (1968) has identified one version of this process as "psychism." I prefer the more colloquial but more descriptive term, "superego-tripping" (Elms, 1972).

Lifton has offered several definitions of psychism, ranging from broad to narrow. The broadest is "a confusion between inner and outer

Cannikin Can
Be Stopped

On Saturday at 2:00 P.M. (P.S.T.) the Cannikin tragedy will be realized. As you may know, the site of this 5 megaton blast is Amchitka, a remote Alaskan island. Traditional channels have been tried in an effort to abort this test but to no avail.

If you now are feeling frustrated, then commit yourself to positive action. At 1:59 concentrate on preventing the detonation of this bomb. Exclude yourself from all external distractions, and direct your thought solely on stopping the explosion.

At the least this psychic sabotage will alleviate your frustrations. At the most it will achieve a triumph over insanity. This will not be a local effort.

PEANUTS

GOOD GRIEF!

4-6

ONE HUNDRED AND EIGHTY-FOUR TO NOTHING!

49

I DON'T UNDERSTAND IT...

HOW CAN WE LOSE WHEN WE'RE SO SINCERE?!

SCHULZ

worlds" (Lifton, 1970, p. 85); the narrowest, "the exaggerated reliance upon will and psychic power to achieve technological goods" (Lifton, 1968, p. xv). An intermediate definition comes closest to what I mean by superego-tripping: "The attempt to achieve control over one's external environment through internal or external psychological manipulations, through behavior determined by intra-psychic needs no longer in touch with the actualities of the world one seeks to influence" (Lifton, 1968, p. 32). My contribution is to point out the particular importance of superego needs: superego-tripping is *acting on the assumption that whatever behavior best satisfies the demands of one's superego will be most effective in attaining one's realistic goals.* In other words, if you judge the effectiveness of your overt acts in terms of whether they make you feel good morally, rather than whether they have changed external reality in the ways you had planned, you're superego-tripping.

Lifton's main example of psychism is the Chinese reliance on Mao Tse-tung's thought rather than on technological skills in trying to achieve a technological "great leap forward" in the late 1950s. Mao's thought may be very helpful in inspiring farmers and soldiers to greater effort; but when you build your own backyard pig-iron smelter out of mud and bricks (as many Chinese did), your virtuous struggle to be worthy of Mao will not keep the smelter from producing shoddy pig iron or from collapsing in the next rainstorm.

Similar examples of superego-tripping are easy to find among American leftist radicals. The Cannikin advertisement is only a small instance of their choosing political strategies that will make them feel better inside, as a substitute for or in preference to strategies that will make the political system better. A more important example comes from Sam Brown (1970), coordinator of the huge Vietnam Moratorium demonstrations in 1969, who complained of a "delusion within the American peace movement . . . that we can retain a private dimension of political morality for ourselves." According to Brown, radicals often engaged in antiwar activities with more concern for exhibiting their moral purity than for gaining broad public support. They felt that "if the war ends, they can take credit for political effectiveness; if it continues, they have personally separated themselves from the war policy."

The common element in Lifton's example and mine is people's assumptions (not necessarily conscious) that if all is right in their inner world—if they feel, in an un-Maoistic image of moral satisfac-

50

tion, that "God's in His heaven"—then all must be right with the outer world as well. At first, this assumption may appear to be another instance of externalization, and indeed there are similarities: in both externalization and superego-tripping, the main positive effects are temporary and are internal to the individual engaging in the practice, while the main external effects are likely to be negative and at times long-lasting. In both cases, people act inappropriately toward reality in order to gain a better feeling toward themselves. But in terms of the processes involved, superego-tripping and externalization work in opposite ways: externalization involves reacting to external objects as if they embodied one's internal problems, while superego-tripping involves behaving as though one's internal state were an accurate index of how well things are going externally.

Superego-tripping also resembles what some social scientists describe as "ritualistic" or "symbolic" political behavior (Gusfield, 1963; Edelman, 1971; Sears and McConahay, 1973), in its emphasis on internal feelings over external effects. Ritualistic or symbolic politics, however, usually involves concerns about social status (of the kind discussed earlier in this chapter in connection with rightist movements) rather than about moral perfection. People may sometimes use moral issues as weapons in their fight to maintain social status, as Gusfield has demonstrated in his analysis of the American temperance movement. But people may also be genuinely concerned about their *moral* status, the distance they feel from the level of perfection their superego demands of them, regardless of their social-status concerns.   51

I chose the term *superego-tripping*, rather than a phrase referring to conscience or the recent cliché *liberal guilt trip*, because Freud's term *superego* connotes more than an internal censor of sinful acts. Freud (1933; English translation, 1964) included within the superego both the conscience, which prohibits us from doing disapproved acts, and the ego ideal, "by which the ego measures itself, which it emulates, and whose demand for ever greater perfection it strives to fulfill." Political superego-tripping, with its insistence on ideological or behavioral purity, seems as often an attempt to attain those high moral goals Freud called the ego ideal as to avoid condemnation by one's conscience.

Superego concerns may play a valuable role in politics. Amoral pragmatism and immoral profiteering have been so common in American politics, culminating in but hardly beginning with Watergate, that a heartfelt stress on high principle is refreshing in any political participant. David Halberstam (1972) has clearly illustrated the dangers of too great an emphasis on political effectiveness at the expense of moral principle, in his analysis of the Kennedy and Johnson Administrations. But as Sam Brown observes, it achieves little to replace this "effectiveness trap" with a "non-effectiveness trap" of going down to defeat "shouting the pure gospel on as many moral issues as possible." If you want to attain political goals, you must keep at least one eye on the political effects of your behavior. You may temper your political objectives with your moral concerns, but you should not operate under the illusion that moral purity alone will get you anywhere. In William Sloane Coffin's (1968) words, "One needs more than simply conscience; one needs to have a great deal of information and a great capacity for rational judgment to take . . . a moral stand."

The term *superego-tripping* is of course derived most directly from a popular slang term of the 1960s, *ego-tripping*. Ego-tripping is behaving in ways that will boost one's own ego, often at the expense of others—for instance, indulging in unnecessarily detailed autobiographical accounts in writing a rock song or a textbook, or elaborately praising the accomplishments of one's own political administration as the greatest in history. Ego-trippers may be rather easily dissuaded, at least temporarily, if you point out to them what they are doing. They have to believe others are both paying attention to them and accepting their statements as credible, or their egos will derive little benefit from this self-generated praise.

52   Superego-trippers may be harder to sidetrack, because their actions are seldom visibly directed toward self-benefit. They are working for the starving masses or for freedom in our time or for participatory democracy; and if the masses suspect the motives, to hell with the masses—the superego-trippers will save them anyway. (The legendary Boy Scout who insists on walking an old woman across the street whether she wants to go or not is taking a brief superego trip.) Self-sacrifice is not as obviously a psychological indulgence as self-admiration.

But indulgence it is. If one could always *both* satisfy one's moral imperatives *and* accomplish one's external goals, the world would be a beautiful place. In a world where we often seem forced to choose one or the other alternative, we are most often concerned with those who try to accomplish their external goals at the expense of their moral convictions. But the reverse can be at least as dangerous. In the process of retaining one's moral purity or of attaining a moral "high," one can lose the world and dash the hopes of all those economically deprived or politically impotent unfortunates one was trying to help save.

How can superego-tripping be distinguished from genuine, realistic, and/or altruistic concern for the masses or for valued political objectives? There is, unfortunately, much room for ambiguity at this point, and I am afraid the term can be used as easily in unjustified name-calling as in honest research. Any sincere resort to principle will involve some superego satisfactions. The crucial factor is the relative importance of feedback concerning the realistic effects of one's actions versus feedback on superego satisfactions. If the latter assumes more weight in influencing a person's behavior than the former (even though he or she claims the reverse is true), the person is superego-tripping.

This proportional relationship between reality feedback and super-ego concerns can be evaluated at least roughly in individual case studies, and indeed biographers of such figures as Woodrow Wilson (George and George, 1956; see Chapter 4 of this book) have implicitly done so. The relationship is difficult to assess at a distance, and claims of making such judgments, particularly of political opponents, should be viewed with much caution. However, when an individual or group repeatedly engages in behaviors whose announced intent is to win the masses or the political leadership to a particular cause, although in fact there is strong evidence (from reliable public-opinion polls or other impartial sources) that the reverse is happening, superego-tripping might reasonably be inferred. Perhaps the people trying to win support are instead stupid or crazy; but since the available evidence shows political activists generally to be at least as intelligent and no more neurotic than the average citizen, superego-tripping may be a good alternative explanation for apparently "self-defeating" behavior.

Are leftist activists more prone to superego-tripping than other people? Their relatively high level of moral development, at least as compared with nonactivists (Haan, Smith, and Block, 1968; O'Connor, 1974), would suggest that likelihood. Leftist activists are more often found at the highest level of Kohlberg's (1969) widely adopted moral development scale than other groups (see Table 1). At that level (Stage 6), individuals presumably rely largely on their own self-chosen principles to make moral judgments, so they have little cause to look

53

beyond their own consciences (and perhaps their most respected friends) for confirmation of the rightness of their decisions. Only one level down (Stage 5), where the main criterion for moral judgment is maintaining the "social contract" with other people, the likelihood that activists will try to ensure close correspondence between the urgings of their conscience and the real needs of other people seems considerably greater.

The possibility does exist that right-wing activists engage in substantial superego-tripping too. They certainly express strong concerns about moral issues (Donovan and Shaevitz, 1973), although their concerns often seem to be voiced at Kohlberg's Stage 4 obey-the-rules level of moral development. Kohlberg's developmental model may, however, be cast in such a way that a genuine rightist simply cannot get beyond Stage 5. According to Silvan Tomkins (1963), the essence of the right-wing orientation (in politics and in other areas of life) is the assumption that conformity to norms or rules defines human worth, whereas the basic left-wing position stresses the value of human beings in and of themselves—a Stage 6 stance in Kohlberg's scheme. Extensive data are not yet available on Tomkins' hypothesis, so he may simply be wrong about the defining characteristics of right and left. But it may also be that Kohlberg's scheme is biased in a liberal direction, with Stage 6 proposed as the highest level because Kohlberg himself is a political liberal who believes a normative orientation is necessarily inferior to an individual-morality orientation. Or it could be that on the average, right-wingers are for one reason or another truly morally inferior to leftists. Whichever is the case, people must *both* have strong moral concerns *and* value those concerns more highly than evidence about the effects of their behavior on other people in order to be frequent superego-trippers. These conditions seem more likely, in the absence of hard evidence, to be found in leftist activists than in rightist activists.

If superego-tripping is in fact widely distributed among both leftists and rightists, I would expect leftists to exhibit it for shorter periods of time on any given issue. This is because, according to at least some evidence (for example, Keniston, 1968), leftist activists are relatively open to self-examination, while according to other data (for example, Adorno et al., 1950), rightists are not. If individuals frequently examine their own motives, or talk about them in enough detail for others to do so, they are likely to discover sooner or later any major self-misrepresentation of the motives, such as that they are seeking superego satisfactions more eagerly than real political accom-

54

Table 1
Classification of moral judgment into levels and stages of development

LEVELS	BASIS OF MORAL JUDGMENT	STAGES OF DEVELOPMENT
I	Moral value resides in external, quasi-physical happenings, in bad acts, or in quasi-physical needs rather than in persons and standards.	**Stage 1:** Obedience and punishment orientation. Egocentric deference to superior power or prestige, or a trouble-avoiding set. Objective responsibility.
		Stage 2: Naively egoistic orientation. Right action is that instrumentally satisfying the self's needs and occasionally others'. Awareness of relativism of value to each actor's needs and perspective. Naive egalitarianism and orientation to exchange and reciprocity.
II	Moral value resides in performing good or right roles, in maintaining the conventional order and the expectancies of others.	**Stage 3:** Good-boy orientation. Orientation to approval and to pleasing and helping others. Conformity to stereotypical images of majority or natural role behavior, and judgment by intentions.
		Stage 4: Authority and social-order maintaining orientation. Orientation to "doing duty" and to showing respect for authority and maintaining the given social order for its own sake. Regard for earned expectations of others.
III	Moral value resides in conformity by the self to shared or shareable standards, rights, or duties.	**Stage 5:** Contractual legalistic orientation. Recognition of an arbitrary element or starting point in rules or expectations for the sake of agreement. Duty defined in terms of contract, general avoidance of violation of the will or rights of others, and majority will and welfare.
		Stage 6: Conscience or principle orientation. Orientation not only to actually ordained social rules but to principles of choice involving appeal to logical universality and consistency. Orientation to conscience as a directing agent and to mutual respect and trust.

55

Source: Lawrence Kohlberg, Moral and religious education and the public schools: A developmental view. In T. Sizer (ed.), *Religion and public education*. Boston: Houghton Mifflin, 1967, p. 171.

plishments. It may be harder to recognize superego-tripping than ego-tripping, particularly if you are surrounded by other people who share your moral concerns (they are unlikely to share your concerns about your ego). But the recognition in either case should come much sooner if you are open to self-examination.

A comparison of leftist and rightist literature in this regard is instructive. There is a great deal more argument in leftist publications about fellow leftists' motives, and a great deal more leftist self-analysis, some of it critical, than is true for the right. This may be one additional reason for the relatively short life of the national leftist movement of the 1960s (and of other leftist movements earlier in our history). That is, the early benefits of superego-tripping petered out as most leftist activists became aware that they were practicing that particular form of self-indulgence; and because they were having little realistic effect on national politics, at least of the kind they wanted, the leftists either gave up politics altogether or turned to more socially acceptable and therefore potentially more effective modes of participation. Rightist activists have been neither as active nor as numerous as leftists in recent years, but their level of political participation seems to have remained relatively stable—perhaps partly because superego-tripping was not a component for many rightists in the first place, and partly because the superego-tripping that was present continues unrecognized and unabated.

In my criticisms of superego-tripping, I have assumed that some kind of effective political action is usually possible. Sometimes none is, in which case a superego trip may be the only consolation a person has. When Aleksandr Solzhenitsyn was still a political prisoner in Russia—and even later when he was out of prison, free to write but not to publish—he seems to have obtained great solace from maintaining an inner feeling of moral purity, through his silent rejection of a psychological union with his masters. He had little else to sustain him, and he did not need to worry that his lack of cooperation would make the political scene in Russia much worse than it was. But as Pauline Kael (1973) has pointed out in a sensitive discussion of *The First Circle*, Solzhenitsyn seems to have come to believe too strongly in "the idea of defeating your enemies by the purity of your suffering," to believe his own undelivered Nobel Prize speech: "One word of truth shall outweigh the whole world." As Kael says: "We respond to the beauty of the message. But we know that when more people actually believed that the poetic truths would conquer, it didn't im-

56

prove their social conditions; it merely helped them to bear their suffering."

Solzhenitsyn appears to have acknowledged this point himself, finally, by accepting exile rather than insisting on death or further imprisonment in Russia. Outside, even though he has in a way co-operated with the Soviet government by leaving, Solzhenitsyn can continue to move others to put whatever pressure they can on the Soviet Union. Inside, he could have retained his moral purity in death, but his influence as a martyr would have been uncertain and probably short-lived. One convenient aspect of martyrdom is that you don't have to assess the realistic effects of your stand for morality—you can just go superego-tripping off into eternity without having to look back at what you have or haven't accomplished. Solzhenitsyn is sufficiently hard-headed to know that the Soviet government will not be reformed or overturned by the death of one man, however morally pure and personally superego-pleasing his martyrdom may have been.

3

plain politicians

the psychology
of the
average officeholder

Are professional politicians different from other people? There are good logical reasons for thinking they must be. "Avocational" or "occasional" politics, to use Max Weber's terms (1918; English translation, 1946), can usually be practiced without much disruption of our ordinary lives. We can go to the polls, or ring doorbells, or even join a demonstration now and then, without giving up jobs, homes, or families. But the decision to run for office, especially at the state or national level, usually implies a willingness to leave behind a good deal of one's previous life. The readiness to work on political matters full-time for years implies an emotional investment in politics that is rare in the United States and most other countries. As Weber says, "Politics is a strong and slow boring of hard boards." The people who take up the tools and go to work might reasonably be assumed to display substantial psychological differences from most of the part-time political participants we have so far considered.

Yet research on politicians does not consistently confirm such reasonable expectations. Just as a wide array of political attitudes may satisfy the same basic psychological function, so running for office, joining the Peace Corps, or boarding a bus for Detroit might all serve the same motive of seeking meaningful work at an adequate salary. Just as a single political attitude may satisfy a wide array of psychological functions in different people, so the holding of political office may, for one or another of the thousands of professional politicians in this country, meet any imaginable combination of human needs. Logical analysis of how politicians as a group should differ psychologically from everyone else must be supplemented by data on how different or similar they really are.

We will review a considerable portion of such data by looking first at motives for seeking election, then at the various personality patterns of several subgroups of politicians already in office, then at the characteristics of those politicians who distinguish themselves enough to be described as leaders. Research on the personalities of the supreme leaders—United States Presidents—will be saved for more detailed consideration in Chapter 4.

political recruitment

The Elgin State Hospital in Elgin, Illinois, is a progressive psychiatric hospital. For some years it has used milieu therapy, a procedure developed by Maxwell Jones in England to increase the usefulness of the mental-hospital experience to patients after their release. In milieu therapy, patients are given substantial responsibility for guiding their own lives within the hospital, including their election of and participation in a ward government. The ward council is responsible for such things as "dispensing funds allotted to the ward, requesting special monies for special projects, organizing and planning social events, making ward regulations, invoking and dispensing sanctions for patients breaking ward regulations, and—in some instances—advising for the discharge of patients" (Rutherford, 1966).

59

Every patient in the milieu-therapy wards is eligible for election to a ward council. But are particular types of mental patients more successful as politicians, at least in terms of being more likely to get elected? Brent Rutherford found this question sufficiently intriguing to collect extensive data on the diagnoses and other individual characteristics of the milieu-therapy population at Elgin State, along with information about their participation in ward councils. One finding was particularly striking: 45.8 percent of the councils' elected officers were paranoid schizophrenics, although only 11.8 percent of the ward population bore the same diagnosis. Manic-depressives were even more overrepresented in percentage terms, but because fewer of them were in the wards to begin with (3.2 percent), their total percentage of council offices (20.8 percent) was not nearly as high as that of the paranoid schizophrenics.

The paranoid as politician: Adolf Hitler.

Does this mean paranoids are likely to become politicians outside of psychiatric wards as well as in, or that most politicians are paranoid? Hardly, although the distinguished historian Richard Hofstadter found enough conspiratorial fears expressed in the Goldwater campaign and similar movements to write a book entitled *The Paranoid Style in American Politics* (1965). Brent Rutherford himself remarks on various scholarly diagnoses of paranoia in Hitler and Stalin and suggests that certain elements of paranoid syndromes, such as feelings of "self-sufficiency, superiority, and certainty," may be very useful in some political environments.

What the findings do tangentially suggest is that not all personality characteristics, whether normal or abnormal, are equally likely to predispose a person for a political career. Every American child may have an equal legal chance to grow up to be a President or a legislator, but it's going to help a lot to possess certain characteristics that appeal either to the people who select nominees for political office or to the people who elect candidates to office. If you are running for office outside a psychiatric ward, you would probably be well advised not to appear overtly paranoid or manic-depressive. But you may be better off with mild versions of those syndromes than with a slight touch of catatonic schizophrenia.

We have now moved into the research area known professionally as *political recruitment*—most broadly, how people are attracted into any kind of political activity, or somewhat more narrowly for our purposes, how they come to seek political office. Much of the research literature in this area is concerned with nonpsychological variables, and the findings are somewhat at variance with the American myth of political equality. Political candidates at any level of office tend to come from the higher socioeconomic classes, to have attained higher than average levels of education, and to be male. There are of course exceptions to all these characteristics, but not many.

Personality research on political candidates has understandably been much more sparse than demographic research. A candidate's sex, educational level, and previous occupation are matters of public record; his scores on neuroticism scales are not. Furthermore, few candidates trust psychologists enough to reveal much about their private selves on request, even if anonymity is promised. Occasional researchers have, however, been able to administer short questionnaires to active politicians, whose responses, if not as revelatory as we would like, are at times sufficiently tantalizing to justify further research.

61

ARE POLITICIANS CRAZY?

Brent Rutherford, in his study of psychiatric patients, was merely continuing to look for answers to one of the first questions posed in political-recruitment research: How much do political activity and mental illness overlap? Harold Lasswell posed that question in *Psychopathology and Politics* (1930), one of the earliest and most influential studies of the psychology of politicians. Lasswell persuaded a variety of current and former political figures (not necessarily elected officials) to undergo lengthy psychoanalytically oriented interviews. On the basis of responses from his somewhat biased sample (several of his interviewees were in mental hospitals at the time), Lasswell proposed a simple formula to summarize the process by which one. becomes a "fully developed political man":

$$p \Big\} \, d \, \Big\} \, r = P$$

That is, one's private and largely "primitive" psychological structures (p) are externalized or displaced (d) onto public objects, and they are then rationalized (r) "in terms of public interest" to produce the political man (P). More specifically, people become politically active largely in order to deal with their unresolved infantile conflicts about sex and aggression. The more conflict-ridden they are, presumably, the more likely they are to move into politics.

This hypothesis received little empirical support other than Lasswell's own initial interviews. But it was so persuasively argued that when other researchers began to examine the psychological health of officeholders more quantitatively, some two decades later, they apparently saw as their first task the establishment of the psychological normality of most politicians. (By that time Lasswell himself [1951, 1954] was arguing that the successful politician in a democracy is necessarily flexible rather than neurotically rigid.) Indeed, the research showed a rebound effect similar to that of the political-extremism research: politicians were seen as not only eminently stable, but often as psychologically superior to the common citizen.

In a small sample of South Carolina state legislators, for instance, J. B. McConaughy (1950) found less indication of neurotic tendencies than in the population at large. Unfortunately, the scale he used to measure neuroticism (the Bernreuter Personality Inventory) is rather primitive and answers to it can easily be faked if a person wants to give an impression of normality. But later studies, using more sophisticated measures, yielded similar results. One summary of this

62

research pictures politically active individuals (party workers as well as candidates) in many of the same terms as the idealized 1960s descriptions of leftist activists: "They feel personally competent; they know themselves and feel confident of their knowledge and skills; their ego is strong enough to withstand blows; they are not burdened by a load of anxiety and internal conflict; they can control their impulses; they are astute, sociable, self-expressive, and responsible" (Milbrath, 1965).

Just as recent studies have shown leftist activists to be less ideal in various ways than many writers had argued in the 1960s, so there has been a rebound from the rebound with regard to the psychological health of politicians. Rutherford's study was, in a way, a part of this double rebound, suggesting as it did that certain characteristics useful in mental-patient self-governance might also be found among some successful politicians in the outside world. The second rebound is softer in a study of "high-ranking officials in the Republican and Democratic parties of Chicago" (Marcus, 1969). On a well-validated measure of psychopathology, it was found that "traditional political participants are no healthier than the population from which they were chosen." That is, they had no fewer pathological symptoms than the general Chicago public; but they didn't have more than the public, either. (They may of course have also possessed positive characteristics not measured by the psychopathology scale, so studies showing the virtues of politicians aren't necessarily wrong.)

Other issues have been pursued in the personality-and-political-recruitment field besides the mental health of politicians. One is 63 whether certain specific personality characteristics (usually not as peculiar as paranoid tendencies) are necessary to push a person into politics. Another issue is whether particular groups of politicians, such as Democrats or men, differ appreciably in their personalities from other groups, such as Republicans or women.

COMPENSATORY POWER AS A POLITICAL MOTIVE

The question of particular motivating characteristics was again raised largely by Harold Lasswell (1948). Lasswell observed that people may enter formal politics for diverse reasons, and that others may seek to play political roles in nonpolitical settings for the same reasons. He then identified the central characteristic of the "basic political type," whether in political office or in a different role, as "the accentuation of power in relation to other values within the personality when compared with other persons." Lasswell further argued that the basic political type regards power as "compensation against estimates of the self as weak, contemptible, immoral, unloved." Again, Lasswell (1954) later revised and clarified this estimate of political motivation, de-emphasizing power-seeking among democratic politicians. But the relationship of power drives to political activity was at the top of the list when researchers began to collect quantitative data on the motives of politicians.

One of the most complex studies of power motivation in political figures was conducted by Rufus Browning and Herbert Jacob (1964). They gave a "test of imagination" (a version of the Thematic Apperception Test, or TAT) to fifty elected local officials in Louisiana, twenty-three businessmen-politicians in an East Coast community, and eighteen politically inactive businessmen in the same community. The imaginative stories these respondents told in response to a series of ambiguous pictures were scored systematically for evidence of unusual concerns with power, with achievement, and with affiliation (positive interaction with other people). The results were varied. Many of the Louisiana politicians showed no concern with power at all, and among the East Coast businessmen, the politicians were not significantly different from the nonpoliticians in power motivation or anything else. On the basis of the simplest data analysis, power needs seemed to explain virtually nothing about political involvement.

However, as Browning and Jacob point out (and as Lasswell would surely agree), political office may be the best way to satisfy one's power needs only in certain social and political settings. Often a business position can provide greater gratification than any available political slot. Even within one geographic area, political offices may vary widely in opportunities for satisfaction of power needs. For instance, in Louisiana, justices of the peace in one of the parishes (counties) under study exercised little power over anything. In another parish, justices of the peace held relatively great power because their decisions influenced the conduct of gambling in the parish. Different sorts of candidates might thus be recruited to what legally is the same position in each parish. Browning and Jacob therefore sorted out, with the aid of political experts in the communities involved, positions in which substantial power could be exercised as contrasted with those in which it could not. They then compared the motivational levels of occupants of these different groups of offices. As anticipated, the holders of the offices with the greatest potential for exercising power were highest in power motivation. This finding was

64

BOOTH

"*Three years in a row, Hoot's lespedeza went moldy. His chickens got sick and quit laying. He tried mixing his own anti-freeze and busted both tractor blocks. Then Coolidge, his favorite mule, slipped in the barn lot and died. It just seemed like one bad omen after another. So finally Hoot says, 'It's either shoot the cattle or run for Congress.' Well, Hoot ain't one to shoot animals, but you can bet your bottom dollar he'll tell those other congressmen what's what up there in Washington.*"

65

particularly evident in the East, where the high-powered offices affected a good deal more than local gambling. The power motivation of those in low-power political positions was even a little lower than among the nonpoliticians. Interestingly, the holders of high-power East Coast positions were also higher in achievement motivation than anyone else (reasonable, since their positions enabled them to achieve the most in terms of actually carrying out policies as well as exercising influence in nonpolicy areas) but were lower on affiliation than low-power officeholders. That is, power-seeking and friendship-seeking tended to be mutually exclusive.

The Browning and Jacob research is particularly valuable in showing the interaction between private motives and the nature of specific political offices. However, it suffers from at least one major weakness, pointed out by Paul Sniderman (1975): their measure of power motivation does not clearly distinguish between a basic *need* for power and an *interest* in holding power as one means to satisfy other needs. Lasswell had originally hypothesized that politicians feel a strong need for power—and therefore go into politics—to compensate for their low self-evaluations. Rather than attempting to measure the power needs of politicians and nonpoliticians as Browning and Jacob had done, Sniderman looked directly at their feelings of self-esteem.

Sniderman found that politicians in his sample (delegates to the 1956 Democratic and Republican national conventions, about 60 percent of whom held elective office) were on the average distinctly *higher* in self-esteem than a representative sample of American adults, even when the samples were matched for social status. The differences were clearest for the particular aspect of self-esteem, feelings of interpersonal competence, that may be most relevant to political activity. (Interpersonal competence, according to Sniderman, involves the ability "to feel at ease and self assured when in the company of others, to be articulate and persuasive, to take the initiative frequently, to be outgoing, active, forceful; by contrast the person who lacks a sense of interpersonal competence tends to be shy, retiring, inhibited, awkward, and anxious when dealing with other persons.") A person high in feelings of interpersonal competence is more likely to learn the ins and outs of politics and to learn the skills needed to succeed as a politician. A person low in interpersonal competence is likely to focus on other kinds of activities and to join the ranks of the politically uninterested or the passive alienated.

The only substantial exception to this general pattern in Sniderman's data involves an interaction between self-esteem and an apparent compulsive syndrome. Politicians in general are hardly more likely than nonpoliticians to possess such personality traits as obsessiveness, rigidity, and desire for fame. But active politicians with low self-esteem exhibit such compulsive characteristics considerably more often than do low–self-esteem nonpoliticians. Sniderman suggests that the "stress on striving, persevering, attaining control, and meeting high standards of achievement and moral character" sometimes found as part of a compulsive syndrome might overcome the usual tenden-

66

cies of the low–self-esteem individual to avoid political activity. People with this combination of low self-esteem and compulsive traits appear from Sniderman's and other data to constitute a minority of active politicians. But they do provide partial support for the compensatory power hypothesis first proposed by Lasswell—who never assumed that *all* politicians seek compensatory power anyway. He did feel that such individuals sometimes attain political importance very much out of proportion to their number, and we will encounter evidence for that proposition in the next chapter.

POLITICAL PARTY PERSONALITIES

In addition to looking at people's motives for becoming politicians, social scientists have occasionally asked whether Democratic and Republican politicians show different patterns of motives or other personality characteristics. Sniderman (1975) found little difference in self-esteem between Democratic and Republican politicians, and "little difference" is the most frequent finding in other comparisons of politicians of the two parties on personality characteristics (Czudnowski, 1975). Like the young radical activists of left and right, Republican and Democratic politicians are more similar to each other on most criteria than they are to nonpoliticians of either (or no) party. But politicians from the two major parties do fall a bit short of being identical, either in personal background or in current personality patterns.

The usual demographic comparisons have been made, this time as high as the office of United States Senator. In a study of all Senators between 1947 and 1957, Donald R. Matthews (1960) found both Democrats and Republicans to be almost entirely from the upper and middle classes, and therefore not distinguishable in gross socioeconomic comparisons. In terms of fathers' specific occupations, however, some differences were evident: Republican Senators were more often sons of ministers, manufacturers, publishers; Democratic Senators' fathers were more often lawyers, doctors, professors, working journalists, merchants, contractors, insurance and real-estate agents, bankers. The slight differences in status perhaps evident in these lists were clearer among those few Senators "born to industrial wage earners." Whereas Republicans' wage-earning fathers were more likely to hold "quasi-middle-class jobs"—printers or barbers—Democrats' fathers held lower-status jobs. (Democratic Senators themselves tended to be more highly educated than Republican Senators, however.) Recent data on Con-

67

gressmen indicate that these rather slight background differences between Democrats and Republicans still hold, although Congress as a whole has become a little less socially exclusive (*Congressional Quarterly*, 1975).

Jeanne Knutson (1974b) studied not only Democratic and Republican politicians but also Peace and Freedom party members and Communists to the left, American Independents and Nazis to the right —107 people in all, identified by their own organizations as "members of the governing bodies" of their parties in Los Angeles County. On a large variety of personality measures, Knutson found the Democrats and Republicans clumping together most of the time, quite distinct from members of those parties either farther left or farther right. Only on two personality variables did she find significant differences between Democrats and Republicans: authoritarianism and "threat orientation," the latter measuring a "paranoid perspective" short of genuinely pathological paranoia. The Republicans were notably more authoritarian and paranoid than the Democrats. But overall, both Democrats and Republicans appeared to be relatively "self-actualizing or at least minimally growth oriented"—that is, psychologically competent—whereas those farther right "are *highly* characterized by a misanthropic, intolerant, dogmatic, threatened viewpoint." The leftist party leaders "can be consistently characterized as cognitively open, tolerant of ambiguity and of others, empathic, unthreatened and trusting."

These descriptions begin to sound like earlier descriptions of rightists as paranoid nuts and of leftists as psychological supermen, except for one final qualification that Knutson makes: the political party leaders she studied are on the whole much less dogmatic, authoritarian, and intolerant of ambiguity than are samples of the non-politician population. Thus, although in comparison with each other the rightist leaders are *relatively* more misanthropic, etc., and the leftists *relatively* more trusting, etc., with politicians of the two major parties falling somewhere in between, no group of political leaders qualifies as truly abnormal on any measures where comparison with the general population is possible. The Nazis come the closest, with distinctly higher scores on both dogmatism and authoritarianism than Knutson's common-man sample; but even the Nazis are, somewhat surprisingly, more tolerant of ambiguity than the population at large.

Another comparison of Democratic and Republican politicians gives a slightly different picture than Knutson's study, partly because different personality measures were used and perhaps partly because

68

a statewide sample, with somewhat more highly placed individuals than Knutson's Los Angeles party leaders, was questioned. Edmond Costantini and Kenneth Craik (1972) persuaded a sample of Congressmen, state legislators, national convention delegates, and county committee chairmen from throughout California to fill out a standard personality measure, the Adjective Check List. Among males, Republicans tended toward a comparatively tightly controlled emotional structure, averaging higher scores than Democrats on scales designed to measure emphasis on self-control, order, endurance, and personal adjustment (as well as, somewhat unexpectedly, nurturance—the desire to help other people). Democratic males were higher on autonomy, lability (emotional changeableness), exhibition, and aggression—mainly indicating relative freedom of emotional expression. In that regard, the average Democrat appears to resemble Knutson's picture of the leftist as being more open and "unthreatened," but the typical Republican politician could hardly be described as paranoid.

POLITICAL WOMEN AND POLITICAL MEN

Costantini and Craik had enough women in the sample to analyze their scores separately and to compare them with those of the men. Most of the personality characteristics measured showed no differences between Republican and Democratic women party leaders; the Republican women were slightly higher on defensiveness and on need for order. In most regards, Republican and Democratic women combined were similar to Republican and Democratic men combined. 69 They all ranked high in confidence, dominance, and achievement motivation (just as influential politicians had ranked high in self-esteem in Sniderman's study, and in power and achievement motivation in the Browning and Jacob research). The women did differ from the men on two measures: they scored higher on a scale called "Counseling Readiness," involving willingness to acknowledge personal problems, and they checked a larger number of positive adjectives as describing themselves. Costantini and Craik interpret these differences (somewhat speculatively) as suggesting that "while both sets of leaders are unusually capable, outgoing, socially skilled, and persistent personas, the female party leaders try harder and worry more." Subtler differences on other scales indicate that the women "tend to express their predominantly forceful, effective, socially ascendant style in a relatively earnest, sobersided, and ambivalent manner, while the male leaders express the same predominant style in a more easygoing, direct, and uncomplicated way." This may, of course, reflect a prevailing assumption among male party leaders that only sobersided and apparently deep-thinking women should be given political responsibility; or it may reflect the unwillingness of direct and easygoing women to subject themselves to the discrimination that women have traditionally faced in politics.

The influence of such differing expectations and social pressures on the careers of male and female politicians is stressed in a recent study by Jeane Kirkpatrick (1974). She compared a sample of fortysix female state legislators from all over the nation with a sample of forty male state legislators. The members of both samples had served at least one term and had been chosen as being "effective" legislators, so they were by no means representative of all male or female politicians. However, their similarities and differences may still be instructive. Both men and women were more geographically stable than the average American, typically having grown up in the town where they were born. About half the members of both samples had parents (often both mother and father) who were active in community affairs —a much higher proportion than for nonpoliticians' parents. Most people in both groups were high in self-esteem, were strongly achievement-oriented, and were concerned with the welfare of their community. However, the women stressed the community-welfare motive for entering politics more exclusively; the men were likely in addition to emphasize the value of political office in advancing their careers. (The men in Costantini and Craik's study were also more likely than the women to mention such motives for entering politics as "to be close to influential people, to achieve power and influence, to make business contacts, and to enhance one's prestige.")

70

Kirkpatrick sees this one major difference between male and female politicians as traceable not to underlying personality differences but to the socially determined life patterns of men and women in our society. Most of the women in the sample were married and had entered politics only after their children were school-age or older. By that time, it was rather late to be considering a career beyond or in addition to political office; and, with working husbands, the women usually had few pressing financial needs. In some ways, as Kirkpatrick notes, these circumstances "protect women from many of the temptations associated with public officeholding," or, in the words of a participant in the study, "We women supported by our husbands are free to be virtuous." But Kirkpatrick further points out that the same circumstances that make economic motives less important to women legislators also make women less likely to *become* legislators. Politics is often a hard life, and the impulse to help advance community goals may not be sufficient motivation to face its demands.

The important role of circumstance in promoting or frustrating women's political activity leads to a more general point: *any* individual's active involvement as a political candidate, particularly for higher office, is in large part a function of circumstance. Few people consciously plot, from an early age, how they are going to become a legislator or Governor or President, and actually achieve that goal. Much more often, a person happens to get out of the army at just the time that a party is looking for a nice young veteran to be a candidate, or he happens to know someone in the right position, or she is beginning to have a little spare time away from the children when a primary contest opens for a seat from which an incumbent is resigning. Under these circumstances, the search for personality characteristics that distinguish politicians from the rest of the population resembles to some extent the search for a clear-cut "criminal personality." Many people break the law; the relative few who get caught and imprisoned may be distinctive not for any particular personality characteristic but mainly for incompetence or sheer bad luck.

Having begun by comparing politicians with paranoid schizophrenics and having almost concluded by comparing politicians with criminals, I do not want readers to forget that, in between, politicians were observed to share many worthy personality characteristics. At the same time, I want to stress that many people outside of political office share any set of personality characteristics that may be found among those in office. Not everyone can become a Senator or a President, and many people whose personalities fit them for the job never get the opportunity.

71

political types

The romance of political campaigning apparently does not extend very far into political officeholding. For every novel or movie on the actual performance of a politician at his job, dozens focus on nominating conventions and campaigns. The same is true of empirical research: we have far more data on the kinds of people who run for office than on the patterns of performance they display once they get into the office.

Performance on the job is crucially important to the operation of our government, and it too is affected in significant ways by the personalities of the officeholders. Politicians do not, once they are elected, all behave in the same way. Nor do their behavioral differences depend entirely on the composition of the constituency that elected them or on the position they hold. The personality characteristics they developed before attaining office will influence their performance while in office; their experiences in office may also affect their personalities in ways that influence their further performance in office or later. How do these mutually influencing processes work?

LASSWELL'S TYPES

The psychological analysis of politicians' behavior in office is yet another research area fathered by Harold Lasswell. In his *Psychopathology and Politics* (1930), he proposed that in terms of their major political concerns, at least three specialized types of political figures can be discerned: the agitator, the administrator, and the theorist. The *agitator*, exemplified by the Old Testament prophets (who were often centrally involved in politics), is concerned with arousing "the emotional response of the public" in regard to public policy. The *administrator*, exemplified by Herbert Hoover, is most concerned with "the co-ordination of effort in continuing activity"—concerned, that is, not so much with obtaining a particular response from the general public as with obtaining an ongoing, smoothly flowing pattern of response from the particular individuals with whom he works. The *theorist*, exemplified by Karl Marx, is never clearly defined, except in describing Marx himself: "Marx wanted unreserved admiration for the products of his mind. . . . It was more important to attain theoretical completeness than to modify his technique of social intercourse." The theorist, that is, is less interested in moving others to immediate action than in developing a distinctive and sound, even "impregnable," set of political ideas.

Lasswell suggested that various combinations of these three types are possible (as with Lenin, who displayed aspects of all three), and that other types may be proposed. But these three appeared to him to be the most useful categories for organizing his studies of politicians. It was into these categories that he assigned the politically inclined psychiatric patients on whom he had data, as well as a number of politicians who were curious enough about psychoanalytic techniques to volunteer to participate in free-association sessions with him. What Lasswell wanted to know was whether politicians who fell into a par-

72

ticular behavioral category shared any aspects of psychopathology, early family history, or general personality traits.

Lasswell's case histories are fascinating. One agitator, who had hated his brother since childhood, repressed the hatred to avoid guilt feelings. He then "generalized his own prohibition against brother-hatred to all society, and identified himself with the workers and with humanity at large, serving a poverty-stricken congregation, spending his own money on the work of the church, adopting the socialist dream of a brotherly state, and demanding the abolition of fratricidal war." Another reported having been seduced by his older brother as a child; as an adult he attained success as a crusading political journalist but began having delusions that "he was a party to the Teapot Dome scandal" and that his house was bugged. A woman active in the early women's rights movement "came to the physician complaining that she was constantly bothered by blushing, stage fright, uncertainty, palpitations of the heart and weeping spells." Her problems were traced to early sex play with a female nurse and to a strong father-identification, both contributing to a powerful penis envy. An administrator Lasswell studied was passive at home and very active on the job. But when a new chief executive limited his scope at work, he took a married woman as his mistress. This man dreamed about himself as "a giant automobile of untold horse-power, whose body was a light French coach of the rococo period."

From these case histories, Lasswell moved to more general psychological characterizations of his types. Agitators are "strongly narcissistic types," typically with "a strong homosexual component" that is displaced onto the community at large. Administrators also displace their emotions, but because of "excessive preoccupation with specific individuals in the family circle," they tend to be more concerned with their relations to specific co-workers, both superiors and underlings, rather than with their effect on people in general. Their sexual problems seem to focus on active heterosexual behavior rather than on homosexual passivity. Theorists remain undiscussed in the abstract, and no clear examples of case histories are provided.

Although Lasswell's attempts to trace political behaviors back to early childhood origins are intriguing, several problems are apparent. One is simply the kinds of subjects he used. Even those he interviewed outside of hospitals seem often to have been quite handicapped psychologically by their repressed conflicts. If neurotic and psychotic symptoms were as widespread among our leaders as among Lasswell's case histories, the government would surely have collapsed long ago.

73

Lasswell did suggest, tantalizingly, that "another group of administrators is recruited from among those who have passed smoothly through their developmental crises" and that these administrators "display an impersonal interest in the task of organization itself." But Lasswell provided no case histories to illustrate his speculation, although in his later writings he often discussed such administrators in general terms.

Another problem is Lasswell's early insistence on reducing virtually all explanation of political behavior patterns to childhood sexual conflict, often involving traumatic sexual experiences. Lasswell in this regard was being more Freudian than Freud. By the time Lasswell's book was published, Freud had recognized both that psychoanalytic patients were inclined to exaggerate substantially the occurrence of childhood seductions and that infantile sexual demands did not remain all-powerful in many adults. Freud came to feel that people were often more oriented toward current external reality, and more capable of dealing with it, then he had originally assumed. Lasswell's later concern with "democratic leadership" (for example, Lasswell, 1948) in some ways reflects this increasing Freudian emphasis on the ego.

Finally, Lasswell's categorizations of political figures never quite attain a solid logical or empirical basis. Some politicians do function to "agitate" the general public more than anything else, and many people spend a good deal of time administrating. But are those the crucial qualities by which political behavior patterns should be categorized? Lasswell himself suggested that "there are thousands of political roles," and he attempted to differentiate a few subcategories of agitators and administrators (for example, the "inventive or driving administrator" versus the "conscientious, overscrupulous official"). But without a sound system for developing categories, whether based on logical organization of behavioral characteristics or on careful and detailed study of politicians in action, Lasswell leaves us with only a few common-sense groupings of rather uncommon cases.

BARBER'S TYPES

James David Barber (1965) has to a considerable degree avoided or coped successfully with these problems. His subjects were currently active state legislators, all serving their first term in the Connecticut House of Representatives. Barber interviewed twenty-seven of them at length concerning their lives and their perceptions of the legislative role. He also obtained answers from more than one-half of the freshman legislators serving in the same legislative session to lengthy questionnaires on personal backgrounds and on attitudes toward legislative activities. Barber relied on a wide variety of psychological concepts, particularly those dealing with the individual's current self-concepts and their origins, rather than depending entirely on early Freudian theory. And he developed, on a logical basis, a system for categorizing legislators that he then substantiated with empirical data. The result is an impressive mixture of quantitative and qualitative approaches to the psychology of political behavior.

Barber's system for categorizing legislators is based on the interaction of two variables: the legislator's *level of activity* in the legislature, and his *willingness to return* for at least three two-year terms beyond the present one. Barber sees the activity–passivity variable as "the one most fundamental characteristic of a person's life style," and it certainly has played a key role in various personality theories. Barber measured it in the legislators by tabulating the number of bills they introduced, the number of comments they made in their own committees and before other committees, and the amount of speaking they did on the floor of the house. He then divided the legislators into high and low participants. The willingness-to-return variable was thought of not as showing whether the legislator really would keep coming back, but as an indication of his general attitude toward legislative participation. It was measured simply by asking the legislator, after his first session in the legislature had ended: "As of today, how likely is it that you would be willing to serve three or more terms in the Assembly in the future?"

75

Barber thus developed a fourfold categorization of legislative types, shown in Table 2 with the percentage of legislators in his sample that fall into each category.

The *Lawmakers* resemble those administrators whom Lasswell (1930) saw as free of major psychological problems and therefore as rather uninteresting. Barber, however, regarded them as in many ways the most interesting of the four types. Most important, they are the people who conduct the main business of the legislature. Their legislative work is one of their central interests, and they do it with care and enthusiasm. They are able to focus on whatever task is at hand, and they show relatively little reality distortion concerning either themselves or their legislative tasks. The Lawmakers typically come from rather large communities with an "active and educated" electorate. Their personal backgrounds often involve parents and other relatives whose political interest and activity are high, and they themselves have long been concerned with elective politics for its own sake, rather than merely as a means of attaining other goals.

Table 2
Barber's categories of legislative types

		ACTIVITY	
		HIGH	LOW
WILLINGNESS TO RETURN	HIGH	Lawmakers (34%)	Spectators (31%)
	LOW	Advertisers (17%)	Reluctants (18%)

Source: James David Barber, The lawmakers. New Haven: Yale University Press, 1965, p. 20.

Much of this description may sound like just what you'd expect of a legislator. But keep in mind that only about one-third of Barber's sample displayed these sterling qualities. Further, that proportion may be exaggerated, since Connecticut has a better-educated and more politically sophisticated populace than many states, and since the particular legislative term during which Barber conducted his research was widely acknowledged as one of the most productive and progressive in many years.

Barber had more difficulty isolating key psychological characteristics in the Lawmakers than in his other categories. The Lawmakers display diverse interests and diverse capabilities, sharing mainly their strong political orientation and their high level of psychological competence. Barber did suggest several important features of Lawmakers' personalities, however. They are very achievement-oriented, with their particular focus being to see that well-thought-out bills are carefully considered and eventually passed by the legislature. They possess "unusual empathic abilities"—that is, they are sensitive to the feelings and perceptions of other legislators. They see their selves as still developing and are therefore willing and ready to profit from experience and from their observation of others' behavior, rather than becoming discouraged or angry at temporary setbacks. They appear not to have carried into adulthood any heavy load of infantile anxiety or

76

displaced hostility. The Lawmakers are not quite perfect; Barber suggested that they sometimes overemphasize reason to the neglect of the emotional appeals that might win followers to their cause, and they may push too quickly to adopt a bill that meets their personal standards of quality even though it has received insufficient consideration by the legislature. But all in all, the Lawmakers are the backbone of good government.

The *Advertisers* superficially resemble the Lawmakers. Indeed, in some respects it is hard to tell the two apart. The Advertisers also are high in legislative activity, although they tend to skimp on their homework and become known more as speechmakers than as authors of significant legislation. They too come from the larger towns, perhaps particularly those with a rapidly expanding electorate. Most often they are young lawyers for whom the legislative post is one of the few legitimate ways of advertising themselves, of letting the world know they're "alive and available," in Barber's words. This is the crucial difference between them and the Lawmakers: the Advertisers are not much interested in making a career of elective politics. They want to increase their law practice or build up their real-estate business or maybe get a nice appointive position later on. They see the legislative office "as a burden, not a prize, a means to self-advancement, not an end in itself."

Psychologically, the Advertisers might be best described as high both in need for achievement (as are the Lawmakers) and in fear of failure (as distinct from the Lawmakers' confidence in their own abilities). The Advertisers are ambitious, but they are afraid others will be more successful than they or that they will fail altogether. Their ambition drives them into politics, but they often feel guilty about the compromises and manipulations that they engage in to attain political success. They alleviate this guilt partly by emphasizing their own suffering, partly by seeing others as sharing their guilt. To maintain their self-esteem, they are highly critical of other legislators: "One looks in vain," Barber wrote, "for compliments of others unmarred by derogatory comments." They also protect themselves by maintaining indifference toward the bills they are working on. The work itself is a good way of coping with anxiety, but if it doesn't produce much, they can always convince themselves that it wasn't very important anyway, and that they are bound for better things than being a legislator.

The *Spectators* are the reverse of the Advertisers in terms of both key variables: they are low in legislative activity, but very willing to return

77

to the legislature again and again. They seem to be in it for fun. They sit back and enjoy the legislative debates; they are charmed by the Governor's inaugural speech; they love the parties and receptions for legislators. They could, of course, go to parties back home and watch the Governor's inauguration on television; but being legislators gives them a special status during all these proceedings, and that status is a major source of their enjoyment. As Barber wrote, the Spectators' "main pleasures in politics seem to come from being appreciated, approved, loved, and respected by others." The office itself is one indication of such approval and respect. Many other indications are likely to come the Spectators' way while they are in office, whether from other legislators, from members of the executive branch seeking legislative support, or from lobbyists and constituents.

Spectators typically come from small towns where candidates for time-consuming political positions are scarce and where the main problem is therefore simply finding someone willing to run. Spectators are not only willing but quite agreeable to whatever the party leaders suggest, in order to gain and protect those sources of appreciation, approval, love, and respect. They are not likely to regard themselves as highly competent in legislative affairs; indeed, they typically have strong doubts about their own worth. But they try to avoid thinking about those doubts. The legislature serves both as a distraction from their private concerns and a source of reassurance, through voter support and through the direct approval of various high-status individuals, that they are in fact better people than they had thought. Spectators need not perform well in order to get this approval; if they try to perform at all, they may display their incompetence. So they keep quiet, do as the party leaders and/or their constituents ask, and devote most of their attention to searching out any indications of approval they can find.

The Spectators' basic pattern of behavior thus appears to be derived from a low need for achievement and a high need for affiliation, distinguishing them from both the Lawmakers and the Advertisers, and from a high fear of failure, shared with the Advertisers. This pattern would not seem at first glance to be a good basis for legislative contributions. But Barber is kind: "Their orientation as applauding members of the legislative audience helps to maintain an atmosphere of affection, esteem, and respect which is encouraging to those who carry on the main tasks." "Their optimism, mild humor and politeness help to smooth over the interpersonal hostilities introduced by con-

78

flicting opinions on bills." The Spectators thus serve, in technical terms (Bales and Slater, 1955; see page 84), as social-emotional facilitators rather than as task specialists. They do not do this intentionally, since their primary concern is to maintain their own self-esteem. At times they may even overdo their enthusiasm for the workings of this marvelous, status-enhancing legislature. But the cynical and aggressive Advertisers will trim their sails. Indeed, if the Spectators did not occasionally bubble over from good cheer into what Barber describes as "maudlin sentimentality," the Advertisers would have hardly any useful role at all.

The *Reluctants,* finally, are those legislators who are both low in legislative activity and little interested in a future legislative career. They are also from small towns where candidates are hard to find, but whereas the Spectators go willingly to the legislature, the Reluctants are typically drafted to serve, and go mainly out of a sense of duty. They are often elderly, retired, or partially incapacitated physically, so that for some time they have played no really useful role in their home communities. They thus have free time for legislative service; they are usually well-known in their hometowns through earlier occupational contacts and community activities; and they feel some obligation to serve if no one else is available to do the job. Their sense of duty seems to stem mainly from their strong identification with the community and its past (including their parents' role in it) and from their concern with maintaining traditional social virtues, including the prevention of conflict. Reluctants disapprove of what they consider political wheeling and dealing, and believe the legislature needs people like themselves who can insist on proper procedure and calm consideration of the issues.

79

The Reluctants are difficult to categorize in terms of achievement or affiliation needs. They are not concerned with advancing their careers, since those careers are already largely behind them. They are concerned that they be respected, but not that they be loved. In psychoanalytic terms, they seem distinctly superego-dominated, but with particular reference to the ego ideal (wanting to live up to the high standards of their parents and to the praiseworthy traditions of their communities) rather than to the conscience (wanting to avoid or alleviate guilt for past transgressions).

The Reluctants may be a special product of the small backwater New England town, and perhaps of similar towns in other regions of the country, where party competition is low or absent. They may even have largely disappeared from those towns, as one-man–one-vote decisions have taken legislative seats away from low-population community preserves and assigned them to larger areas where Reluctants would have few personal acquaintances. Perhaps they will not be much missed, since they find it difficult to keep up with the speed and complexity of modern legislative processes and are rarely able to do more than "restrain those who are in a hurry to get things done." But Barber sees such restraint as, in its own limited way, a useful function. The Spectators and the Advertisers are not much concerned with the rules; they have their own gratifications to obtain as best they can. The Lawmakers learn the rules in order to get their bills adopted as speedily as possible, but they may manipulate the rules unfairly for the same purpose. The Reluctants, without being overly passionate about it but with a persistence rooted in their own characters, insist that the rules be obeyed, that debate be fair and honest, and that conflict center on the issues rather than on personalities. Perhaps in view of all the contrasting examples in state and national government in recent years, citizen groups should back a few Reluctants for each legislative session, just to provide a reminder to other legislators of the standards they themselves should be observing.

Barber's categorization of legislative types cannot be taken as a model for all legislative or governmental participants. The Connecticut legislature and the Connecticut electorate differ from those of other states in many ways, including legislative roles; length of legislative term; economic, educational, and ethnic backgrounds of voters; and community and statewide political traditions. The particular legislature Barber studied was unusual even for Connecticut, in terms of its increased number of Democrats and of first-termers as well as in terms of its legislative output. Also, the neatness of Barber's categorizations is somewhat suspect. As he himself commented, "At a certain stage in the development of a typology . . . the world begins to arrange itself in fourfold tables." There is surely more diversity among legislators than those tables and their author are able to accommodate.

KIRKPATRICK'S TYPES

Some of this diversity is suggested in another fourfold table of legislative types, this one devised by Jeane Kirkpatrick (1974) to categorize her women legislators (Table 3). Kirkpatrick found no one resembling

Table 3
Personality and role: a typology

POLITICAL TYPE	PREFERENCE VALUE	GOAL	INTERPERSONAL STYLE
Leader	Power	Impact on total process	Eclectic
Personalizer	Affection	Acceptance and approval	Ingratiation
Moralizer	Rectitude	Increased righteousness of political process and output	Ideological affirmation
Problem-Solver	Multi-value (affection/ rectitude/ power)	Community service	Purposive socializing

Source: Jeane J. Kirkpatrick, *Political woman*. New York: Basic Books, 1974, p. 174.

Barber's Advertisers in her sample, apparently because none of the women she interviewed were young lawyers who needed publicity to advance their careers. Her *Personalizers* are very much like Barber's Spectators in their search for affection from other legislators. They are apparently somewhat more serious about their legislative duties than the Spectators, but that may only be because Kirkpatrick, in selecting a sample of *effective* legislators, got the most serious Personalizers available. The same explanation may apply to Barber's Reluctants and to Kirkpatrick's *Moralizers*: both stress superego concerns (the Moralizers often to the point of superego-tripping), but the Moralizers seem to pursue their moral goals in the legislature much more energetically than the Reluctants. Kirkpatrick probably would not have considered as effective enough for her study any female Reluctants who were as limited by age and infirmity as Barber's sample. Also, as previously noted, women who have no financial worries or outside career goals may feel more free to stress their moral concerns, even at the expense of reelection, than male legislators of comparable age.

Kirkpatrick's remaining categories appear to be subdivisions of

81

Barber's Lawmakers. Kirkpatrick noted that her subjects, who had already served at least one legislative term and sometimes several, would have had more time to find a comfortable legislative role than would Barber's first-term legislators. Some of Barber's highly capable Lawmakers, we might speculate, would realize after a term or two that they function best and feel most gratification in directing the efforts of other legislators; they would thus become *Leaders* in Kirkpatrick's typology. Other Lawmakers might find continued attention to legislative issues, at the committee or individual level rather than in a leadership role, to be most satisfying; they would be Kirkpatrick's *Problem-Solvers.*

Barber's and Kirkpatrick's tables in combination appear to be a good beginning in organizing our understanding of what it means to be a practicing politician. As other researchers begin to devote a similar degree of psychological sensitivity to the study of diverse political roles, the number of identifiable categories will surely increase along with our understanding of the personal significance of political officeholding.

political leadership

"Our leaders" is an honorific title more than a descriptive one. Many of the public officials grouped under that title seldom or never lead at all. They may serve useful functions, or they may sit quietly collecting salaries, but by and large they don't bother even trying to summon the citizenry either to engage in common cause or to support major public endeavors.

Research such as Barber's and Kirkpatrick's tells us what sorts of legislators are likely to work hard and why. Beyond that, however, it tells us little about the characteristics that may transform some of those hard-working legislators into outstanding public leaders.

Political scientists are by no means unaware of the importance of leadership, having theorized about it since the earliest days of the field. (Political leadership is one of those topics first given theoretical form by Plato.) But they have done hardly any empirical research on it. Psychologists have done only a little more, although they have collected a great deal of data on leadership in artificial laboratory-formed groups and in business organizations. A few attempts have been made to relate the psychological research findings to the theories of the political scientists (most notably by Verba, 1961), but the results are limited by the remoteness of the original research situations from the actual political scene.

Early leadership research was aimed mainly toward relating specific personality variables to specific displays of leadership, in the hope that the qualities broadly characteristic of leaders in general would thereby be revealed. Following this research strategy, each new study seemed to reveal yet another list of leadership qualities, usually different from and often contradictory to previous lists. By the time such simple correlational studies were abandoned, only a few personal qualities still appeared likely to be found in most leaders: a high rate of energy output, alertness, originality, personal integrity, self-confidence, decisiveness, knowledge, fluency of speech (Gibb, 1969; Stogdill, 1974). Leaders are likely to possess these qualities to a higher degree than followers; but how much of each a person needs in order to be a leader, and which qualities need be present only in minimal amounts, is not clear from the research. Nor is it clear whether leaders simply need more of each quality than anyone among the led, or whether particular combinations of certain intensities are necessary. Furthermore, active political participants generally are likely to share these qualities; do political leaders then come from those with even higher amounts than most politicians?

A strong reaction against this disappointing leadership research developed during the 1950s. Personality differences were denounced and ignored; the *situation* was proclaimed the dominant force in determining who would lead. The earlier research had been akin to the "great man" line of historical thinking; the reaction more nearly resembled "impersonal historical force" theories. No one, according to this approach, could be considered a natural leader because no particular individual qualities were distinctive of all leaders. Craft unions demand one kind of leader, industrial unions another, the navy yet another (Stogdill, 1974). The sort of person who leads in the Connecticut legislature may be a failure in South Carolina or in the White House. This view of leadership makes considerable sense, and research showed its validity in a wide variety of instances. But it rapidly became as overstated as the original personality-oriented research. There was, after all, that small but consistent list of psychological characteristics that recurred in leaders whatever the situation being studied. There were some qualities a leader just could not get along without. Not many groups are likely to choose as their leader a stupid, inde-

83

cisive ninny who never does a lick of work for the group unless he is selling them out. If they do choose him, out of their own stupidity or ignorance, they are not likely to keep him long.

Almost inevitably from the two extremes a middle view of leadership has emerged, emphasizing the interaction of personality and situation (Gibb, 1969). This revised view includes among other things an appreciation of the diverse roles of leaders and a recognition of how certain leadership traits promote greater group effectiveness in some circumstances but not in others (Fiedler, 1965). It also allows for the possibility of more than one kind of leader in any particular group. Indeed, at times this view not only allows but insists on the presence of two leaders per group, their functions suitably differentiated.

TASK AND SOCIAL-EMOTIONAL SPECIALIZATION

The basic differentiation in group leadership, first clearly expressed in the work of Robert F. Bales and Philip Slater (1955), is between the *task specialist* and the *social-emotional specialist*. Repeatedly in studies of laboratory-formed small groups, one person has emerged as most likely to determine the direction of activities involved in the performance of the group's assigned tasks; another person typically has emerged as being responsible for promoting positive social relationships and alleviating negative interactions within the group. Furthermore, the task leader and the social-emotional leader often seem to acknowledge the usefulness of one another's roles (as do other members of the group) and more-or-less consciously reinforce one another's functions. Getting the job done is enough work for one leader, the early work on the Bales-Slater differentiation indicated. The task leader can't spend much time placating the group members on whose toes he steps in the process, so he needs someone else to cope with hurt feelings and momentary surges of hostility. The two leadership roles are seldom formally recognized, but in the laboratory groups they usually emerge whether or not anybody identifies them.

84

The applications of this differentiation to political leadership seem readily apparent. Some Congressmen acquire reputations as experts on taxes or armaments; others are known as "Great Compromisers" or as inspiring speakers. Barber's Lawmakers and Kirkpatrick's Problem-Solvers are clearly task specialists, while Barber's Spectators and Kirkpatrick's Personalizers function mainly as social-emotional specialists.

But it doesn't take long to see the limitations in such applications of the double leadership role to politics. Many Congressmen can be cited who have been widely regarded as both task specialists and social-emotional specialists. Sam Ervin, authority on the Constitution and skilled moderator of the Senate, is one outstanding recent example; the few legislators categorized by Kirkpatrick as Leaders are others. Most twentieth-century Presidents have to a considerable degree fulfilled both roles—as a truly effective national leader must. What special dispensation frees political leaders from the apparent rule that the two leadership functions must be served by separate individuals, or perhaps requires that the two functions must be so united in political leaders?

Rather than special dispensations for politicians, what seem to be involved are special circumstances within the artificial groups originally studied. Sidney Verba (1961) describes the situation in these initially leaderless groups as follows:

. . . individuals who do not value highly interpersonal control by others [that is, young adult college students] are brought together in groups where the exercise of such control has no external backing from some extra-group hierarchy. The members are unknown to each other and have no apparent status differences such that one member would be expected to exert more influence in the group than another. Under these circumstances it is no wonder that the most active group member, even if he contributes the most to group performance, will tend to be rejected by the group on socio-emotional criteria. His control attempts are viewed as arbitrary and as direct personal challenges.

85

LEADER LEGITIMACY

Peter Burke (1972) has demonstrated that if the experimental situation is changed so that the task emphasis of a small group's emergent leader is *legitimized*, in the sense that the group task he is trying to get accomplished is recognized as important and appropriate by the group as a whole, no clear differentiation develops between task-oriented and social-emotional roles. Only if the group cares little about its assigned task does it seem to resent a taskmaster enough to need a separate social-emotional specialist as well. Studies by Hollander and Julian (1970) further suggest that if a leader is elected rather than appointed, therefore presumably giving him greater legitimacy in the group's eyes, the group is much more favorable to his being a tough taskmaster—thus again not requiring an additional leader to soften the blows of the whip.

Our political leaders are, of course, usually elected through a process widely recognized as legitimate. They are often engaged in business that the public itself regards as very legitimate, in terms of its being necessary to the functioning of the Republic and important to the satisfaction of their own needs. We should not be surprised, then, that the task-versus-emotion differentiation is much less clear among public leaders than it is in small experimental groups of college students.

One further complication in all this, however, is the margin of victory in the leader's election. Hollander and Julian have shown experimentally that when a leader is elected with strong backing from his constituents, he not only can function without having a social-emotional leader to supplement his guidance; he also *feels* able to get away with plenty more, and operates on that basis. Strongly backed elected leaders in Hollander and Julian's laboratory groups were significantly more likely than either appointed leaders or weakly backed elected leaders to ignore group sentiments in making decisions. They were also less likely even to "show a recognition of the viewpoint of the team and to conciliate differences." And they used fewer words in justifying their unilateral decisions to the group.

That is how the concept of an "electoral mandate" is translated into laboratory behavior. The absence of such a mandate is probably even more important in real life than in the lab, because heated disputes and strong ideological convictions among at least some of the electorate may further confuse the interpretation of whatever messages a winning candidate tries to get from a close victory margin. On the other hand, the presence of an "electoral mandate," as the winning candidate sees it, is doubtless reinforced in real life by the easy availability of campaign money, enthusiastic hangers-on, and other prerequisites of a popular candidacy. The results are different in intensity and importance, but not apparently in their basic nature, from those observed in the laboratory. Whether it is called "the arrogance of power" (Fulbright, 1966) or "idiosyncrasy credit" (Hollander and Julian, 1970), the leader's feeling of freedom to ignore his followers' opinions seems to have been sharply intensified by the Johnson landslide of 1964 and the Nixon landslide of 1972.

The motives of Presidents and other major political leaders are difficult to assess quantitatively. In lieu of adequate quantitative

86

data, most studies of genuine political leaders (particularly of the sort that Max Weber originally identified as *charismatic* leaders, those who arouse strong emotional responses in their followers [Weber, 1918, English translation, 1946; see also Katz, 1973]) will probably continue to be conducted on an individual, biographical basis, as in the next chapter. What we need most from quantitative researchers to supplement these psychobiographies are not more lists of the necessary personality characteristics for a good leader—prepackaged media campaigns can fake those characteristics enough to befuddle many voters anyway—but more studies of the Hollander and Julian sort, showing how the processes through which a person becomes and continues as leader affect the expression of his personality characteristics in behavior. We have seen in our recent history not only how landslide-elected leaders may feel free to expand undeclared wars and to shape the American government in their own image, but also how an appointed President may feel sufficiently free, through sheer public acclamation, to pardon a disgraced ex-President of all criminal wrongdoing. We could use better ideas on how to find good leaders, but even more we need better ideas on how to make them simultaneously responsive to their own inner standards and to the highest impulses of their followers.

87

4

great men.

psychobiographies
of outstanding
politicians

During the 1964 Presidential campaign, *Fact* magazine published what it called "the most intensive character analysis ever made of a living human being." The "analysis" consisted of questionnaire responses from 2417 United States psychiatrists, who responded to the question, "Do you believe Barry Goldwater is psychologically fit to serve as President of the United States?" Every psychiatrist in the country was sent the questionnaire; four-fifths chose not to answer at all. Of those who did reply, slightly less than one-half said Goldwater was not fit; slightly more than one-quarter said he was; and the remainder said they didn't know. In their comments, the psychiatrists ranged from calling Goldwater a "compensated schizophrenic" and a "megalomaniac," to describing him as an "anal character" or as merely "immature," to complimenting him for being a "thoughtful, capable person" who was "well adjusted and attuned to reality." The psychiatrists were not asked to comment on the psychological fitness of Goldwater's opponent, Lyndon Johnson, but a few did, usually negatively. One remarked that whichever candidate won, "It is certain that we will have an immature, unstable, exhibitionistic, unpredictable, and probably dangerous man for President for the next four years."

Fact's character analysis of Goldwater had several results. Goldwater's overwhelming loss to Johnson was probably not one of them,

Senator Barry Goldwater speaks to a divided crowd during the 1964 Presidential campaign.

although the *Fact* analysis may have contributed a little. *Fact's* own collapse can be attributed in part to Barry Goldwater's libel suit against the magazine; he eventually collected $75,000 (Rogow, 1970). A further consequence was that several psychiatric and psychological professional associations and journals issued statements highly critical of "mail order psychiatry." This last effect may have been the most significant one, since (depending on one's perspective) the professional groups' statements may well have either discouraged the writing of a number of serious analyses of our political leaders' personalities or encouraged the writers of such analyses to be more careful in their assessments.

Several public statements about the *Fact* treatment of Goldwater were so hostile in tone that they seemed to oppose all psychological studies of prominent individuals. Unless a person spent a good deal of time on a psychotherapist's couch, the argument went, the psychotherapist was in no position to draw inferences about his personality. And if the person *did* spend time on the therapist's couch, professional ethics would prevent the therapist from publishing any identifiable information about him. Thus the public would be effectively barred from reading any psychological study of any well-known political leader.

Fortunately in certain cases and unfortunately in others, these strictures have not been observed by all professional analyzers of personality. (They appear to have been pretty much ignored by non-professional analyzers of personality.) It is fortunate that some such analyses have continued to be written because we badly need to increase our understanding of how our top leaders function on the job, particularly in the role of President, and what kinds of leaders are likely to function best. The argument has even been made that we should use such information to screen candidates for the Presidency and other high offices. It is unfortunate that certain other analyses have been written, both because they have been done so poorly as to bring this general approach to political personality into even more disrepute than did the *Fact* poll, and because they have unfairly injured the politicians on whom they focused.

Detailed psychological case studies of individual politicians—*psychobiographies,* as they are now often called—do have advantages not enjoyed by the more quantitative approaches of the previous chapter. But the psychobiographer also faces particular problems that are much less formidable in other types of research on personality in politics. The advantages and the problems are best understood through detailed consideration of individual cases; and the individual cases most often studied by psychobiographers, probably because the importance of understanding these cases well somewhat offsets the difficulties involved, are United States Presidents. We will therefore examine the major studies of the two most "popular" psychobiographical subjects among United States Presidents, Woodrow Wilson and Richard Nixon; then we will consider some of the general issues involved in conducting such research.

psychobiographies of Woodrow Wilson

THE FREUD-BULLITT ANALYSIS

Thomas Woodrow Wilson: A Psychological Study, by Sigmund Freud and William C. Bullitt, was first published in 1967. David Levine's caricature of Woodrow Wilson crucified on a psychoanalytic couch epitomizes public reaction to the book. One might think that a full-scale study of a great American President, co-authored by the founder of psychobiography, Sigmund Freud, would be greeted with acclaim. Instead the book was denounced almost as bitterly as the *Fact* magazine treatment of Barry Goldwater. The prominent psychoanalyst Erik Erikson (1967) agreed with former CIA head Allen Dulles (1966) that the book never should have been written. Pulitzer Prize winning historians Richard Hofstadter (1967) and Barbara Tuchman (1967) described it, respectively, as "a disservice to history" and as "lamentable." At least one official psychiatric journal attacked the book editorially, just as *Fact* magazine had been criticized for the Goldwater attack.

A summary of the book's main themes may not sound all that outrageous. According to Bullitt and Freud,* Wilson had an accepting but rather colorless mother and a demanding but magnificent father. Because the father was such an impressive speaker, so handsome, so well respected as a minister, Wilson identified strongly with him and made him "his great love-object." But since the father sternly insisted that Wilson speak, write, and behave perfectly, Wilson also hated him while completely repressing the hatred: ". . . in all the sixty-eight years of [Wilson's] life we can find no hostile thought or act" directed toward his father. As an adult, Wilson was driven, because of this repressed hostility, "to violent and unreasonable hatreds of men who were to him father representatives . . . he found it difficult to maintain friendly relations with men of superior intellect or position, and preferred to surround himself with women or inferiors." Wilson's identification with his magnificent minister-father gave him a tremendously powerful and "exalted Super-Ego," "made in the image of the Almighty." This superego simultaneously demanded an impossible perfection from Wilson and assured him that "In his unconscious he himself is God. Whatever he does is right because God does it." In addition, because he also had unconsciously identified his father with God, Wilson came to see himself as Christ, the Son of God, and saw his duty as submitting to God's will. "He fears to fight. Therefore, through his identification with Christ he convinces himself that he does not need to fight, that by submitting he will achieve his aims."

Having set forth this basic character structure, Bullitt and Freud went on to discuss Wilson's political behavior in the same terms. Wilson's choice of politics as a career came from his adolescent identifica-

91

* There is considerable controversy as to how great a role Freud had in co-authoring the book. See Erikson (1967) and Strickland (1967) for opposing views.

tion with Gladstone, whom he saw as an even more exalted version of his speechmaking father. His lifelong delight in drawing up organizational constitutions, beginning in boyhood with the Lightfoot Baseball Club, came from his father's insistence on "rules of orderly speech. . . . From the Lightfoots to the League of Nations is a clear line." Wilson's major defeats in life came when his hostility toward father figures drove him into rigidity: first his struggles with Dean West at Princeton, which brought about Wilson's forced resignation from the college's presidency; then his battle with Senator Lodge over the League of Nations Covenant, which ended in Wilson's achieving "almost the exact opposite of that which he wished to accomplish" and his total physical and psychological collapse. "He had never solved the major dilemma of the Oedipus Complex, and in the end he was destroyed by the same incomparable father who created him."

In its bare bones, this analysis of Wilson's character makes a good deal of sense. Every major biographer of Wilson has noted the unusual influence of his father on the young Wilson. His choice of career as a "Christian statesman" was not identical to that of his father but was strikingly similar. Wilson's own later speeches and writings are filled with statements identifying himself as the instrument of God or almost literally as another Christ: for example, "We knew that an altar had been erected upon which that sacrifice could be made more gloriously than upon any other altar that had ever been lifted among mankind, and we desired to offer ourselves as a sacrifice for humanity." Wilson's hostility toward West and toward Lodge seems clearly stronger than the men deserved, and his behavior in the struggle for approval of the League of Nations Covenant was so self-defeating that a psychological explanation seems essential. Why, then, was the Bullitt-Freud analysis greeted with general animosity?

Bias and Unsupported Inference

One reason is the book's hostile tone. Although its central theme is Wilson's difficulty in managing his hostility toward his father, the book itself is suffused with anger. In Erikson's (1967) words, "The items are strung together relentlessly on a thread of vindictiveness which does not let 'little Tommy' [Wilson] get away with anything." As Erikson pointed out, Freud "at least fulfills the first rule of a psychohistorical study" by openly avowing his personal antagonism toward Wilson in his introduction to the book. But Freud added that in studying Wil-

92

son's life he developed "a measure of sympathy . . . mixed with pity" and that his feelings of antipathy "underwent a thorough subjugation." Perhaps, then, it is Bullitt's anger rather than Freud's that permeates the book. Or perhaps Erikson's "first rule" of psychohistory should be broadened from simply admitting bias to avoiding psychohistorical subjects about which one's biases are too one-sided to permit fair treatment.

The authors' anger results not only in the repeated choice of a negative adjective or interpretation when a neutral one would do, but in the virtual omission of Wilson's positive characteristics and achievements. When potentially positive material is mentioned, it is always accompanied by qualifications that yield an overall negative effect:

> Thanks to his early education, Tommy Wilson always tried to be on the side of the angels; he endeavored to think about serious matters; and he attempted to express his thoughts in distinguished phrases. Those were exceptional attributes in the United States after the Civil War, when most men of ability were concentrating on the acquisition of wealth. They gave Tommy Wilson both prestige and an endearing idealism. He was so serious about himself that others took him seriously. To make fun of him was easy; to ignore him was impossible. He was a prig; but a prime prig.

In 1910 (English translation, 1957), Sigmund Freud summed up the reaction of "readers today" to the primitive psychobiographies of the time:

93

> They clothe their aversion in the complaint that a pathographical review of a great man never results in an understanding of his importance and his achievements; and that it is therefore a piece of useless impertinence to make a study of things in him that could just as easily be found in the first person one came across.

According to Freud, such criticism was manifestly unjust, but the Wilson book certainly does not help his case. Although Wilson may have been a "prime prig," he nonetheless made important contributions as a political scientist, classroom teacher, college president, state Governor, and United States President. A book that almost completely ignores the background of these achievements in favor of magnifying Wilson's weaknesses is pathologically pathographic.

Another reason for the book's negative reception is its tone of absolute confidence in describing aspects of Wilson's inner life that can, at best, only be guessed at. "The Civil War left scars in the souls of almost all Southerners of his generation. It left no scar in him." This unsupported statement is flatly contradicted by Wilson's most thorough biographer, Arthur Link (1947). Other inferences about Wilson's thoughts and unconscious impulses are so fanciful that refutation is neither possible nor necessary. For example, when Wilson's proposal of marriage was rejected by a cousin on his mother's side, Hattie Woodrow, "he dropped Thomas—the name of the father of the girl who had rejected him—and became unadulterated Woodrow. Thus he identified himself with his mother and satisfied his need for a mother representative by becoming himself his mother." One wonders why he did not instead drop both Thomas *and* Woodrow and become just plain Wilson, thus identifying himself even more closely with his beloved father.

Frequently the reasoning follows a circular path often found in psychobiographies: if *this* is true now, then *that* must have happened earlier, which explains why *this* is true now. For example, Bullitt and Freud observed that "in later life Thomas Woodrow Wilson always needed to have at least one affectionate relationship with a younger and physically smaller man, preferably blond," whom he ultimately cast "into the outer darkness as a Judas." They suggested that such relationships repeated Wilson's experience with his ten-years-younger brother Joe, although "we have no evidence as to Tommy Wilson's emotions at the time of the birth of his brother Joe, and we know little about their future relations." Then Bullitt and Freud sewed up their argument in a neat circle: "When one considers Wilson's later relations with his brother Joe, Hibben, House, Tumulty and others, one is driven to conclude that the birth of the infant Joe Wilson must have aroused far stronger emotions in the ten-year-old Tommy Wilson than are usual in a child of that age confronted by an infant brother" —namely, "much hostility and a paranoid sense of betrayal." In other words, Wilson loved and then rejected small blond men because he had loved and rejected his brother Joe, and we can infer that he had loved and rejected Joe because he later loved and rejected small blond men.

This kind of "if this/then that/therefore this" reasoning suggests a second "rule of psychobiography": *Don't move very far out in front of your data.* The information on Wilson's later relationships with small blond men might lead one to investigate his early relationship with his

94

brother; but if data about the early relationship are sparse, one should draw back before the abyss of sheer speculation.

Analytical Oversimplifications

The most substantial basis for criticism of the Freud-Bullitt study should be evident by now: its excessive reliance on simplistic explanations of Wilson's later behavior in terms of his early childhood experiences, particularly those involving his father. An emphasis on the importance of childhood in personality development is of course a hallmark of psychoanalytic theory and has led to some of its greatest contributions. But by the time the manuscript of *Thomas Woodrow Wilson* was completed, Freud had begun to acknowledge the significant role of later experience as well; and other psychoanalysts have carried the developmental process much further into adulthood. Bullitt and Freud did note an intensification of Wilson's identification with Christ at age sixteen and of his identification with God in middle age. But these were presumably variations in the strength of trends established much earlier. Throughout his life, according to Bullitt and Freud, Wilson was wrestling with—and losing to—his childhood superego; he was trying both to identify actively with and to submit passively to the father-image of his earliest memories; he was handling the problems of the nation and the world in terms of his infantile narcissism. In view of the neurotic element clearly expressed in some of Wilson's behavior, such an account of his motives may be more appropriate than it would be for many adults. But it is far from being the whole story. 95

A major part of the story that it omits is the social and cultural milieu within which Wilson moved. Bullitt and Freud rarely mentioned such factors, and when they did, they again seized on the opportunity to belittle Wilson:

> Moreover, Wilson's neurotic character was well suited to the demands of his time. First America, then the world, needed a prophet who could speak as if he were God's mouthpiece on earth. . . . Yet a neurosis is an unstable foundation upon which to build a life. Although history is studded with the names of neurotics, monomaniacs and psychotics who have risen suddenly to power, they have usually dropped as suddenly to disgrace. Wilson was no exception to this rule. The qualities of his defects raised him to power; but the defects of his qualities made him, in the end, not one of the world's greatest men but a great fiasco.

But would those "defects" be defects at any time, or did they lead to fiasco only in the context of a particular historical situation? Did the demands of Wilson's time present him only with opportunities, or with pressures and frustrations added to those he carried within himself from boyhood? Richard Hofstadter (1967) suggests the latter:

> Wilson was trying to cope not simply with the demands and the smothering love of [his father] but also with the problems of male identity in the America of the Gilded Age, the problems . . . of the balance between his native conservatism and the appealing moral upsurge of American Progressivism as he saw it, of presidential power, of neutrality and national security, of the European balance of power, of the wartime collapse of the nineteenth-century bourgeois world.

Wilson may have become "a great fiasco" in the end, but his failure must be seen in broader terms than his family relationships—as important as those relationships may have been.

One other aspect of the Freud-Bullitt study detracts considerably from the main line of their argument, although it probably could have been easily corrected in the right hands: the pseudotechnical language. I say "pseudo" because the book often fails to use the technical language of psychoanalysis, much of which has become familiar to the general reader. We read of "psychic accumulators" and "physical generators," of Wilson's libido as "charging aggressive activity toward his father," and of Wilson seeking "outlets for his passivity to his own father," as well as of the more usual "unconscious identifications," "reaction-formations," and the like. Woodrow Wilson emerges from all this as a clanking, wheezing mechanical man, with a heart full of hydraulic fluid and a head full of mush. In part, Bullitt's inept translation of Freud's German is probably responsible; Freud was usually cautious in his use of technical terms, particularly in works intended for the general reader. In part, Bullitt's and Freud's shared animosity toward Wilson may have made them reluctant to put any effort into explaining Wilson's emotional problems in ordinary human terms.

THE GEORGES' ACCOUNT

Just such an effort has made Alexander George and Juliette George's *Woodrow Wilson and Colonel House* (1956) a much more successful psychobiography. Also working within a psychoanalytic framework, but without knowledge of Bullitt and Freud's conclusions, the

Drawing of Woodrow Wilson by David Levine. Reprinted with permission from The New York Review of Books. Copyright © 1967 N.Y. Rev., Inc.

Georges arrived at strikingly similar explanations of much of Wilson's behavior. Given the peculiarities of Wilson's background and personality, it would probably have been difficult to arrive at a radically different set of conclusions. But in trying to make sense of Wilson's behavior in ordinary language rather than in the technical and pseudotechnical vocabulary of Bullitt and Freud, the Georges identified a considerably more complex interaction of influences in Wilson's life. They were also helped by their greater distance from Wilson's successes and failures, as well as by their broader perspective on psychoanalytic theory itself.

George and George covered familiar territory, but their stress was often different from Bullitt and Freud's. In the Georges' account, Wilson's father is a stern and commanding figure, the object both of Wilson's loving identification and of his repressed hostility. But Wilson's behavior in response was not merely an expression of the passive (feminine) and active (masculine) tendencies that Freud assumed to be present in all humans. Rather, Wilson the boy was made to feel terribly inferior to his magnificent and critical father, and he could relieve that feeling of inferiority only by striving to be a great man. (The Georges have here drawn directly on Lasswell's [1948] compensatory-power hypothesis.) Father Wilson's religious messages strengthened those tendencies in Wilson: "Man is innately depraved, a corrupt sinner who deserves eternal punishment," but "good works and pure thoughts are signs of election" by God Himself "to a state of grace and eternal life." Those who later interfered with Wilson's plans were not seen simply as father figures; the father, after all, engendered both love and hate. They were seen specifically as blocking the good works Wilson needed in order to maintain his fragile self-esteem and to ensure him God's grace, and they thus earned the full force of his repressed hostility toward his demeaning father.

The Georges did not speculate as to whether Wilson from an early age unconsciously identified his father with God and himself both with God and with Christ. They did point out his need to rationalize all of his overt expressions of hostility as moral acts. In this instance, they were applying Lasswell's (1930) early externalization formula for the "political man"—private motives displaced onto public objects and rationalized in terms of public interest. The virtue of the Georges' analysis is in pointing out what kind of rationalization Wilson found acceptable, and what sort of public object was therefore likely to be the occasion for expressing his hostility. Just any rationalization would not do; it had to be congruent with the self-concept modeled on his father's character and on the teachings of his church. Neither Wilson's self-interest nor a materialistic public interest were sufficient grounds for such rationalization. Only a "moral crusade" could justify his anger toward those who got in his way.

Wilson's Successes

Wilson rarely found a moral crusade both necessary and feasible. The Georges cited repeated instances in which, through a combination of his own talents and fortuitous circumstances, Wilson fulfilled his ambitions without serious or sustained opposition. After a brief failure as a lawyer, for which he could hold no one but himself accountable, Wilson moved quickly to prominence as a scholar, to successively more prestigious jobs as a college teacher, and to the presidency of Princeton College. For several years he enjoyed great success in the latter position, making innovations that strongly influenced American higher education thereafter. Only when he encountered stiff opposition to one of his proposals did Wilson begin to show the angry rigidity so evident later in the League of Nations battle; and only when he found a truly moral issue within the Princeton controversy did he become really savage toward his opponents. A frustrating father figure was an essential part of the controversy, according to the Georges, but the father figure alone was by no means sufficient to provoke Wilson's public rage.

The Princeton controversy was conveniently resolved for Wilson by the availability of the Republican candidacy for Governor of New Jersey. During and after his successful campaign for Governor, Wilson showed a degree of flexibility—in terms both of his willingness to seek support from diverse quarters and of his changes in political position to meet the prevailing ideological winds—that appears in flat contradiction to his final Princeton days. Indeed, he practiced this flexibility to such a degree that the newspaper publisher William Randolph Hearst, angered by Wilson's abandonment of an earlier conservatism, described him as "a perfect jackrabbit of politics, perched upon his little hillock of expediency, with ear erect and nostrils distended, keenly alert to every scent or sound and ready to run and double in any direction." Hearst's characterization was, as a general description of Wilson's personality and behavior, as erroneous as its opposite. Wilson was expedient (or flexible, depending on one's political viewpoint at the time) only when moral issues were not of central concern, or when "expediency" appeared likely to advance him to a position that would even more strongly assure him of his worth. At this point, Wilson was already looking forward to the Presidency of the United States.

Both as Governor of New Jersey and in the early years of his Presidency, Wilson enjoyed political success and moral acclaim such as few men in the history of America have experienced. The Georges suggested that "the extraordinary energy with which he applied himself to the task of making his will prevail was supplied . . . by the pent-up aggressive impulses which could find expression at last through his leadership tactics," given a set of praiseworthy goals. But they also argued that Wilson brought much besides neurotic energy to his work:

> In selecting the projects by means of which to satisfy his ambitions for idealistic achievement, Wilson was a hard-headed realist. They were always practicable possibilities likely to attract widespread public support and capable of realization within a reasonable time. It was the core of the man's genius to be able to choose his issues wisely and to crystallize public opinion in favor of them. . . . He was boldly inventive and skillful in devising techniques for creating support, for bringing the wavering to his side, for holding his ranks firm.

In addition, Wilson benefited each time he gained a major executive post from "an initial period during which the type of leadership he exercised in response to his inner needs coincided with the type of leadership the external situation required for impressive accomplishment." Wilson might have encountered disaster immediately if he had been confronted by a Congress, a Supreme Court, or a public solidly committed to self-interest or to "normalcy." Instead, he found the nation's majority waiting to be led to great things—to political reform at home and to moral leadership in the world. For a time, Wilson could make the nation's goals his own, and his private goals the nation's.

Wilson's unconsciously self-serving idealistic visions carried him and the nation safely through the First World War. He was reluctant to abandon American neutrality, even under considerable provocation; he could not agree to fight a war only in the self-interest of America and the Allies. But once Wilson had developed a moral rationalization for the expression of American hostility—a "war to end all wars"—no pacifist tendencies or presumed cowardice held him back. (Bullitt and Freud insisted that "little Tommy Wilson" was always afraid to fight. The best explanation they could devise for those occasions when he *did* fight was that a father figure provoked him; but they made no effort to identify a father figure in the First World War.)

Wilson's Greatest Failure

Wilson's great hope in entering the war was that he could play the leading postwar role in giving the world everlasting peace. That would surely show him to be worthy of his father and of God; it would be the greatest deed any man had ever done. The Georges suggested that

100

Wilson in fact had a realistic basis for expecting to mediate among the European powers, since American interests were not as directly involved in a war settlement and since the American public (responding in part to Wilson's persuasive skills) was willing to accept a relatively altruistic outcome to the war. Wilson at that time was also exceedingly popular in Europe: "Men who witnessed the triumphal entry of Woodrow Wilson into Paris said that never before on this earth had one human being been so revered by his fellows." But, seemingly with everything in his favor, Wilson marched steadfastly into the greatest failure of his lifetime.

He failed, according to the Georges, for the same reasons that he had received temporary setbacks earlier in life. But this time the disaster was so much greater because the stakes were so much higher, and because Wilson had nothing beyond the United States Presidency to salvage his self-esteem when he met frustration in Paris. He might have been willing to accept the title "Ruler of the World," but the rulers of Europe were in no mood to give it to him. Wilson wanted to settle the war and to end war forever by establishing a morally impeccable League of Nations, with himself recognized as virtually its sole founder. The European diplomats wanted to protect their self-interests and to punish their enemies; the United States Senate wanted to play some role in establishing the terms of any treaty into which the United States entered. Wilson responded to the European demands with his usual rigidity under attack; and although the European leaders grew scornful of his self-righteous moralizing, they finally acceded to his wishes in establishing the League of Nations Covenant. It was his insistence on sole authorship of the Covenant, without contamination or glory-sharing by anyone else, that brought him low in his own country.

101

Henry Cabot Lodge, the principal opponent of the League Covenant in the Senate, seems to have understood a good deal of Wilson's psychology—enough, at least, to use it to lead Wilson into self-defeat. Lodge criticized the quality of Wilson's intellect, his use of language, his selfish motives.

> Lodge trained all [his] capacity for sneering sarcasm against Wilson.
> . . . Once before, long ago, Wilson had had to endure barbed criticism. Once before, long ago, he had been sent in humiliation to revise and re-revise some carefully wrought composition. And long ago, overwhelmed by his masterful father, he had submitted to sarcastically made demands and to aspersions on his moral and

intellectual worth. He had submitted in seeming docility. Perhaps the rage that he had suppressed then emerged in full force against those he encountered in later years who reawakened the disagreeable sensations of half a century and more before.

All Lodge needed to do, in the face of Wilson's uncompromising rage, was to attach a few minor amendments of his own to the League Covenant, and Wilson would never accept the revised version. Wilson never did accept it, even when more sympathetic Senators substituted still weaker amendments for Lodge's, even when European leaders assured Wilson that the amendments were so trivial as to be meaningless. Wilson would not be dictated to by others, and he would not share authorship in what was to be his final triumph. The uncontaminated Covenant was defeated soundly in the Senate.

A Complex but Cautious Analysis

The Georges marshaled a great many facts in support of their psychological analysis of Wilson. They were careful to detail the circumstances that led to one kind of behavior rather than another at different times in Wilson's life, and to integrate his personal development with the course of the historical events within which he was operating. They speculated about his early life and his later unconscious motives, but with a caution and an appeal to the evidence of his letters and personal remarks that made their speculations reasonable. They nowhere resorted to Bullitt and Freud's "If this is so, then that must have happened, which explains why this is so" circularity, or to Bullitt and Freud's eager imputation of elaborate private dramas to Wilson's unobserved unconscious.

102

The Georges' analysis of Wilson is not a perfect psychobiography. A perfect psychobiography would include a much more detailed factual account of the subject's early life than they were able to supply. It would consider alternative explanations of the subject's major behavioral peculiarities in considerably more detail than they did. For instance, immediately prior to every instance in which Wilson exhibited his rigidity and public rage, he experienced a series of major successes. An account of this behavior in terms of positive reinforcement schedules or rising expectation levels might be worth pursuing.

The Georges' analysis does, however, have the advantage of overall cohesiveness. They tried an explanation based directly on available information about Wilson's background; they used it successfully to account for Wilson's successes *and* failures; and they appear to have omitted nothing of major importance from their account. They have shown us persuasively how the personality of one individual, operating within the context of a particular political era, could have momentous consequences for the history of our nation and of the world. I am sure they themselves would not claim perfection for their book; they know well enough the dangers of an insistence on perfection. But they have given us the best psychobiography of an American politician that anyone has written so far.

psychobiographies of Richard Nixon

Richard Nixon's formal statement of resignation from the Presidency was a calm and controlled performance. He had decided "that I no longer have a strong enough political base in the Congress" to avoid impeachment. He wished Gerald Ford well. He wanted people to remember how hard he had worked for peace. It could almost have been a retirement speech by a respected President turning over the reins to his elected successor, or perhaps a State of the Union oration designed to comfort more than to inform. It certainly informed the audience very little about Nixon's internal state.

Nixon's informal farewell to his staff, on the other hand, was a psychobiographer's dream. With sweat and tears streaming down his face, Nixon praised the staff for not having robbed the public till and pitied himself for having to "find a way to pay my taxes." He remembered "my old man," who moved from job to job and who sold "the poorest lemon ranch in California . . . before they found oil on it," but who was nonetheless "a great man, because he did his job and every job counts up to the hilt regardless of what happens."

Then Nixon, in the most emotional part of the speech, recalled his mother:

> Nobody will ever write a book probably about my mother. Well, I guess all of you would say this about your mother: my mother was a saint. And I think of her two boys dying of tuberculosis, nursing four others in order that she could take care of my older brother for three years in Arizona and seeing each of them die. And when they died it was like one of her own. Yes, she will have no books written about her. But she was a saint.

103

This was followed by an odd combination of self-deprecation and implied self-praise, as Nixon launched into a story about the death of Theodore Roosevelt's wife with the statement, "I'm not educated, but I do read books," and then finished the story by noting that as an ex-President, Roosevelt "served his country, always in the arena, tempestuous, strong, sometimes right. But he was a man."

Finally, the concluding homilies:

> Because the greatness comes not only when things go always good for you, but the greatness comes when you're really tested, when you take some knocks and some disappointments, when sadness comes. . . . Always give your best. Never get discouraged. Never be petty. Always remember, others may hate you, but those who hate you don't win unless you hate them. And then you destroy yourself.

Exit Richard Nixon, destroyed.

If a skilled psychobiographer had sat down to write a farewell speech for Nixon that would incorporate in dramatic form the major psychological themes of Nixon's life, he would have written just such a speech. That Nixon did it himself, apparently with little advance preparation and under great emotional stress, makes it one of the prize psychobiographical documents of modern times.

NIXON'S EARLY HISTORY

Most good psychobiographies have dealt with individuals already studied exhaustively by conventional biographers. A thorough biography of Richard Nixon has yet to be written, although several campaign biographies (pro and con) are available. The several Nixon psychobiographies to be discussed here would all have benefited from the reliable detail of a good biography, particularly since none of the three authors involved appears to have collected any original biographical information either from Nixon himself or from his current and former associates. Nor has Nixon yet published a genuine autobiography, another major basis for psychobiographical inference in works such as Erikson's *Gandhi's Truth* (1969). But Nixon did write (with some help) his selection of autobiographical highlights, *Six Crises* (1968), and in spite of his usual public reserve, he supplied psychobiographers with many revelations of his psychological world long before his resignation. The themes expressed in his farewell speech were familiar themes, gratifying for their confirmation of previous inferences rather than for their revelation of a previously unknown Nixon psyche.

The farewell speech is particularly striking for its attention to Nixon's early life. He was the second son of a serious but sympathetic Quaker mother and a blustery father, whom she converted from Methodism to a loose version of her own faith. Nixon's father Frank had a hard time keeping the family above the poverty line, partly because of bad luck, partly because of his harsh temper and lack of foresight. Nixon's mother Hannah worked long hours to help out, and placated those whom Frank angered by his political bombast or his general irritability in the family store.

The death of children was a recurrent theme in Richard Nixon's own childhood. He was almost killed in a carriage accident at the age of three, nearly died of an illness at four, was seriously ill during much of his senior year in high school. (Yet as President, he claimed that he had never been ill a day in his life.) His younger brother Arthur died suddenly of tubercular encephalitis when Richard was twelve. His older brother Harold died of tuberculosis when Richard was nineteen, after a long struggle in which Hannah Nixon took Harold to Arizona for two years (not three, as Nixon said in the farewell speech) in hopes of a cure. The reference in the farewell speech to her watching "four others" die as well is to the other tubercular children she took care of in order to support herself and Harold away from the family. Richard joined them for a time, working at odd jobs and then as a pitchman at a carnival gambling booth to help lighten the financial burden.

Nixon grew up in small-town Southern California, and he stayed there through college—Whittier College, a small Quaker institution that he noted "did not offer a course in political science in the years I spent there." (He added that he got a good education, but that if he *had* been "exposed" to a political science course, he might have defeated John F. Kennedy in the 1960 election.) Nixon worked hard to maintain his grades and his scholarship assistance, was a successful debater and a campus leader, and served as a second-string tackling dummy for the first-string football team to practice against. He continued to work hard at Duke University Law School, where an older student assured him that he needn't worry about competing with all the Phi Beta Kappas because the basic requirement for learning law was "an iron butt."

Nixon's career as a lawyer began badly. He tried and failed to get either a job in a New York law firm or a position in the FBI. He returned to his hometown, where his mother persuaded a family friend

105

to take him into a local law firm. Nixon did well in the firm, but failed dismally at a business effort in which he headed a frozen-orange-juice venture. After five years of law practice in Whittier, Nixon went to Washington in 1942 for an unhappy eight months as a junior-grade bureaucrat with the Office of Price Administration. He joined the navy, served as a supply officer in the South Pacific, and won several thousand dollars at poker. After the war, he was asked to run for Congress on the recommendation of the Whittier College president. The rest is well-known history.

MAZLISH'S ANALYSIS

In the most detailed psychobiography of Nixon yet written, *In Search of Nixon,* Bruce Mazlish (1973) emphasized much the same material as Nixon did in his farewell speech. Mazlish worked within a loosely psychoanalytic framework but generally avoided the Freud-Bullitt–type analysis of narcissistic gratifications, energy distributions, and so forth, in the absence of psychoanalytic interviews with Nixon. He did stress the powerful influence of Nixon's early family life; but even

Richard Nixon concludes his farewell address to his staff, August 9, 1974.

106

here, Mazlish's analysis is often no more psychoanalytic than that of much earlier biographers who attributed one set of characteristics to the subject's father, another to the mother, and noted the clash between them.

Mazlish saw Nixon's "Protestant Ethic" traits, his emphasis on planning, hard work, and persistence, as coming from his mother and his maternal grandmother. Mazlish seems to have carefully avoided any statement about Nixon's identifying with the mother but instead wrote of Nixon's "resembling" the mother or "acquiring" these traits from her—perhaps by simple learning or by imitation rather than by an emotional identification, although Mazlish himself did not attempt to specify the process involved. The mother's other major role in Nixon's character development, according to Mazlish, was a negative one: at various times Nixon presumably felt he had lost her affection, particularly when she spent two years away from the family nursing brother Harold. Nixon thus acquired "feelings of the precariousness of life and love," as well as feelings of "betrayal."

Mazlish described Nixon as identifying with his father in a number of ways: his love of argument, his interest in politics, his being a "loner," his fear of failure. Mazlish speculated that Nixon "sought to redeem his father by being successful" and used his mother's "traits of hard work and persistence" in the service of that goal. Nixon also tended to identify more with his father's fundamentalist version of Quakerism than with his mother's pacifist and relatively liberal version, although he continued to feel ambivalent about war and peace throughout his life.

Nixon's brothers were also important to him, mainly in negative ways. They aroused in him "the natural emotions of sibling rivalry"; they took his mother away from him, in one way or another; and the deaths of two brothers must have aroused powerful emotional responses. Mazlish speculates that the major responses were "a threat and fear of his own death," as well as "strong unconscious guilt feelings" over having survived when they died and over having resented them when they were alive. Nixon's later pattern of seeking out crises, or at least of glorying in the appearance of coping with a crisis, was proposed as being "partly motivated by the need to confront his death fears, repeatedly and constantly."

Nixon's own childhood illnesses presumably exacerbated this fear of death. Nixon was not only seriously ill a number of times during childhood; he was also physically clumsy and socially inept, and seems

107

to have developed the assumption (we are not told on what basis) that he was not terribly bright. But the emphasis on hard work and persistence that he had gotten from Hannah Nixon, as well as the argumentative skills acquired from Frank Nixon, brought him success in spite of these handicaps, in what Mazlish calls "an almost classic case of compensation for inferiority." (Note the Lasswell formula again.)

Mazlish by no means stopped with Nixon's childhood. One of the virtues of his analysis is that he paid considerable attention to Nixon's behavior as a young man and then as a successful and unsuccessful politician in adulthood. Nor did Mazlish limit himself to an analysis of the developmental themes already cited; they are simply the most obvious among many. Indeed, the major drawback of Mazlish's analysis is that he presents *too many* themes, without fully developing the evidence for any of them and often without directly relating apparently very similar themes that may well have the same developmental antecedents.

Weaknesses of the Mazlish Approach

The successful psychobiographer must steer carefully between two dangers: the rock of reductionism and the sands of overcomplexity. Reduction of a major political leader's behavior to a handful of early determinants is likely to omit much of his humanness and to ignore the sources of much of his adult success, as we have seen in Bullitt and Freud's treatment of Woodrow Wilson. On the other hand, an attempt to list the full range of an individual's adult behaviors and to relate each only to its most obvious antecedents is likely to leave us more confused about the individual's underlying psychology than we need to be. People are generally complex, and their behaviors often seem inconsistent or little related to each other. But if common themes can be found, if apparently diverse behaviors can be marshaled as support for the existence of these common themes, and if seemingly irreconcilable behaviors can be accounted for by the interaction of common themes and varied situations, then the individual's complexity becomes much more understandable and the psychobiographical effort becomes worthwhile.

Table 4 is my attempt at a rather loose organization of most of the Nixon personality themes cited by Mazlish. I could have gone further, either by relating clusters to other clusters or by tabulating the number of items of support Mazlish cites for the elements in each cluster.

108

Table 4
Richard Nixon's predominant psychological characteristics

Denial

Avoidance of introspection

Daydreaming

Fear of failure

Fear of death

Fear of loss of love

Fear of dependency

Fear of seeming weak or unmasculine

Ambivalence about passiveness and strength

Ambivalence about peace and war

Difficulty in decision-making

Depressive moods

Low self-esteem

Compensation for inferiority

Rootless American

Ambivalence between rural California and New York City

Desire for warmth and approval of crowds

Desire for respect

Need for weaker men around him

Role-playing or acting

Verbal ability

Interest in argument

Concern with form rather than substance

Compulsiveness

Anality

Need to control situation

Need to be strong

Learned self-control

Lack of affect

Careful planning

Persistence

Identification with strong enemy

Need for strong people around him (particularly women)

Projection of negative feelings

Need for emotional enemy

Repressed hostility

Competitiveness

Sibling rivalry

Unconscious guilt feelings

Resentment of Eastern Establishment

Death-wishes toward father figures

Orality

Need to be dependent

Social isolation

Suspiciousness, lack of trust

Identification with (or imitation of) mother

Compassion

Emphasis on work ethic

Need to be hard on self and others

Identification with father and with authority

Desire to redeem father by proving himself

Need to risk failure to prove himself

Need for crises as means of confronting death fears

Interest in politics

Liberal beliefs

Conservative beliefs

Religious fundamentalism

Identification with national interest

Self-image as "great" and as "totally right"

109

Based on Bruce Mazlish, *In search of Nixon*. Baltimore: Penguin Books, 1973.

I also could have sorted individual themes into groups on somewhat different principles. But my main intent in making up the table is served by noting the sheer number of elements Mazlish recorded as being identifiable features of Nixon's personality and by indicating that these fifty-nine or more features can be grouped and interrelated rather more economically than Mazlish has so far done. In some instances he himself made an effort to identify relationships between personality elements, but in many others he left it to the reader's creativity.

The Table 4 groupings may also suggest to author or reader the need for a clearer explanation of why some items are on the list at all. Each of the larger groupings suggests at least one important common theme in Nixon's personality, and some items from the smaller groups can easily be related to these larger clusters (as, for instance, we might match "Identification with mother" with the list headed "Compulsiveness"). But in certain instances, one item or a short list of items appears from the evidence Mazlish gave us to be little related to any major cluster in the table—for example, "Daydreaming" or "Orality." Are these merely isolated features of Nixon's personality, acquired by chance; are they related to other features at some deeper level not yet made clear to us; or are they perhaps items imposed on the Nixon personality by Mazlish, but not really deserving of inclusion?

"Daydreaming" was indeed a characteristic of the very young Nixon, which might with some effort be related either to the "Role-playing" list or to the "Desire to redeem father" item. "Orality" seems to be the real ringer. After considering Nixon's anal tendencies, for which there is a good deal of trivial and some substantial evidence, Mazlish tried briefly to build a case for the importance of orality in Nixon's character. He cited these items in support: Nixon "has little interest in 'good' food"; his mother was an expert cook, but he gave away her pies and sandwiches to his college friends; "he seems almost to feed on a crisis"; the words he uses to describe his crises "are basically 'oral' images, relating to his 'insides' "; speech is his "preferred mode of releasing aggression."

The last item is the only one that might stand up as evidence for a general characteristic of orality, and even it is used very speculatively. Nixon's father offered such an emphatic model of verbal skill, and Nixon was so physically inept and so frequently ill as a boy, that his aggressive use of speech may well have had very different functional bases than satisfaction of the infantile-dependency orality needs to which psychoanalytic theory usually refers. Nixon's lack of interest in

110

good food or in his mother's cooking suggests, if anything, a corresponding lack of oral orientation, although again other factors could well be involved. His tendency to "feed on a crisis" is Mazlish's image, not Nixon's. Consider instead the images Nixon himself has used to describe his crises: "the intense desire . . . which I had kept bottled up inside myself"; "not being able to act is what tears your insides out"; feeling "drained . . . emotionally" at the end of a crisis. These are far from being "basically 'oral'" images, as Mazlish describes them; they are gut images, or what psychoanalysts would usually call "anal" images. Anality fits very nicely into Table 4; orality might better be saved for a study of Hubert Humphrey.

Mazlish is very familiar with the theoretical literature on psychobiography, having written some of it himself, and he is usually more cautious than the orality example suggests. But he is rarely as cautious as he should be in his treatment of data. Caution in psychobiography involves more than the insertion of "maybes" and "I would suggests" into one's discussion. It centrally involves, as Mazlish himself observed, "the *density* of material, building up a conclusion as one builds up a puzzle . . . not mere agglomeration of data but their accumulation in a definite configuration." Mazlish assembled the beginnings of a good psychobiography in his treatment of Nixon, but his hypotheses are spread so widely that the density is still very thin, and the configuration has yet to emerge clearly.

CHESEN'S ANALYSIS

111

Eli Chesen, in *President Nixon's Psychiatric Profile* (1973), tried the opposite tack. Chesen was familiar with Mazlish's analysis of Nixon and criticized it as too much of a classic psychoanalytic interpretation for the available data to support. But Chesen's own interpretation, which appears to have drawn heavily on selected points from Mazlish, is even more traditionally psychoanalytic, arriving in the end at a diagnosis of Nixon as a standard obsessive-compulsive neurotic. It is a simple diagnosis, easily understood and capable of being neatly diagramed. But in fitting Nixon into the diagnosis, Chesen often found it necessary to overinterpret the data or to read them in questionable ways. Mazlish left too many loose ends for anyone to diagnose *him* as an obsessive-compulsive; Chesen is so tidy that one sometimes wonders whose characteristics he is really describing in his diagnosis of Nixon.

Chesen wrote that rather than discussing sibling rivalries, Oedipal conflicts, and such, he wanted "to present insight merely into a young, insecure boy growing up in early twentieth-century California." This would have been a valuable achievement, since Mazlish, although he frequently mentioned the circumstances influencing Nixon's behavior, admittedly failed to give the historical and cultural context its proper due. But Chesen swiftly moved to a description of Nixon's father as "quite a violent man," frightening Nixon by his "wrath and authoritarianism" and thus preventing the young Richard from gaining self-confidence; to a view of Hannah Nixon as a domineering matriarch; and to Nixon's problems in trying to identify with the stronger, more competent parent. In Chesen's version, Nixon certainly did not resolve the identification dilemma in the classic Oedipal way; but neither did some of Freud's most famous cases (including the psychobiographical "case" of Leonardo da Vinci).

According to Chesen, Nixon's primary identification was with his mother. This led to "significant feelings of uncertainty about himself as a male," to "considerable sexual confusion," and thence to "over-concern with the important task of proving himself manly." Since "unconsciously he is *helpless, dominated, and weak,*" but doesn't want anyone to know it, Nixon moves to "shut the world out" and to seek total control over every situation. This total control is made even more necessary by his need to repress his hostility toward mother, father, and brothers ("Nixon's unconscious is a vault bulging with aggression") as well as his need to conquer the insecurity feelings aroused by his brothers' deaths and his own illnesses. His mother's behavior and her religion's emphasis on planning provided him with models for control. Chesen regarded Nixon's "robotized arm movements," "ambivalent smile," "limited voice range," and absence of humor as evidence of his attempts at self-control. His establishment of the White House Plumbers' unit to deal with security leaks is "an inevitable extension of Nixon's psychological need to have total control over himself and his environment." He has newsmen's phones tapped "to monitor closely . . . the degree to which his protective shell is being penetrated. He can then fortify any weakness before things get out of control." His repeated tendency toward "overkill" in preparing for crises is one of the clearest indications of his need for control: "Overkill is a theme woven through the fabric of Watergate and the life of Richard Nixon."

Chesen's analysis often seems persuasive in light of Nixon's public behavior. At times, he clarified relationships between data that Maz-

112

lish had sketched in but left unconnected in separate regions of the total Nixon picture. But Chesen was too eager to prove his case. His description of the Nixon household is more like an evil fairy tale than like the real family we know from other sources. Nixon's father *was* easily angered, loudmouthed, argumentative; but was he so "violent" and "authoritarian" that Richard "was unable to gain confidence because he could not argue with the man and occasionally win"? Richard's mother could not recall that her husband ever spanked the boy. More important, Nixon himself told one of his biographers (Kornitzer, 1960) in reference to his father that "when you got into mischief, you had to be pretty convincing to avoid punishment. . . . He had a hot temper, and I learned early that the only way to deal with him was to abide by the rules he laid down. Otherwise, I would probably have felt the touch of a ruler or the strap as my brothers did." Here we have a young Nixon learning to get along with authority and to profit from his own verbal skills—learning to win, not lose, in conflicts with his father.

Chesen also described Hannah Nixon's Quakerism as demanding "stringent literal acquiescence to such unfaltering respect of all authority. This is suggested by the fact that Nixon's grandmother frequently used 'plain speech,'" the old-fashioned "thee" and "thou." But as Stanley Renshon (1975) has noted, the fact that Nixon's mother never used plain speech when talking with her children made her "a 'liberal' by church standards." Chesen is hardly justified in assuming that "Nixon grew up in a kind of microcosmic 'police state.'"

Chesen went on to explain Nixon's anti-Communism and hawkishness in terms of his identification with his father (although Frank Nixon was apparently a political liberal in most respects), Nixon's peacemaking efforts in terms of the maternal identification, and so forth—until the "Nixon identification" and the "Milhous identification" are popping up and down like Punch and Judy. Even Nixon's reluctance to meet with Senator Sam Ervin during the Watergate hearings was explained by Nixon's transference of his childhood fears from his father to Ervin. Frank Nixon's outrage over the Teapot Dome Scandal during the Harding Administration led the ten-year-old Richard Nixon to announce, "Mother, I would like to become a lawyer—an honest lawyer, who can't be bought by crooks" (Kornitzer, 1960). But, concluded Chesen, "now it is Frank Nixon, poorly disguised as Sam Ervin, who is outraged over President Nixon and *his* corrupted administration. . . . The reawakening of repressed unconscious fears in Nixon's mind are indisputable."

113

Possible, maybe; indisputable, hardly. Chesen has been ship-wrecked on that psychobiographical rock of reductionism, emphatic oversimplification. Sam Ervin may have been something of a punitive father figure for Nixon, but other reasons existed, sufficient unto them-selves and rather more easily established, for Nixon not to want to discuss Watergate with Sam Ervin.

BARBER'S ANALYSIS

The observant reader may have noticed, among all these "facts" and speculations about Richard Nixon's psychology, certain resemblances to Woodrow Wilson. They shared at least some compulsive charac-teristics; they both had eloquent fathers; they both fought on long after their last battle had been decisively lost. Wilson described his mother as "saintly" eighty-five years before Nixon gave his farewell speech. Wilson "shrank from reflecting about his inner motivation," according to the Georges; Nixon avoids "turning inward," according to Mazlish. Wilson spent many childhood hours drawing ships and daydreaming that he was their captain; Nixon dreamed of being a train engineer and traveling to faraway places. Wilson's major extra-curricular interest and the source of his earliest successes in college was the debating society; so was Nixon's. During his first year of law practice, Wilson's only client was his mother; Nixon had to turn to his mother to obtain his first position as a lawyer. And so on. Nixon recognized a certain similarity between himself and Wilson, and at one period in his life he talked of Wilson as a personal hero, although in the final days of Watergate he preferred to compare himself with Harry Truman and Theodore Roosevelt.

114

James David Barber, in *The Presidential Character* (1972), devel-oped such similarities between Nixon and Wilson into a lengthy analy-sis of Nixon's personality. Barber began by applying his fourfold table of legislative types to American Presidents. He found that with some modifications and elaborations of detail, it worked well. He again used level of activity and attitude toward elective office as his major cri-teria for categorization, although his judgments of Presidents' attitudes toward the Presidency appear to be more impressionistic than his criterion of legislators' willingness to serve three terms in office. He dropped such descriptive terms as *Lawmaker* and *Spectator* as names for the categories, identifying them instead by their defining character-istics. George Washington was a passive-negative President, dutifully serving his country and guarding "the right and proper way" but not enjoying the job. John Adams was "an active-negative President, a compulsive type," "much given to work and worry." Thomas Jefferson enjoyed his work and strove to realize "his vision of what the country could be"; he was active-positive. Of the first four Presidents, James Madison comes closest to the passive-positive, or compliant, type, interested in the possibilities of the position but giving in too readily to public demands. Barber's categorization of Presidents since Theodore Roosevelt is shown in Table 5.

These are categorizations of Presidential *character,* or "the way the President orients himself toward life" in a broad sense. Barber also considered each President's *world view,* consisting of "his primary, politically relevant beliefs," and his *style,* or "habitual way of performing his political roles." But the major emphasis is on character. Barber's analysis of Woodrow Wilson's character is very similar to the Georges' analysis, to which he frequently referred. Wilson began with low self-esteem, for which he compensated by hard work and by "dominating his social environment with moralistic rhetoric." He repressed his hostility toward his demanding and critical father, turning it against himself or redirecting it onto a selected enemy. He feared self-gratification because it would violate the demands of his "perfectionistic conscience" and would mean he had failed in his efforts to control his emotions. Wilson feared compromise or surrender as "an admission of guilt and weakness." His core feeling, basic to the active-

115

Table 5
Barber's categorization of modern United States presidents

| | | AFFECT TOWARD THE PRESIDENCY | |
		POSITIVE	NEGATIVE
ENERGY LEVEL	ACTIVE	Franklin Roosevelt Harry Truman John Kennedy	Woodrow Wilson Herbert Hoover Lyndon Johnson Richard Nixon
	PASSIVE	William Howard Taft Warren Harding	Calvin Coolidge Dwight Eisenhower

Based on James David Barber, *The presidential character.* Englewood Cliffs, N.J.: Prentice-Hall, 1972.

negative category, was "I must." This led him at first to great success and then to increasing rigidity, as he saw himself increasingly forced to compromise and strove to avoid it.

Nixon's core feeling, according to Barber, is not simply "I must" but "I must make my own way." This comes from two major sources in his childhood: his need to "wend his way cautiously between Frank and Hannah," pleasing one without annoying or driving away the other; and his need to "develop an identity of his own which would confirm his manliness." Nixon had identified strongly with his "calm, reliable, and repressed mother," but had also come to feel that "manliness meant being like his father—impulsive, aggressive, surprising, unpredictable."

Barber largely avoided hypothesizing about Nixon's early unconscious life beyond these basic themes, although he still made a few unnecessary and unsupported assumptions, such as that Nixon's eleven-pound weight at birth meant "the delivery was difficult." Whether or not Nixon felt strong sibling rivalries or survival guilt with regard to his dead brothers, Barber reasonably suggested that "out of his childhood Nixon brought a persistent bent toward life as painful, difficult, and—perhaps as significant—uncertain." Under these circumstances, Nixon found it gratifying to follow his mother's injunctions to "work hard and be prepared."

Working hard and being prepared were particularly useful for Nixon in certain school activities: "speaking, debating, play-acting." Those activities also helped him to unload his repressed anger in a socially acceptable way. During Nixon's first Congressional campaign, the same activities worked again. The campaign "was overwhelmingly rhetorical, an exercise in impression management, innuendo, and dramatic debating . . . backed up with very intensive homework." According to Barber, a politician's first independent political success is crucial in understanding his character, because it usually presents the major themes of his political career in somewhat simpler form than his later victories and because it helps set the politician firmly in his winning pattern of behavior. When Nixon won his Congressional seat largely by his own efforts (including considerable financial help from his wartime poker winnings), "the infusion of confidence must have been massive." He thereafter followed a pattern not only of angry rhetoric and careful role-playing but of isolation from most advisers and of insistence on total control of campaigns and eventually of the government itself.

116

Weaknesses and Strengths in Barber's Approach

Barber established rather well that Nixon fits the active-negative category on the basis of the principal criteria. Nixon has certainly been an industrious laborer in the political vineyards throughout his career; and the reports of relatives, friends, his football coach, his own semi-autobiography, all stress Nixon's lack of easy enjoyment in the tasks he has set for himself. If anything, he gets his pleasure from the suffering his work induces, rather than from the work itself. (The White House tape transcripts [Nixon, 1974] include, in a discussion of the Watergate cover-up:

> *President:* [Sighs] This is hard work. . . . But I've got to do it. Got to do it. And it's best for me to do it, too.)

But is such evidence enough to categorize Richard Nixon with Woodrow Wilson as Presidential equals in their active-negativism? Even taking into account the various other similarities between Nixon and Wilson, the two seem hardly to be in the same league. Probably the crucial difference is Wilson's moral compulsiveness versus Nixon's apparent dearth of moral concerns. Wilson was the supreme superego-tripper of modern times; Nixon appears to have been almost as supreme an ego-tripper. This is not to say that elements of self-regard were unimportant to Wilson's psyche or that Nixon is devoid of a superego. It is to say that there is a big difference between basing one's behavior in large part on uncompromising moral principles and basing it largely on getting ahead in the world as expeditiously as possible—even if the ultimate outcome is disaster in both cases. 117

Barber recognized that Nixon does not altogether fit the Wilson mold. Rather than abandoning his fourfold categorization, however, Barber invented for Nixon a special subcategory of active-negativism. Whereas Wilson felt personally threatened by defeat on those issues on which he had taken a moral stand, Nixon feels threatened mainly by "threats to his independence." The difference is reflected in Wilson's "I must" becoming Nixon's "I must make my own way." The difference began, perhaps, in the differences between the Presidents' fathers (although Barber did not make the comparison). Wilson's father was frightening, frustrating, but also a magnificently good and moral man. Nixon's father was frightening, frustrating, worth identifying with in some ways but (as Mazlish suggested) an appropriate figure to identify *away* from in others. The mothers complicated the situation, by presenting the question of feminine sex-role identification in different ways to Wilson and to Nixon.

Barber's suggestion that Nixon would feel most threatened (and therefore would be most likely to show behavioral rigidification) by threats to his independence is very useful in understanding Nixon's behavior after Barber's analysis was published. Nixon had earlier shown amazing flexibility in his dealings with Communist nations, essentially reversing his position on one of the most important issues of his early political life. But his rigidity in dealing with Watergate was just as amazing, leading finally to an even more spectacular downfall than Wilson's defeat over the League of Nations. The necessity to place Nixon in a subcategory of his own is not, however, particularly encouraging with regard to the fate of Barber's fourfold categorization of Presidential types. Are activity level and degree of occupational enjoyment really the crucial dimensions for describing Presidential character, or do we need to pay more attention to such issues as superego-versus-ego dominance? Having recognized the basic features of the active-negative Presidential character in the person of Woodrow Wilson, must we then devise individual subcategories of active-negativism for every other President who loosely fits the main defining characteristics?

Barber did not propose subcategories for the other modern activenegative Presidents, Hoover and Johnson. But Alexander George (1974) argued that the categories as they stand do not accommodate Hoover and Johnson any better than Nixon, since all differ in significant ways from Wilson and from each other in terms of motives, goals, and the ability to shape their motives to attain those goals. George also argued that Barber's main defining criteria are so imprecise that it is impossible to determine the accuracy of even the broad categorizations and that Barber often molded data to fit the categories—thus succumbing as others have done to that great psychobiographical temptation.

Barber's problems derive in considerable part from the ambitious task he set himself. He developed psychobiographical analyses of not one but eleven Presidents and made frequent comparisons between one President and another. I don't know enough about most of those Presidents to be sure of Barber's accuracy; but he can easily be forgiven for relying heavily on the Georges' own authoritative account of Wilson's psychology, and he was certainly more careful in handling the details of Nixon's life than, for instance, Chesen was.

Regardless of his deficiencies, most of which appear remediable,

118

Barber has performed an important service for psychobiography. Mazlish raised the question of whether certain Nixonian characteristics are uniquely Nixon's or are common among American Presidents, American politicians, or just plain Americans. It is often hard to know how much weight to place on an apparently crucial item of data when only a single individual's life is being studied. But comparisons across a number of Presidents, similar at least in general form to those Barber has made, should eventually go a long way in showing us what is crucial and what is coincidental, what is unique or limited in distribution and what is common. Here we are moving back in the direction of the quantitative studies of the previous chapter. But as long as we retain the psychobiographical method's advantages of detail, longitudinal consideration, and seeing personality whole, this apparent regression should really be a methodological advance with major implications. Barber's four categories may not survive further comparisons either of the Presidents he has studied or of others. (Is Gerald Ford really a passive-positive?) But they should be an inspiration and at least a preliminary guide for future psychobiographers.

psychobiography: perils and rewards

Psychobiography is a recent word, but people have been doing something like it ever since Thucydides. Rarely has a biographer ever even tried to give an account of an individual's life without dwelling on the subject's motives, emotional responses, patterns of temperament, and other psychological processes. The history of a war or of a nation's development may be useful even though it says little about human psychology, but a biography that omits consideration of the protagonist's inner life seems hardly worth writing.

119

Until the twentieth century, however, biographers were seldom systematic in their interpretation of the subject's personality. They preferred to apply whatever common-sense explanations were available for the subject's most prominent behaviors, and to ignore "minor" examples of behavior or to apply still other common-sense interpretations to them.

Sigmund Freud changed all that. Most notably in his study of Leonardo da Vinci (Freud, 1910; English translation, 1957), Freud argued that his psychoanalytic theory of personality could be usefully applied to the outstanding figures in history, and that the research techniques he had developed in face-to-face interactions with

Sigmund Freud at work on a manuscript.

psychiatric patients could be adapted to the study of secondhand biographical data. Freud was in certain regards cautious about the process of writing a psychological biography. He suggested that his study of Leonardo might reasonably be regarded as a "psychoanalytic novel" rather than as a scientific study, and he warned that the role of sheer chance in a person's life seriously limits the degree to which a psychoanalytic interpretation of behavior can be definitive. Nonetheless, Freud was quite willing to draw dramatic conclusions about Leonardo's personality, and later about the personalities of such individuals as Fyodor Dostoyevsky and Woodrow Wilson.

Psychobiography has, in the hands of such researchers as Alexander and Juliette George, James Barber, and Erik Erikson, made substantial advances since Freud's early work. But several problems continue to bother the conscientious psychobiographer and to supply ammunition for unsympathetic critics. We have already encountered specific examples of some of these problems; others arise so frequently in psychobiographies that they merit more general discussion.

AVAILABILITY OF DATA

One of the most obvious psychobiographical difficulties is obtaining enough information of the right kinds to do a thorough personality study of a prominent individual. The psychotherapist who wants to develop a detailed picture of a patient's personality can ask for intimate descriptions of the patient's present and past behavior, for reports of dreams and free associations to those dreams, and—if the therapist is so inclined—for answers to various kinds of personality tests and psychological questionnaires. The therapist can also observe at first hand the patient's *transference reactions,* the ways in which the patient transfers long-standing patterns of emotional reactions from important figures in the patient's earlier life to the therapist. Not all of what the patient tells the therapist about himself will be accurate; he may consciously or unconsciously conceal his true feelings. But out of the massive amount of information accumulated about a patient over a course of treatment, an observant and thoughtful therapist should come to know the patient rather well.

Politicians are inclined to be secretive about their private thoughts and private lives, for fear of losing votes. Most successful politicians are experts at impression management, the deliberate shaping of other people's views of them. And few will make themselves available to the psychobiographer so that he may penetrate the public mask. Often, the politician is dead before the psychobiographer even begins to work on the "case," so that only written documents or, at best, interviews with others who knew the politician are available. How, then, can the psychobiographer ever presume to know his subject as well as the psychotherapist knows his?

In the first place, the psychobiographer may not *need* to know his subject as well. As the Georges (1964) point out, the psychoanalytic patient's broad personality pattern typically emerges during the first few interviews, "which usually consist largely in the patient's account of his difficulties and an initial narrative of significant life experiences." Most of the later sessions, constituting the bulk of the psychotherapeutic interaction, are taken up with treating the patient's problems. The psychobiographer has no obligation to relieve his subject's psychological distress, so he can get along on much less information.

Further, the psychobiographer often does have access to a good deal of information, including some that would not usually be available to the psychotherapist. Letters and diaries as well as public statements may be available even for long-dead politicians. For those still alive or recently deceased, the psychobiographer may be able to make direct behavioral observations, in person or from filmed appearances, and to interview the subject's family and associates. The psychobiographer may well have an advantage over the psychotherapist in this

121

regard, since the therapist is almost always limited to the patient's own account of his experiences, without knowing what actually took place or how others saw the same events.

VALIDITY OF INTERPRETATIONS

Once the psychobiographer has amassed enough data to begin working out a coherent picture of the subject's personality, another problem presents itself: How does he know the interpretation is right? The clinician again has advantages here: he can check his developing interpretation with the patient, either by asking the patient for additional information that may help to confirm the accuracy of the interpretation or by assessing the patient's sense of "therapeutic conviction" that the interpretation is correct. The therapist can also observe the effect of the interpretation on the subsequent course of therapy and on the patient's behavior to see whether it had the intended effect in terms of giving the patient greater insight into and control over his motives.

The psychobiographer usually is not able to observe the effects of an interpretation on the subject (although some psychobiographers dream that their work will have a reforming influence on the living politicians about whom they write). Nor does he usually get any feedback from the subject regarding the interpretation, except perhaps in the form of a libel suit or an outraged protest about "glaring errors." Nonetheless, the psychobiographer can make a number of checks on the validity of the interpretation, some of them similar to what clinicians do or should do with the data from their patients.

One such check is what George and George describe as an "iterative process" of successive approximations. That is, the psychobiographer begins framing hypotheses about the subject fairly early during data-collection and then checks these hypotheses against later data. Since he is unlikely to have guessed completely right the first time, he will have to revise the hypotheses to take account of the new data and to check the revised hypotheses against still further data. Sooner or later, if the psychobiographer is sensitive to the implications of the data, an interpretation should emerge that works well with whatever additional data become available.

It is important, however, that the psychobiographer not stop in the middle of this process by concluding that the most recently revised hypotheses fit the data so well that they need no further checks. The hypotheses *should* fit the data on which they were based, since they have been custom-designed to do so. The real test is whether they also fit data that the psychobiographer had not collected at the time the hypotheses were developed. He should go even further, by trying to find and to account for information apparently contradictory to the hypotheses, before he rests reasonably confident in the accuracy of an interpretation. (If he doesn't go this additional step, the psychobiographer can be sure that a critic will do it for him after he publishes his work.)

Although psychobiography rests more on qualitative than on quantitative criteria, the psychobiographer does need to support any interpretation with certain kinds of quantitative information. He should never base a hypothesis on a single piece of data, since by itself it may express many unknown influences or circumstances other than the one he identifies as important. A bulwark of psychoanalytic method, often ignored in casual attempts at parlor psychoanalysis of public figures, is the building up of an intricate framework of internally consistent, mutually supportive bits of data to sustain any specific interpretation. A personality-based interpretation of an individual's behavior is much more reasonable if based on a demonstrated underlying consistency across a variety of situations than if based on the occurrence of a single dramatic behavior on a single occasion. The individual need not (and indeed, will not) behave the same way on all occasions, since different situations demand different responses; but the psychobiographer should demonstrate a commonality of behavior within somewhat discrepant circumstances, unless he wants to offer a strictly environmental explanation of the person's behavior. Similar behavior on several very similar occasions is not enough to support a personality hypothesis, unless the behavior is quite unusual for those occasions. Most Americans stand every time the "Star-Spangled Banner" is played in public, but that repeated behavior doesn't say much about their level of patriotism.

123

PSYCHOBIOGRAPHER BIAS

We have assumed so far that the psychobiographer (as well as the therapist) is conscientious, motivated to seek the truth, and willing to revise hypotheses as the data demand. This is, of course, not always true; some therapists impose a standard interpretation on every unsuspecting patient who enters the office, and psychobiographers may

begin with strongly held hypotheses for which they seek only supportive data. In dealing with these extremes, it is not much use to
suggest self-applied remedies; more responsible professionals can
only try to warn the potential audience. But even the responsible
psychobiographer will have personal biases toward subjects, and he
needs ways of dealing with them directly, in addition to the data-
analysis precautions already mentioned.

Personal bias first becomes evident in the selection of the psychobiographical subject. According to Freud (1910),

> biographers are fixated on their heroes in a quite special way. In
> many cases they have chosen their hero as the subject of their
> studies because—for reasons of their personal emotional life—they
> have felt a special affection for him from the very first. They then
> devote their energies to a task of idealization, aimed at enrolling the
> great man among the class of their infantile models—at reviving in
> him, perhaps, the child's idea of his father.

Such idealization obviously makes for bad biography; but so does the
opposite situation, probably more frequent in psychobiography, where
the subject is chosen because of the psychobiographer's special hostility toward him. Whether this hostility comes from the psychobiographer's need to express aggression toward a substitute parental figure,
or from opposition to the subject's political position, or from both and
more, fair treatment of the data is as improbable as for the uncritically
loved subject.

124   One might therefore recommend that the psychobiographer deal
only with subjects toward whom he is completely neutral. But such
psychobiographies are unlikely to be completed in the first place, or
read in the second. As I suggested earlier, the psychobiographer's best
choice may be subjects about whom he is consciously ambivalent.
They are likely to prove the most interesting subjects for him and his
readers in the long run anyway; he is more likely to handle the data
honestly; and he should be more open to revision of his hypotheses as
he goes along than he would be if he began with the assumption that
the subject had a heart either of gold or of obsidian.

Once a subject has been chosen, personal bias can be tempered by
the previously discussed iterative process, by tests for internal consistency, and by laying one's scientific cards on the table. The latter
duty of the psychobiographer is summarized by Betty Glad (1973):

> The sources of his data must be given, so that his facts are susceptible
> to an outside check; and his explanatory framework should be ex-

plicitly presented, so that it may be judged by other scholars in terms of its ability to handle the data in an economic and internally consistent way that accords with the broad body of social science theory and data.

AVOIDING REDUCTIONISM

The most frequent criticisms of psychobiography (for example, Barzun, 1974) deal with a particular kind of interpretative bias: reductionism. Readers are still complaining, sixty-five years after Freud tried to respond to the issue, that psychobiographies tend to be too "pathographic" in orientation, that they concentrate excessively on individuals' infantile motives and neurotic conflicts, with little reference to the surrounding social and political conditions. I have made such complaints myself, in discussing several psychobiographical treatments of Wilson and Nixon.

A reductionist or pathographic orientation is not characteristic of all psychobiographies, however. Some psychobiographers—most notably Erik Erikson, in his studies of Martin Luther (1958) and Mahatma Gandhi (1969)—have begun to stress the individual's sources of psychological strengths, the means by which he has been able to attain "greatness" despite his human failings, and even the positive contributions of his childhood experiences to his growth into competent adulthood. Robert Coles (1973) sensitively suggests some such possibilities:

> It may be that certain friends or teachers or events or sets of circumstances have specially touched a life here, another life there— bringing out traits otherwise dormant, initiating perceptions, supplying understanding, furthering awareness. And as to those mothers and fathers whom we have all learned to approach with such foreboding, perhaps their influence is indeed decisive. Perhaps Leonardo, Conrad, Abraham Lincoln or Gandhi, Zapata or Cesar Chavez, Mao or de Gaulle, slowly learned much from their parents: determination and patience; a capacity for deep attachments or passionate involvements; glimpses into all sorts of things; suspicions about how corrupt a given society is; a store of knowledge; a host of skills or talents; an appreciation of the world's complexity; encouragement to stretch the imagination; an aptness for words; a sharpness of vision; a readiness to listen or speak in such a way that others listen; a turn of mind that is a bit different; a taste for the nuances of meaning or emotion.

125

A psychobiographer who paid attention to all these possibilities would clearly not be concerned only with the primitive psyche or with the individual's infantile conflicts. But he might still be too closely focused on the narrow circle of the individual's family life and not sufficiently alert to the pressures of the individual's culture or the political structure within which the individual's political behaviors must be expressed. When such an overemphasis on the subject's private circle of influences is found, it can be attributed largely to the clinician's habit of focusing on the patient both as a source of information and as a target for change. This is often a necessary focus in therapy, in order to build a trusting therapeutic relationship and to exert influence where it is most efficacious, but it is hardly essential to psychobiography. Indeed, because the psychobiographer's information about a subject's early life is usually so much more limited than the clinician's, the psychobiographer cannot afford to ignore information about influences outside the family even if he thinks the family context was more important.

Here again, Erikson has provided the model for other psychobiographers. Repeatedly, both by maxim and by illustration, he has emphasized the psychobiographer's obligation to place the individual's innate biological and acquired psychological characteristics within the social context as the individual himself experiences it. Erikson has pursued this obligation under the most difficult circumstances, writing about individuals remote in time or in cultural tradition; his success should encourage those who deal with the comparatively easy (although still terribly difficult to do well) analysis of recent American politicians. As Erikson (1974) put it in discussing a prominent American politician of another day, Thomas Jefferson: "What we must vigilantly pursue is the relationship of man's deals with his archaic inner life . . . and those political deals which mark the system of privileges and duties in his expanding world." Erikson is referring not only to "shady" deals, of course, but to the full range of the individual's efforts to cope with his psychological needs in the ways his political world permits.

The psychobiographer has the opportunity to do what few other researchers on personality in politics can ever even hope to accomplish —to give a thorough account of at least one personality and a thorough account of the political context within which that personality operates. Whether he makes full use of the opportunity is a function of his own personality and its context. He cannot fairly blame the nature of psychobiography itself for his failures. It can be done well, and it is worth the effort to do it better.

126

5

behind
the throne

the psychology
of the
nonelected politician

Eli Chesen (1973) claims to have based much of his analysis of Richard Nixon's personality on the televised Senate Watergate hearings. He could not have formed any direct impression of Nixon during those hearings, since the star witness failed to appear. But millions of Americans watched the testimony of the men closest to Nixon and wondered what lay behind John Ehrlichman's cockiness, H. R. Haldeman's humble manner, John Mitchell's grim smile.

Chesen briefly attempted to characterize the Presidential advisers as well as the President. He saw Haldeman's personality as similar to Nixon's, but as more compulsive than obsessive. Ehrlichman shared "a sense of superhumanness" with Nixon. Billy Graham, "the 'Chaplain' of the Nixon inner circle . . . uses massive amounts of projection to relieve his tremendous unconscious storehouse of hostilities." But these are merely casual sketches. As Chesen wrote about Graham, "It would take another book to document this analysis fully."

Full documentation of a Presidential adviser's personality has seldom been tried. The President is a more obvious target for psycho-

127

President Richard Nixon meeting with aides H. R. Haldeman, Dwight Chapin, and John Erlichman.

biography, and his behavior is likely to be more visible. Cabinet officers, government bureau heads, Congressional aides—hundreds of nonelected individuals powerfully influence the nation's political processes, and they are in turn influenced by private motives and individual quirks. But they usually remain quiet enough to escape the attention of personality researchers or inaccessible enough to give the researchers little reward for their efforts.

The few studies available of Presidential advisers or other non-elected political figures have almost without exception focused on foreign-policy experts. Perhaps domestic-policy advisers are considered less influential; or perhaps foreign policy, less restrained by structural checks and balances, offers more fertile ground for the action of personality variables. Whatever the reason, there are at least two detailed psychological analyses of Secretaries of State (Glad, 1966; Ward, 1975), one of a Secretary of Defense (Rogow, 1963), and one of a principal foreign-policy adviser who had no official title (George and George, 1956), as well as several studies of groups of foreign-policy advisers at various levels of government—but hardly anything, as far as

I know, on the personalities of Attorneys General or other cabinet officers, domestic bureau chiefs, or major legislative appointees. So this chapter's broad concern with nonelected politicians will most of the time be somewhat narrowed to the role of personality in American foreign-policy decisions.

In most of the studies just mentioned, an attempt was made to consider the total personality of a particular foreign-policy adviser. But attention has more frequently been directed at a particular personality process or characteristic as it influences foreign-policy decisionmaking. This chapter will therefore be organized around three such research focuses: misperception, Machiavellianism, and groupthink.

misperceptions among foreign-affairs advisers

John Foster Dulles once served for a few months as a United States Senator from New York, having been appointed to fill out a term vacated because of illness. When Dulles ran for election to the office in his own right, he was handily defeated. Other than this brief encounter with elective politics, Dulles served his country mainly as a diplomat. His diplomatic career began when his uncle, the Secretary of State under Woodrow Wilson, sent the twenty-nine-year-old Dulles on an "unofficial" mission to Panama, and ended with Dulles' own term as Secretary of State under Dwight Eisenhower.

Dulles participated in the Paris Peace Conference that initiated Wilson's downfall. While agreeing with Wilson's general goals, Dulles was dismayed by Wilson's inflexibility, and for years thereafter he condemned "the assumption that any difference between ourselves and a foreign nation is due to the inherent righteousness of our cause and the inherent perverseness of our neighbors" (quoted in Guhin, 1972). He was even accused of being pro-Nazi for refusing to join in moral condemnation of the German government prior to the Second World War.

Nonetheless, by the time he became Secretary of State in 1953, Dulles had adopted a harsh moralistic stance toward the Soviet Union. British Prime Minister Anthony Eden later described him as "a preacher in a world of politics," and Dulles' own statements as well as those of staff members indicate that he believed the Soviet government was not just wrong but thoroughly evil (Holsti, 1967). Ole Holsti conducted an extensive content analysis of Dulles' writings, in which

129

several consistent themes emerged: Soviet policy as the expression of an atheistic and materialistic creed, directly opposed to Dulles' own religious views; the Soviet government as the instrument of an aggressive and expansionist worldwide Communist conspiracy; and Soviet leaders as holding views radically different from those of the ordinary Russian people, with whom the United States had "no dispute."

These basic beliefs led Dulles to make further assumptions that had important implications for American foreign policy. He thought the only Soviet statements that could be trusted were those indicating aggressive intent, since "atheists can hardly be expected to conform to an ideal so high" as telling the truth. He assumed until his last year in office that the Soviet economy was on the verge of collapse because the Russian people were unwilling to work hard for their Communist masters. He believed that Soviet promises of aid to underdeveloped countries were merely propaganda, and he canceled a United States agreement to finance the Aswan Dam in Egypt so that the Russians would be forced to put up or shut up. (The Russians put up; the Egyptians became decidedly more pro-Russian and seized the Suez Canal; and the English, French, and Israelis seized it back again, in a move that had major international repercussions.)

Many of Dulles' judgments on foreign affairs are still debated, with evidence for and against their soundness. But in these and related instances, Dulles appears not to have perceived the circumstances nearly as accurately as he could have had his basic beliefs been different. He was receiving a large amount of information about the Soviet Union that could have led to more realistic conclusions, but he seems often to have processed the information badly.

TYPES OF MISPERCEPTIONS

Dulles was hardly alone, however. This idea of poor information processing—of *misperception,* as it is most often called—is central to many psychological discussions of foreign relations (for example, Pruitt, 1965; de Rivera, 1968; White, 1970). Ralph K. White has categorized the major types of misperceptions, of which several seem characteristics of Dulles as Secretary of State. The *diabolical enemy-image* and the *moral self-image* are perceptions of the enemy government as totally bad and of one's own government as totally good: the Communists are atheists, and God is on our side. The *black-top enemy image* is the particular subcategory to which Dulles was partial: the

"Don't You Ever Have Anything Fresh?"

From *Herblock's Special For Today* (Simon and Schuster, 1958).

assumption that only the leaders of the enemy country are really bad, while the people want peace. A *virile self-image* involves a perception of the enemy not only as bad but as weak, and of one's home country as strong and manly. (Dulles had no problem in believing that the Russian arsenal of airplanes and missiles was growing rapidly—that proved, after all, how aggressive the Communists were. But he assumed the whole military structure would collapse like a house of cards when the Communist economy failed.) A related misperception is *military overconfidence*, the inaccurate assumption that you have much greater fighting capacity than the enemy. *Selective inattention* involves focusing on those aspects of reality that best support one's prior assumptions. *Absence of empathy* is a particular kind of selective inattention in which the enemy's emotional responses (such as fear of one's own potentially aggressive moves) are ignored.

White demonstrated convincingly that United States government statements and policies during the Vietnam War were thoroughly grounded in these kinds of misperceptions. Indeed, he did the same for Austrian policy toward Serbia at the beginning of the First World War and for Hitler's perceptions of Germany and Poland at the beginning of the Second World War. Further, he pointed out the existence of a "mirror image" in North Vietnamese perceptions of the United States during the Vietnam War: just as we assumed we were stronger and they were weaker than was really true, so they assumed *they* were stronger and *we* were weaker. (Their misperceptions were apparently not as extensive as ours, however.) Urie Bronfenbrenner (1961) made a similar but less detailed analysis of American and Soviet mirror images. Gamson and Modigliani (1971) have ingeniously shown, through an elaborate statistical treatment of *New York Times* foreign affairs stories between 1946 and 1963, that leaders of the United States and the Soviet Union not only shared but *behaved* as if they shared mirror-image perceptions of their own and the opponent's intentions. Each leadership group regarded itself as consolidationist (interested in maintaining but not expanding its current holdings) and assumed it was seen by the enemy as consolidationist, but saw the enemy as expansionist—a set of misperceptions whose results were deplorable.

132

ORIGINS OF MISPERCEPTIONS

What causes such misperceptions? They have often been attributed to common human feelings, either unspecified or else specified only in the broadest sense—for example, "fear." Such explanations are properly categorized as part of the social psychology of politics rather than as an expression of personality in politics, because the assumption is that given certain situational factors, everyone will react equally with misperceptions. Gamson and Modigliani, for instance, cited "mutual insecurity and fear" as a likely source of the joint Soviet and American misperceptions they found in their *New York Times* analysis. But they saw no need to consider whether some individuals feel more insecure than others at the contemplation of Soviet power, or whether perhaps one American Secretary of State or Soviet Foreign Minister might have more difficulty controlling his fears than another one. Their model of international misperceptions works rather well over eighteen years of Soviet-American relations without any attention to individual variations in misperception levels or their causes.

One wonders, however, about the occasional stretch of time for which this impersonal model doesn't quite fit. Here, as in other areas of psychological research, the best predictions seem likely to come from a simultaneous consideration of situation *and* personality. A Secretary of State may have to operate within a certain pattern of national expectations or to struggle with a State Department bureaucracy ingrained with certain shared misperceptual patterns, but he usually has room to shift official policies and public opinion at least a little way out of their previous ruts if he wishes. And the psychologist who wishes to help shift people out of such ruts needs to know not only that misperceptions do occur, but to whom they are most likely to occur and why.

We don't know much about the particular misperceptual susceptibilities of John Foster Dulles. Holsti argued that Dulles' religion had much to do with his misperceptions of the Communists: Dulles was the devoted son of a Presbyterian minister (as was Woodrow Wilson). But a more sympathetic student of Dulles' life (Guhin, 1972) argued that Dulles' father and Dulles himself were far from fundamentalist in their beliefs, and that Dulles was more interested in using the church to advance international order than in using international relations to advance his religious views. Some of Dulles' statements as Secretary of State don't seem to square entirely with that view (Finer, 1964; Hoopes, 1973); a good full-scale psychobiography of Dulles is needed to help resolve the argument.

Ralph K. White (1970) did cite several individual personality factors in misperception, as well as such social factors as communications problems and the economic interests of the military-industrial complex. He considered desires for "power, prestige, and possession" as paramount, with motives for aggression, consistency, and anxiety reduction as also important. White easily demonstrated how such desires *could* produce misperception, and anyone studying misperception in specific instances should consider their possible functioning. For example, the desire for prestige or self-esteem can be met in part by identifying oneself with one's country and then coming to perceive that country as both strong and good, while perceiving others as weak or evil. But

133

White did not present any detailed examples of how individual variations in such desires might influence the development of misperceptions in a particular instance. We are left with the possibility that things happen this way, rather than with the evidence.

MISPERCEPTION AND PERSONALITY PATTERNS

Lloyd Etheridge (1975) has given us such evidence. He asked a random sample of State Department foreign-policy specialists to consider several hypothetical international crises and to indicate their choice of an American response, which could but did not have to include the use of force. Responses to these scenarios presumably were influenced by the diplomats' usual patterns of perception or misperception in foreign affairs: whether a Soviet naval buildup was likely to indicate a serious threat to national security, whether a small country's "move to the left" implied the falling of a domino to the Communists or something less drastic, and so on. Etheridge also gave the diplomats a series of personality tests, and then related willingness to use force in international affairs with specific personality characteristics.

Etheridge found several consistent differences. Desire for power over others, general mistrust of others, and enjoyment of competition with others were all positively related to willingness to use force in international affairs; that is, the higher a diplomat scored on one or more of these personality characteristics, the more likely he was to regard force as an appropriate response in the scenarios. (Competitiveness, however, was positively correlated with preference for force only in cases where the United States was dealing with smaller countries. Etheridge suggested "that people of competitive bent are still constrained by the danger of nuclear war" with regard to treatment of the Soviet Union. This speculation, correct or not, is a useful reminder that a reasonably sane diplomat will consider much more than his personal motives in deciding whether to advocate military action.) Diplomats with high self-esteem were in general less likely to recommend force than those with low self-esteem. However, those who had both high self-esteem *and* a high power need showed "an unusually powerful tendency to advocate force."

So far, Etheridge's results could be explained in either of two ways. First, certain personality patterns may be associated with particular patterns of misperception that lead to greater or lesser use of force.

134

Second, there may be a direct relationship between personality and preference for force. The latter possibility could mean that some diplomats would enjoy attacking other countries whatever their perceptions or misperceptions. Etheridge found support for this possibility when he asked his subjects to describe their images of other countries. The power-oriented and competitive diplomats, who were more likely than the others to recommend force, were also more likely to see the Soviet Union as "active and menacing." They did not, however, display a generally more paranoid view of the world; personality patterns had no effect on perceptions of England. Etheridge suggested that this is because "English policy is much more open to scrutiny than Russia's." It's presumably easier for people to warp their views of a country to fit their own needs if they know relatively little about the country. That seems to be a sensible explanation, but I'd feel better about it if Etheridge had asked his diplomats how much they actually knew about English and Russian foreign policy. Does one view Afghanistan with fear and hostility, and Cuba with disinterested objectivity, because one knows so little about Afghanistan and comparatively so much about Cuba?

Assuming that misperception does play an important role in foreign policymaking, as several of these studies suggest, will we be able to solve all our foreign-policy problems by eliminating such misperceptions? Bringing policymakers' perceptions into line with reality is a pretty tall order in itself; but even if we manage to make the world safe from misperception, we'd still have plenty of problems. One of John Foster Dulles' problems, according to Holsti, was his assumption that genuine conflicts of interest would cease to exist between the Soviet Union and the United States if only the Communist leaders would straighten their thinking and stop seeking world rule. But real bases for conflict would indeed remain, in terms of resource allocations, disagreements on the functioning of the world economic system, and so on. Elimination of misperceptions is a worthy goal, and we should all be better off for achieving it. But once we can see clearly, we'll still see some things we won't like. Psychologists misperceive too, when they focus on perceptual processes to the exclusion of other factors in international relations—of which there are many.

Nonetheless, it should help us to have a Secretary of State and a sturdy crew of foreign service officers whose perceptions are relatively unbiased, who can keep their emotions out of the way of their

135

decisionmaking. For that matter, it should help to have equally clear-headed and unemotional domestic advisers. Or so it may seem, until we consider the Machiavellians of the next section.

Machiavelli as foreign minister

According to his Harvard roommate, Henry Kissinger at one time "contemplated going to medical school and becoming a psychiatrist" (Blumenfeld, 1974). That was only a temporary aberration from Kissinger's interest in government, and he has since then shown little patience with psychological interpretations of his own behavior. However, he has written one semipsychobiography, a thirty-five-page study of Otto von Bismarck published shortly before Kissinger joined the Nixon Administration (Kissinger, 1968).

Kissinger spent less than a page on Bismarck's childhood. Instead, much of the paper is devoted to discussing and illustrating the relationships between Bismarck's adult personality and his achievements as "Germany's greatest modern figure." Bismarck's "first major diplomatic document" was a letter to the deeply religious father of his prospective bride, acknowledging that Bismarck had a bad reputation as an irreligious rake but that marriage to the gentleman's daughter could help "to awaken and to strengthen my faith." He followed this carefully phrased appeal with a visit to the family estate, where (in his own words) Bismarck "moved the whole affair to a different plane by a decisive embrace of my bride, immediately upon seeing her, to the greatest astonishment of the parents." After describing this episode, Kissinger noted Bismarck's "mastery in adapting to the requirements of the moment. . . . [H]e was finely attuned to the subtlest currents of any environment and produced measures precisely adjusted to the need to prevail."

As a Prussian ambassador and later as Foreign Minister, Bismarck developed what Kissinger called a "matter-of-fact Machiavellianism," urging that "foreign policy had to be based not on sentiment but on an assessment of strength." Or in other words (still Kissinger's), "Policy depended on calculation, not emotion." Although Bismarck was nominally a conservative, he could tough-mindedly consider replacing conservative Cabinet members with liberals in order to gain a foreign-policy objective. For the same purposes, he could raise the possibility of a Prussian alliance with a traditional enemy, Russia: ". . . it is

136

nonsense always to swear at once that we will never go with Russia. Even if it were true we should retain the option to use it as a threat." Because of such attempts to base foreign-policy moves only on utilitarian considerations, Kissinger noted, Bismarck was often accused of being "above all an opportunist. The charge of opportunism, however, begs the key issue of statesmanship. Anyone wishing to affect events must be opportunist to some extent."

Through his masterfully expedient statesmanship, Bismarck united Germany and helped to maintain a peaceful Europe for decades. Kissinger clearly admires Bismarck's achievements; but he has emphatically denied that he identifies either with Bismarck or with Bismarck's earlier Austrian counterpart, Metternich, about whom Kissinger wrote his doctoral dissertation. Still less does Kissinger wish to be identified with Machiavelli, although he described Bismarck in apparently approving terms as Machiavellian. When an interviewer (Fallaci, 1972) wondered "to what extent you have been influenced by Machiavelli," Kissinger replied:

> To none whatever. There is really very little of Machiavelli's one can accept or use in the contemporary world. . . . Most people associate me with Metternich. . . . There can be nothing in common between me and Metternich. He was chancellor and foreign minister at a time when it took three weeks to travel from Central Europe to the ends of the continent. He was chancellor and foreign minister at a time when wars were conducted by professional soldiers and diplomacy was in the hands of the aristocracy. How can one compare such conditions with the ones prevailing in today's world, a world where there is no homogeneous group of leaders, no homogeneous internal situation and no homogeneous cultural background?

137

Metternich would probably have laughed at the description of the nineteenth-century German states as a "homogeneous internal situation." But Kissinger seems, intentionally or not, to have missed a more important point: a Foreign Minister of today may face very different external problems than those faced by Machiavelli or Metternich, yet he may deal with them through very similar internal processes. Kissinger identified Bismarck as "Machiavellian" not because nineteenth-century Prussia and sixteenth-century Italy presented identical problems that could be solved by following the same rules of statecraft, but (I assume) because Bismarck's usual approach to a problem broadly resembled the patterns of thought and behavior recommended by Machiavelli.

THE MACHIAVELLIAN PERSONALITY

Machiavellianism as a personality pattern, rather than as adherence to a fixed set of rules, has been studied for the past twenty years by Richard Christie and many others (see Christie and Geis, 1970, for a summary of research). From the time Christie began thinking of Machiavellianism as a distinct personality syndrome, he placed it firmly within a political context. Initially, Christie was seeking ex-

Niccolò Machiavelli.

138

planations for the behavior of certain extremist political leaders, as well as for a way to extend and improve on the "authoritarian personality" research. He found ideas not only in the writings of Machiavelli but in *The Book of Lord Shang,* written by a pragmatic Chinese politician more than two thousand years ago, and in the *Arthasastra,* written in India at about the same time by the "remarkably utilitarian" Prime Minister of an Indian province.

From such sources Christie and his collaborators developed a pool of statements to be used in a personality questionnaire. The final version of the questionnaire, after considerable statistical and conceptual refinement, included such items as:

It is wise to flatter important people.
Most men forget more easily the death of their father
    than the loss of their property.
Anyone who completely trusts anyone else is asking
    for trouble.

Agreement or disagreement with such items yields rather consistent patterns of test-score differences between individuals, and these patterns are associated with certain behavioral differences. Christie identifies the basic characteristics of the highly Machiavellian individual as: "1. *A relative lack of affect in interpersonal relationships.*" The Machiavellian tends to view others "as objects to be manipulated rather than as individuals with whom one has empathy." "2. *A lack of concern with conventional morality.* . . . [T]hose who manipulate have an utilitarian rather than a moral view of their interactions with others." Machiavellianism is in this sense at one extreme of a continuum with superego-tripping at the other, and with most people falling somewhere in between. "3. *A lack of gross psychopathology.*" Machiavellians need to be at least enough in contact with reality to evaluate accurately the information that will help them manipulate others. "4. *Low ideological commitment.* The essence of successful manipulation is a focus upon getting things done rather than a focus upon long-range ideological goals."

139

The Machiavellian's behavior patterns have been observed extensively, inside the laboratory and out. Highly Machiavellian individuals lie more plausibly, and look members of their audience in the eye more often while lying, than do low Machs. Assigned the role of a psychological experimenter, high Machs manipulate their subjects more than lows do, and are particularly good at "devising innovative manipulations." In several different kinds of games involving bargaining skill, high Machs "won overwhelmingly," apparently both because they can keep their own emotions out of their decisionmaking and because they can take advantage of other people's emotional responses. Individuals in personal service occupations tend to be more Machiavellian than those who work mainly with nonhuman objects; psychiatrists are more Machiavellian than surgeons; urban residents are more Mach than rural ones, the young more than the old. From all these data and others, Christie and Geis (1968, 1970) suggested that Machiavellians require several situational factors to make the most effective use of their personality characteristics: face-to-face interaction with those they wish to manipulate, latitude for improvisation, and stimuli that will arouse "irrelevant affect" in their opponents. If they cannot directly influence others, or must adhere to a rigid regulatory structure, or are dealing with issues that are no more emotionally arousing to others than to themselves, Machiavellians will fail to show any unusual degree of success.

Finally, high Machs seem to *enjoy* manipulating others. Their enjoyment is not malicious or psychopathic; they are interested in exercising their skills and winning the game rather than in demeaning their opponents. When instructed to deceive others in an experiment, low Machs ask if they really have to, high Machs devise new deceptions and ask if they can use those too. Low Machs may spontaneously apologize afterward to the people they've deceived; apology doesn't seem to occur to high Machs.

140

KISSINGER'S MACHIAVELLIANISM

International diplomacy seems an ideal situation for the Machiavellian individual—as Machiavelli himself demonstrated. Top diplomats frequently negotiate face to face with their counterparts, are usually permitted substantial improvisatory elbowroom (if their chief executives have any sense), and often deal with issues of national honor, ideology, and tradition that arouse "irrelevant affect" in their opponents, in the sense that it is irrelevant to the material advantage of either party. Bismarck certainly fits the major criteria of the Machiavellian personality: a "utilitarian rather than a moral view" of international relations; little ideological commitment in any traditional sense, much to the dismay of his original conservative allies; the ability to stand back and view his relationships with others, even with his new bride, in the coldest practical terms; no notable psychopathology; and apparently a great delight in the exercise of his manipulative skills. Kissinger correctly identified Bismarck's "matter-of-fact Machiavellianism," although he probably had only a portion of these characteristics in mind. Are we right in identifying Kissinger himself as highly Machiavellian, in terms of his personality as well as his tactics?

Consider Kissinger's self-description first. He is emphatic about his lack of affect in situations where affect would place him at a disadvantage: ". . . I'm not one of those people that allow themselves to be swayed by their emotions. Emotions are of no use. Least of all are they of any use in helping one to attain peace." "To me women are no more than a hobby. Nobody devotes too much time to a hobby. . . . The fact that I don't live with my children doesn't give me any guilt complexes." His discussion of Bismarck indicates the value Kissinger himself places on a utilitarian rather than a moral view of international politics. Kissinger's ideological commitment has always been vague. He has served as an adviser to Kennedy, Johnson, Rockefeller, Nixon, and Ford and says his position "towards all presidents has always been the same: . . . When they asked for [my opinion], I gave it to them, telling them all, indiscriminately, what I thought. I was never concerned with what party they belonged to." And Kissinger's enjoyment of his manipulative success is obvious:

> The main point stems from the fact that I've always acted alone. Americans admire that enormously. Americans admire the cowboy leading the caravan alone astride his horse, the cowboy entering a village or city alone on his horse. Without even a pistol, maybe, because he doesn't go in for shooting. He acts, that's all; aiming at the right spot at the right time.*

141

Other information about Kissinger provides similar insights into his character. Kissinger was a refugee from Nazi Germany, and many of his friends and relatives were killed or imprisoned by the Nazis. Yet when he returned to Germany at war's end as an American soldier, assigned to track down and arrest Nazis, he became known both for his effectiveness in getting the job done and for his "objectivity," his "even-handedness," in doing it. He later told one of his aides who protested the intense bombing of North Vietnam on humanitarian grounds, "Sentimentality would not have saved the European Jews. If

---

* All the quotations in this paragraph are from Oriana Fallaci's 1972 interview with Kissinger, who seems to have temporarily blown his Machiavellian cover in order to impress an attractive young woman journalist.

we had been tough with the Nazis when they moved into the Rhineland, that might have stopped them. It is not your morality but my toughness that will save the world" (Blumenfeld, 1974).

The latter statement underlines not only Kissinger's emotional control but his emphasis on utility over morality. Marvin and Bernard Kalb (1975), who have probably been closer to Kissinger than any other journalists, summarized Kissinger's general approach to foreign affairs in almost those words: "a global *realpolitik* that placed a higher priority on pragmatism than on morality." The utility-over-morality emphasis is reflected in another view of Kissinger's army experience, recounted by an acquaintance from his Harvard student years: "He told complicated stories about how he would get women who wanted to ingratiate themselves to those in authority. He always talked in manipulative terms. He was the man with the gun, the jeep, the coffee, stockings, chocolate . . . those were important things" (Blumenfeld, 1974).

The utility-over-morality emphasis apparently united with Kissinger's lack of ideological conviction in his decision to join the Nixon Administration. During the primary campaign of 1968 Kissinger worked hard for Nelson Rockefeller's nomination and told people that Nixon was "the most dangerous" of all the potential nominees. When Nixon won the nomination, Kissinger reportedly wept and said that "that man Nixon . . . doesn't have the right to rule" (Kalb and Kalb, 1975). Yet the same day, Kissinger agreed to work as a foreign-affairs consultant to candidate Nixon, and within a month after the election he had accepted a major role in the administration. According to the Kalbs, "Kissinger accepted the opportunity to work at the White House because his misgivings about Nixon were overcome by the prospect of exerting that much power." Kissinger also decided, after talking with Nixon, that his views and Nixon's were not so different after all. Nixon appeared to be an eminently practical man.

Kissinger loved his job from the beginning. A prominent foreign adviser does not publicly admit his pleasure at manipulating the leaders of other nations, but Kissinger's staff members (quoted by the Kalbs) suggested how he felt about it: "He thrives on adversity, even at the White House. He needs to feel challenged, admired, put upon, despised, loved; he needs to feel cornered so he can outperform everyone, almost as though he enjoys overcoming adversity and showing off his brilliance and subtlety." "You can see that it's in his life's blood. He's more relaxed, tanned, happier . . . since he's been in this job.

Secretary of State Henry Kissinger is greeted by Soviet Communist Party General Secretary Leonid Brezhnev in Moscow, October 1974.

Anybody else right now would be a wan, shaken wreck. He thrives on it. And I think he knew he'd thrive on it." Despite occasional signs of nervousness, Kissinger appears to enjoy manipulating reporters at televised press conferences as much as he apparently enjoys handling Foreign Ministers at secret meetings.

MACHIAVELLIAN ORIGINS

In many ways, therefore, Kissinger fits the Machiavellian pattern. But how deep does the pattern run in his personality? Is it mainly a veneer, coming from a surface identification with the great European Foreign Ministers Metternich and Bismarck, or does it grow from deeper roots? Unfortunately, the information we have both on Kissinger's childhood and on the childhood of the typical adult Machiavellian is very sparse in comparison with our knowledge of their adult behaviors. But as far as can be told, Kissinger fits the Machiavellian developmental pattern fairly well.

Some data indicate that children tend to resemble their parents in level of Machiavellianism (O'Kelly and Solar, 1971); others suggest the opposite relationship (Braginsky, cited in Christie and Geis, 1970, 335–36). Kissinger's father, a reportedly "soft-hearted" schoolteacher who kept hoping the Jewish situation would improve in Nazi Germany even after he was fired from his job solely for being Jewish, was notably un-Machiavellian. Kissinger's mother was tougher and more resourceful, managing to get the family out of Germany before they were arrested and then supporting them when they first settled in New York. Her behavior is not conclusively Machiavellian, but it is suggestive.

Stanley Guterman (1970) has found evidence that high adult Machiavellianism tends to be related to low "perceived rapport with parents," particularly with the father, during the subject's adolescence. Guterman measured "perceived rapport" by asking subjects how frequently each parent had participated with them in leisure activities, how much the parent had helped them with adolescent emotional crises, and how frequently they had confided in their parents as teen-agers. Kissinger reported having had "a very close family relationship" during his adolescence (Kalb and Kalb, 1975), but there is evidence that his relationship with his father was a difficult one. One German friend remembered Kissinger telling him "more than once that he couldn't discuss anything with his father, especially not girls" (Blumenfeld, 1974). The father was an Orthodox Jew, as was Kissinger as a child. But in New York, Kissinger began to drift into more liberal religious circles, at least partly through his mother's influence. Most important, Kissinger had seen his father fail to cope with the Nazis in Germany and then fail to cope with life in America. The father dropped from the prestigious role of German schoolteacher to a poorly paid bookkeeper's job in New York. Kissinger described him later as "a man of great goodness in a world where goodness has no meaning" (Kraft, 1971). In other words, Kissinger's father lacked just those Machiavellian characteristics that Kissinger believes are essential to survival.

Perhaps here we have a clue as to what the researchers on Machiavellianism should be looking for in their developmental studies, rather than for such indirect variables as rapport with parents. When and under what circumstances do children learn that it is good to control their own emotions in order to control other people? Richard Nixon seems to have learned such self-control very early, in navigating between an aggressive father and a pacifist mother, although he never learned to do it as well as Kissinger. Although Kissinger probably

144

learned some emotional restraint during childhood in response to his father's Orthodoxy and schoolteacherish demands for control, his big lesson must have come in adolescence, when he saw what happened as his father lost control of his life. Kissinger showed little sign of being a Machiavellian as a child, but by the age of twenty-one, he was in control and loving it. Later, whenever he voices any goal other than that of coping with the immediate situation, the goal is "order," "international stability," "a structure of peace." Kissinger has repeatedly denied that his family's treatment by the Nazis had any real impact on his own later thinking; he does not want to be accused of bearing grudges against Germany. But he seems to have worked very hard, in those years after his father's "goodness" became meaningless, to shift emphasis from goodness to control.

KISSINGER'S OTHER QUALITIES

I am not proposing Machiavellianism as a total description of Henry Kissinger's personality. People really should not be labeled "Machiavellians," any more than they should be labeled "oral personalities" or "racists" or "active-negatives," with the idea that the label says it all. Machiavellianism may appropriately describe the form of a person's behavior, but it says little about the content. Kissinger appears adept at controlling his emotions and at controlling others in order to obtain his goals. But his goals—public adulation, compliant women, world order, or whatever—may be very different from the goals of other Machiavellian personalities.

145

In a brief psychobiography of Kissinger, preliminary to a full-scale one, Dana Ward (1975) identified Kissinger as a "depressive personality" and tried to match his characteristics at every point with those of the typical depressive. In certain regards the analysis seems to work well. Ward is not the first to note a depressive theme in Kissinger's writings and in some of his personal behavior. However, the fit is considerably less than exact. We are told (in a quotation from Frieda Fromm-Reichmann) that "the typical depressive personality 'seeks and quickly forms superficial relationships and tends to be clinging and exploitive.'" It would be hard to show that Kissinger is "clinging"; the other qualities fit the Machiavellian pattern as well as the depressive one. We are further told that depressive neurotics (in Benjamin Wolman's words) "are full of tabloid wisdom and express their cliché statements as if they were great and original ideas," and that Kissinger's writings and cocktail party discussions are similar to the depressive's—this about a man regarded even by his enemies as one of the most brilliant foreign-policy analysts of the century. We are offered a damned-if-you-do-or-don't speculation that even Kissinger's sense of humor shows he is a depressive personality, "since 'megalomania is a defense against feelings of inferiority.'" (There is some indication [Blumenfeld, 1974] that Kissinger developed his self-deprecating humor in the army for the same reason that many bright young people learn a similar style—in defense against accusations of egotism.) Depressive tendencies and Machiavellianism may be related, or in some individuals at least complementary; but I am not persuaded that a diagnosis of "neurotic depression" explains any more about Kissinger's personality than an analysis of his Machiavellianism. In some ways it does not explain as much.

MACHIAVELLIAN STRENGTHS AND WEAKNESSES

Ward's analysis of Kissinger's depressiveness is rather negative, even pathographic, in tone. I do not intend to convey a similarly negative judgment in describing Kissinger as Machiavellian. Christie and Geis (1970) noted that when they began their research they thought of Machiavellians as "associated with shadowy and unsavory manipulations." But they came to develop "a perverse admiration for the high Mach's ability to outdo others in experimental situations," and they concluded that high Machs can play various useful roles in society. Very high Machs are recommended for positions in which "they are sent on what amounts to detached service in which there is freedom to wheel and deal to both their own and [their] organization's benefit."

146

Christie and Geis did not specify any jobs that would fit this description. But Kissinger's position fits it to a "T." As already noted, the high Mach's special skills at self-control and at manipulating others are supremely fitted to the demands and the opportunities of the senior diplomatic post. However, Kissinger would for the same reasons be quite inappropriate as a President. High Machs can wheel and deal with relative impunity on the international scene, confident that their success in defending their country's interests will excuse any moral transgressions in their compatriots' eyes, and that their international opponents' personal attitudes toward them will have little effect on their tenure in office. But high Machs on the domestic scene may soon find that even minor moral lapses, even for what they identify as reasons of national security—such as the tapping of telephones to detect leaks of confidential information—are not excused by all their constituents. They may find, as Christie and Geis put it, that a "cool cognitive analysis of the needs of the organization coupled with a disregard for the individual needs of those within it could quite easily lead to disaffection and problems of morale which can cripple the organization."

The highly Machiavellian individual may sometimes cause problems even as a Foreign Minister. It is tempting to reject the rigid moralism of John Foster Dulles or of Woodrow Wilson in favor of the brilliant flexibility of Henry Kissinger. The nation may gain from flexibility a détente with its former enemies, Russia and China; the world may get a settlement between the Arabs and the Israelis. But we may also get a brutal bombing campaign against North Vietnam and an "incursion" that leads to the destruction of much of Cambodia, because these seem like good tactical moves at the time and because they are unrestrained by any substantial moral concerns. We may get a Foreign Minister who, in addition to his Machiavellian characteristics and his willingness to serve the country, has a private agenda coming from other motives that are hidden until it is too late to stop him. Bismarck believed in the principle of "restraint," for reasons never explained by Kissinger, and carefully restrained his nation from trying to take over Europe for as long as he could. Kissinger believes in the concept of "order" and apparently refrains from certain easy opportunities for *realpolitik* because they would visit more disorder on the world—disorder perhaps painfully reminiscent of what he experienced as a child in Germany. Another Machiavellian Foreign Minister might believe in the concept of "American empire" or of "racial purification" and behave accordingly.

In his analysis of Bismarck, Kissinger himself identified one other major drawback of the Machiavellian Foreign Minister. If the nation or the world depends on one brilliantly manipulative individual to maintain peace, rather than on international structures that can be operated by less than brilliant men, the whole international balancing act may collapse when that one man grows tired or dies. That's what happened when Bismarck was gone, and it may happen again when Kissinger steps down. Reliance on one person's Machiavellian skills may even leave the situation worse off after he is finished than before he began, since other less talented people will in the meantime

147

have been discouraged from trying to compete with him or will have been persuaded that their efforts are not needed. They may also learn the wrong lessons from their subtle master, as Kissinger noted with regard to Bismarck's successors: "They remembered the three wars that had achieved their unity. They forgot the patient preparation that had made them possible and the moderation that had secured their fruits."

In 1973 Kissinger won the Nobel Peace Prize. In 1974 the "peace" he had negotiated in Vietnam collapsed completely, to be replaced by the imposed peace of the North Vietnamese victors. But Kissinger had long since moved on to other arenas. Let us hope that as a good Machiavellian interested in practical results, he has learned some cautionary lessons to apply during the remainder of his service and to pass on to his less brilliant successors.

groupthink in the highest groups

"The best and the brightest" David Halberstam (1972) called them. The talented young men of the Kennedy Administration, they seemed too bright to get bogged down in moralistic misperceptions of the world outside our borders, too sincere and high-principled to become totally Machiavellian. And yet three months into Kennedy's Presidential term, they were in the midst of one of the biggest foreign-policy fiascoes of the century, the attempted invasion of Cuba at the Bay of Pigs. Although they recouped their losses the following year in the Cuban Missile Crisis, several remained at the center of American foreign-policy planning during what Halberstam, in another book title, called "the making of a quagmire"—the Vietnam War. How did they go wrong?

Various explanations for the Bay of Pigs debacle have been proposed by both participants and nonparticipants. Some explanations (for example, Schlesinger, 1965) pin the blame at least partly on individual personality characteristics of specific participants, although no participant seems to have displayed the personality extremes of a Wilson or a Kissinger. Irving Janis (1972) argues instead that in this instance and in a number of similar ones, the whole was greater than the parts: certain rather ordinary personality tendencies working within the context of a face-to-face planning group summated to produce a decisionmaking disaster.

148

Janis calls this phenomenon *groupthink*. For many years he has studied the dynamics of small groups, ranging from classroom discussions to gatherings of overweight or cigarette-addicted men and women brought together to help each other with their problems. While reading Schlesinger's account of how the Bay of Pigs invasion plans were developed, Janis was struck by the apparent similarities between the Kennedy foreign-policy–planning group and the small groups he had been studying, particularly in terms of certain group processes that interfered with realistic decisionmaking. Janis began to investigate the Bay of Pigs decision in greater detail, as well as other major foreign-policy decisions of the twentieth century, both successful and unsuccessful. From this research, the groupthink hypothesis was born.

Groupthink, according to Janis, is "a mode of thinking that people engage in when they are deeply involved in a cohesive in-group, when the members' strivings for unanimity override their motivation to realistically appraise alternative courses of action. . . . Groupthink refers to a deterioration of mental efficiency, reality testing, and moral judgment that results from in-group pressures." The basic groupthink hypothesis is: "The more amiability and esprit de corps among the members of a policy-making in-group, the greater is the danger that independent critical thinking will be replaced by groupthink, which is likely to result in irrational and dehumanizing actions directed against out-groups."

Group policymaking is not all bad, as Janis recognizes. Numerous experimental studies have found groups to be more effective than single individuals in at least some kinds of problem-solving, usually because the assortment of group members assures a greater array of skills or knowledge than any one group member possesses. Government policy decisions are often subjected to group discussion, both because of this obvious advantage of groups and because groups are assumed to be less likely than individuals to fall prey to the kinds of personality-based aberrations discussed earlier in this book.

But the gains from group decisionmaking do not always exceed the losses. Individual decisionmakers often have their weaknesses as well as their talents, and Janis argues that the weaknesses in particular are likely to be exaggerated by group interactions. To see how this might happen, let's consider the *origins* of groupthink, the *processes* involved, and the *results* in terms of defective decisionmaking. The examples I use are drawn mainly from Janis' discussion of the Bay of Pigs decisionmaking process, although he also closely examined Amer-

149

ican foreign-policy planning prior to Pearl Harbor and during the Korean and Vietnam wars.

GROUPTHINK ORIGINS

Janis does not go into detail on the origins of groupthink, beyond his specification that it derives from deep involvement in a cohesive in-group and becomes more likely as the group members become more dependent on each other for mutual support in coping with the stresses of decisionmaking. An individual's deep group involvement may come from a variety of motives. He may want the friendship of others within the group, thus satisfying his need for affiliation or love. He may seek positive feedback from group members about himself, thus building or maintaining self-esteem; or, having joined the group for other reasons, he may seek to remain on friendly terms with group members to keep from suffering a loss of self-esteem. He may feel that membership in the group is prestigious or that group membership will lead to still more prestigious positions in the larger organization of which the group is a part—as members of Presidential policymaking groups probably often assume. He may even be afraid, as Mary Mc-Grory (1973) has suggested, that he will lose his chauffeur-driven government limousine if he antagonizes other group members.

The diverse motives of the Kennedy, Johnson, and Nixon planning groups have been speculated on by Halberstam and others. It would be worth studying them in detail, since some motives (such as the need for affiliation) may lend themselves more easily to sustained groupthink than others, or may produce somewhat different emphases within the general groupthink process. The common element in all these motives is that they lead group members to try to *maintain the existence of the group and their membership in it,* regardless of whether or not the group is really solving any problems. Indeed, some things that might actually promote more effective problem-solving are avoided because they could lead to disagreement and thus to the dissolution of the group.

GROUPTHINK PROCESSES

What are the processes by which this general desire to maintain the group's existence results in poor decisionmaking? Janis lists several, of which the main ones are: suppression of personal doubts; suppression of others' doubts; development of an illusion of unanimity; development of an illusion of invulnerability; and leadership-fostered docility.

Suppression of personal doubts. This appears to be the basic inner response to the desire to maintain a cohesive group. Without its widespread functioning, all the other processes would fail to produce groupthink. Janis described it as "self-censorship of deviations from the apparent group consensus . . . each member [minimizes] to himself the importance of his doubts and counterarguments." As an example, Janis quoted from Arthur Schlesinger Jr.'s (1965) description of his experience in Kennedy's inner circle:

> In the months after the Bay of Pigs I bitterly reproached myself for having kept so silent during those crucial discussions in the Cabinet Room, though my feelings of guilt were tempered by the knowledge that a course of objection would have accomplished little save to gain me a name as a nuisance.

Theodore Sorensen (1965) wrote that "doubts were entertained but never pressed, partly out of fear of being labelled 'soft' or undaring in the eyes of . . . colleagues." If you want to preserve the group *and* your reputation in it, obviously one of the first things you can do is to keep your mouth shut if by opening it you might disrupt a developing group consensus.

Suppression of others' doubts. Sometimes not everyone connected with a group values his membership enough to keep quiet about errors that appear to be creeping into the group's judgments. But if he begins to express his doubts, according to Janis, other group members may decide to appoint themselves as "mindguards" who take steps to "protect the group from adverse information that might shatter their shared complacency about the effectiveness and morality of their decisions." For instance, Janis noted Undersecretary of State Chester Bowles' experience after he sat in on a Bay of Pigs planning session as a substitute for Secretary of State Dean Rusk, who was out of town. Bowles was appalled at what he heard, and when Rusk returned, Bowles asked him for permission to discuss his negative reactions with President Kennedy. Rusk told Bowles in effect to forget it, since the invasion plan was going to be dropped anyway "in favor of a quiet little guerilla infiltration." (Rusk seems to have taken his mindguarding task very seriously with respect to protecting the Kennedy Administration from Bowles. According to Halberstam, "when Bowles returned from Southeast Asia in 1962 and suggested the neu-

151

tralization of Vietnam, Rusk turned to him, quite surprised, and said, 'You realize, of course, you're spouting the Communist line.' ")

Development of an illusion of unanimity. With everyone in the group either suppressing his private doubts or determined to protect the group from hearing about the private doubts of others, it's not surprising that soon everyone comes to feel that the group is totally agreed on the rightness of the majority's preferred plan. As Janis suggests, this illusion of unanimity may be seen by each group member as very persuasive evidence that the decision must be the correct one. Even though most members of Kennedy's foreign-policymaking group apparently held at least "vague reservations" concerning the Bay of Pigs invasion plan prior to its final adoption, they came to agree that it was the best plan possible after they observed everyone else in the group either promoting it or at least not speaking against it. After all, every group member was a highly capable and intelligent individual, and if they could all agree on a plan, what could be wrong with it?

Development of an illusion of invulnerability. This is similar to one of the frequent foreign-affairs misperceptions categorized by Ralph K. White (1970) as "military overconfidence," except that Janis doesn't limit it to military misperceptions. It is the feeling that "if our leader and everyone else in our group decides that it is okay, the plan is bound to succeed. Even if it is quite risky, luck will be on our side." That is, the plan is not only right, it's fail-safe—it will work, no matter what.

Janis suggests that such a feeling often arises when a group first becomes cohesive. The members see that they have succeeded in the difficult task of forming a group that builds their self-esteem, gives them prestige, and offers them opportunities for friendship with all these other intelligent people who agree with them; so why should the group not accomplish everything else it tries? Various people have reported on the tremendous confidence felt by Kennedy's top men in the early days of his administration. Schlesinger described the dominant mood in the White House then as "buoyant optimism," and wrote, "Euphoria reigned; we thought for a moment that the world was plastic and the future unlimited."

As part of this illusion of invulnerability, group members are likely to begin feeling that their opponents are "stupid, weak, bad guys," since who else would oppose their magnificent plan? What Ralph K. White called the diabolical enemy-image and the moral and virile self-images seem to be entering at this point—not just to maintain the

152

President Ford and advisers react to news that the U.S.S. *Mayaguez* has been rescued off Cambodia.

group's cohesiveness, according to Janis, but also to reduce group members' incipient feelings of anxiety and guilt about making decisions that could affect a lot of people very adversely. It's easier to cope with your worries by insisting that your group has all the right answers and that everyone else is wrong or evil, than to admit that maybe somebody else could be right about some things and that you could be making a terrible mistake.

Leadership-fostered docility. Janis has argued that when group members strongly want to maintain the group's existence and cohesiveness, they may permit themselves to be manipulated more easily than usual by a leader who wishes to exaggerate the operation of the processes already mentioned. The leader may be able to promote suppression of personal doubts, for instance, by conducting open straw votes with the most prestigious group members voting first. During the rapid expansion of the Vietnam War, Presidential Assistant Bill Moyers sometimes objected to the escalation decisions of the White House policymaking group. Lyndon Johnson began greeting Moyers' arrival at group meetings by calling out, "Well, here comes Mr. Stop-the-Bombing" (Thomson, 1968). Johnson seems to have not only been trying to shut Moyers up, but to serve as a mindguard for the whole group and to establish a norm for the group to follow in the future. A leader may also give the clear impression that he wants specific group members to serve as mindguards, for instance by delegating to them the responsibility to sift through incoming information or to screen the leader's daily appointments, as Nixon did with Haldeman and Ehrlichman. Obviously, how the group leader responds to people in the group who are worried about their prestige, their self-esteem, and so forth, can considerably exacerbate any groupthink tendencies already existing within the group.

Just as group members with certain needs may be more open to groupthink, so may certain kinds of leaders be more likely to encourage it. In terms of Barber's four types of Presidents, the passive-positives and the active-negatives appear to be the most likely prospects. The passive-positives may submerge themselves in the group, becoming fully subject to groupthink and setting an example for others to do the same, since in Barber's (1972) description, "This is the receptive, compliant, other-directed character whose life is a search for affection as a reward for being agreeable and cooperative rather than personally assertive." President Harding's twice-weekly poker games with his Cabinet members and other cronies, for instance, must have been magnificent displays of groupthink, presided over by the man who (according to Charles Evans Hughes' funeral oration) "literally wore himself out in the endeavor to be friendly."

Active-negative Presidents are less likely to be found in the midst of the groupthinking group, and may even prefer to make major decisions alone. But when they do work with a policymaking group, they are likely either to encourage the members directly toward groupthink or to instill in them a fear of recrimination that deters critical thinking just as effectively. In Barber's conceptualization, the typical active-negative President tends to see any conflict in moral terms, and transforms policy problems "from a matter of calculation of results to a matter of emotional loyalty to ideals. . . . [H]is view of reality must be accepted, else the cause fall apart." George and George (1956) noted just such a pattern in Woodrow Wilson:

> One of the most disastrous consequences of Wilson's personal insecurity was his inability to consult about matters which had become emotionally charged for him except with those upon whose ultimate approval he could count, or with those who, in the last analysis, were not in a position to exert pressure upon him to adopt their views.

Under such extreme circumstances, policy groups would be so specifically designed to encourage either groupthink or anxious conformity that they might as well not exist.

Active-positive Presidents are apparently susceptible to group-think too, as Janis' numerous examples from the Truman and Kennedy Administrations indicate. They would have the natural human tendency to want their ideas accepted with as little criticism as possible and would initially encourage their policymaking groups in that direction. But if they are as open to learning from experience as Barber suggested, they should approach the next round of policy-making after the first major groupthink-induced disaster much more cautiously, perhaps deciding either to dismantle the group entirely, to change its procedures, or to revise its membership. Examples of active-positive Presidents' attempts to combat groupthink will be given shortly.

GROUPTHINK RESULTS

Do all these uncritical decisionmaking processes really result in bad decisions? Janis presents a great deal of evidence that they do. A groupthinking group typically limits itself to considering only a small range of alternatives, fails to examine nonobvious risks in the chosen alternative, and fails to develop contingency plans in case that alternative doesn't work. If group members instead made a point of considering other alternatives or looking for flaws in the chosen one, they would have to engage in an uncomfortable amount of self-criticism and would probably destroy any developing illusions of unanimity and invulnerability—illusions that satisfy important psychological needs for them. Likewise, the group will typically make little effort to obtain information from outside experts who might disturb the group's coziness, and members tend to show selective bias in processing the information the group does have available, by emphasizing supportive information and ignoring contradictory data. 155

The Bay of Pigs invasion plan is a good example of a bad decision based on just such a series of groupthink-induced errors. The policymaking group seriously considered only two possibilities, either an invasion of Cuba with full American air support or an invasion without identifiable United States involvement (but not a guerrilla infiltration or a halt to invasion plans). They chose the plan that included no recognizable United States involvement and therefore changed the landing site to the Bay of Pigs to make the invasion look more like a local uprising, but they did not then reexamine the original plan, which called for invasion troops' escape to the mountains, to take account of the swamp between the Bay of Pigs and the mountains. Even after American complicity in the training of invasion troops became widely known, the planning group failed to reconsider the other major option of total United States involvement in the invasion. They relied for information largely on one set of military men and top CIA brass, and failed to consult with knowledgeable State Department experts and British intelligence agents. They ignored contradictory information that Senator Fulbright, reliable newspaper reporters, and others tried to bring to the planning group's attention. They failed to alter invasion plans even after several important assumptions—including the high morale of the Cuban refugee invasion force, the likelihood of internal uprisings against the Cuban government, and the ability of a small force of obsolete American bombers to destroy the entire Cuban air force—were thrown into serious doubt. The planning group members must have gotten a lot of nice strokes from each other along the way, but the way led straight to a stunning defeat that should have been obvious all along.

GROUPTHINK REMEDIES

What can be done to ensure that groupthink does not seriously interfere with the development of major policy decisions? A President could simply resort to one-man decisionmaking, but in several recent instances that has not proved notably effective either. Or a President could try to make sure that policymaking group members never develop any interest in maintaining the group. That would be hard to do if he wanted the group to accomplish anything; members who would rather be doing something else could hardly be expected to engage in creative decisionmaking, as anyone who has sat on several university administrative committees already knows.

Janis suggests several ways to combat groupthink by changing the group structure or the functions of group members. Just as the group leader can exaggerate groupthink effects, so he can diminish them by his own actions. He can initially present the problem at hand in an unbiased way, avoiding any indication of where he would like the group's discussion to go. He can emphasize that he expects and accepts criticisms of his own statements as well as those of others. He can frequently absent himself from group meetings to permit honest criticism, as Kennedy often did during the Cuban Missile Crisis. He can appoint a group member as a temporary devil's advocate (perma-

156

nent ones tend to pull their punches or to be ignored). He can bring in outside experts and encourage them to challenge the views of core group members, as was again done during the Cuban Missile Crisis. He can break up the planning group into temporary subgroups or establish several completely independent groups and assign each group or subgroup to develop its own solution to a problem and then to hammer out a final solution with the other subgroups at a later meeting. Janis prefers the establishment of temporary subgroups, since the independent-group arrangement is likely to result in each group developing its own cohesiveness, beginning its own groupthink patterns, and then defending its own solution bitterly against the "enemy" groups. The final choice of a solution in such circumstances may be determined more by the power and political skill of the groups than by the quality of the individual plans.

Temporary subgroups were used during the Cuban Missile Crisis, apparently to good effect—counteracting groupthink rather than promoting it in several different groups. A system of relatively permanent and competing subgroups seems to have developed almost accidentally in the top echelons of the Nixon Administration, with bad effects for everyone concerned. According to Bertram Raven's (1974) analysis of the basic Nixon planning group (responsible for domestic political decisions rather than for foreign-policy decisions, which were handled largely by Nixon or Kissinger), hiring patterns and personal animosities resulted in the set of relationships diagramed in Figure 2. Mitchell, Dean, and Kleindienst were pitted against Haldeman and his close associates, with Magruder trying to pursue an uneasy middle course. The subgroups were so mutually hostile that, rather than helping to correct each other's groupthink errors, they either totally ignored or destructively criticized their competitors' proposals. Eventually, the two subgroups did find a use for each other: as a target for blame when the Watergate cover-up fell apart.

Janis' recommendations for reducing groupthink appear to be based on the assumption that a group's personnel are relatively fixed. He therefore directs most of his attention toward changing group interaction patterns. However, it should also be possible to combat groupthink by careful attention to the composition of the group itself. We could obviously begin by trying to elect a President who is less likely than his opponent(s) to encourage groupthink among his staff members. The President could himself select staff members who can work effectively together but who are unlikely as a group to be groupthink-

157

Figure 2
Sociometric diagram of Nixon and his men

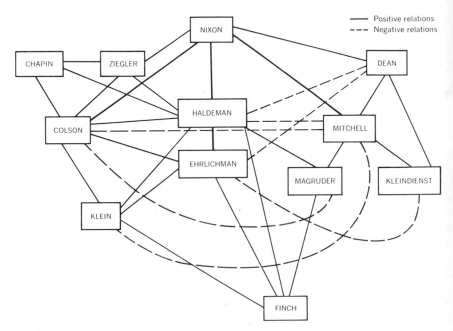

NOTE:
President Nixon has positive relationships with nearly every one on the chart.
Only the most significant of these are illustrated.

Source: Bertram H. Raven, The Nixon group. *Journal of Social Issues*, 1974, *30* (4), 307.

prone. Franklin D. Roosevelt seems to have had just this consideration in mind, according to Richard Neustadt's (1960) description:

> Not only did he keep his organizations overlapping and divide authority among them, but he also tended to put men of clashing temperaments, outlooks, ideas in charge of them. Competitive personalities mixed with competing jurisdictions was Roosevelt's formula for putting pressure on himself, for making his subordinates push up to him the choices they could not take for themselves. It also made them advertise their punches; their quarrels provided him not only heat but information.

John F. Kennedy, however, seems to have made his initial selections of foreign-policy personnel in such a way that groupthink was inevitable. As David Halberstam (1972) described the search for a Secretary of State:

> What it came down to was a search not for the most talent, the greatest brilliance, but for the fewest black marks, the fewest objections. The man who had made the fewest enemies in an era when forceful men espousing good causes had made many enemies: the Kennedys were looking for someone who made very small waves.

Adlai Stevenson was regarded as too soft to be Secretary of State. (The desire to appear tough was an important source of groupthink in the early Kennedy foreign-policy group, as later on under Lyndon Johnson.) Chester Bowles was, among other things, too idealistic. J. William Fulbright was unsatisfactory to the Democratic left. And so on. The same selection process continued through a number of other appointees beyond Secretary of State; an important criterion was whether a person would be a good "team player." Good team players often turned out to be good groupthinkers.

Even if groupthink is effectively eliminated from the deliberations of our top policymaking groups, whether by personnel changes, structural revisions, or simple awareness of the dangers of groupthink, our problems will by no means be over. Even if we also eliminate major misperceptions of other nations and somehow manage to put a leash on our Machiavellian Foreign Ministers, and if other nations simultaneously do the same, we will not have reached Utopia. As I noted in discussing John Foster Dulles' assumptions about the Soviet menace, psychological problems do not cause anywhere near all our difficulties. Real shortages of resources, real economic crises and border conflicts and population explosions will continue to exist regardless of psychologists' efforts to change people's ways of thinking. In trying to deal with these difficulties, our leaders and their advisers will continue to make errors of judgment even when they are doing their best, as a result of inadequate information, human information-processing limits, and just plain wrong guesses. But that is no reason to ignore the improvements that *can* be made through the elimination of groupthink. A better understanding of the role of personality dynamics in political decisionmaking falls far short of telling us everything we need to know; but it can help.

159

6

psychopolitics

personality
researchers
in political roles

"This analysis of groupthink is vital reading for Washington decision-makers." "Professor Janis' book should be placed in the hands of every government official in the land." "Every thinking citizen should read *Victims of Groupthink*." These are the kinds of testimonials many researchers on personality in politics dream of getting, and indeed Irving Janis got an unusual number of them. I would have written one myself if anyone had asked me.

Few personality researchers admit publicly to any larger political ambitions. They want their work read and taken into account by political leaders and concerned citizens; otherwise, their political activism rarely extends beyond their local precinct. An occasional social scientist actually runs for political office, but those who do have seldom if ever been particularly interested in the role of personality in politics. (Eugene McCarthy is the only one I can think of, and his interest has been expressed in poetry rather than in scientific research.)

At least two active political roles may be open to the personality researcher who wants to go beyond writing and teaching but who doesn't want to run for office. One role, that of campaign adviser, has been practiced by social scientists at various levels of politics for some years, although never nearly to the extent that popular media descriptions of "scientific" campaign techniques have suggested. The other role, that of screening candidates for office in terms of their psychological qualities, has only been proposed and not practiced. The first role focuses on how knowledge of voter characteristics may be used to increase the persuasiveness of campaign messages. The second role focuses on the relationship of candidate characteristics to the satisfactory performance of public office. In both cases, the social scientist intervenes directly in the choice of political candidates, rather than merely standing on the sidelines trying to get voters and officeholders to think more clearly and knowledgeably about the political process.

Direct intervention raises serious questions as to whether the social scientist is scientifically, ethically, or politically justified in engaging in these forms of political activism. After considering personality-based campaign strategies and psychological screening techniques, we will conclude with a brief look at such questions of ethics and justification.

influencing the voter

The Barons of Behavior, by Tom Purdom (1972), is a psychopolitical science-fiction novel. It isn't very strong either as science or as fiction, but it gives more attention than any other book I've read to the use of individual personality data in manipulating political campaigns. The story takes place in New Jersey a little less than thirty years from now. United States Representative Martin Boyd rules the Fifth Congressional District of New Jersey, not with an iron hand but with a crew of "psychotechnicians." To continue getting elected term after term, Boyd has his psychotechs devise psychological appeals that will motivate virtually everyone in the district to vote for him. Among other things, the psychotechs design a residential development that appeals strongly to oral personalities, advertise it with oral themes, and screen out anybody with pronounced anal or phallic tendencies. That way, political messages can be shaped exactly to fit the community's uniform psychological dimensions, with no worry that a message aimed at oral personalities will offend or bore anals and others.

161

Onto this scene comes Ralph Nicholson, a nationally known psychologist who fears that Boyd's rule over the Fifth District may gradually extend to all of America, and who wants to make the world safe from psychopolitical manipulations. Using psychological techniques himself, Nicholson selects the most appealing possible opposition candidate in the Fifth District and goes to work on the voters. He creates incidents intended to arouse them to seek a law-and-order candidate, and trains his own candidate to give the right sort of law-and-order response. He uses advanced propaganda and entertainment techniques (but no hot dogs) to gather crowds for his candidate's rallies. He generates synthetic odors, including the smell of a woman's breast, to calm the crowd when Boyd's psychotechs try to disrupt it. He manipulates hired role-players in the audience (people used to call them "shills") to influence both the audience's and the candidate's behavior, while he collects detailed minute-by-minute data on crowd reactions from assistants who circulate through the crowd, wired with remote telemetry devices that feed back their own physiological and emotional responses as they encounter the same stimuli as everyone else attending the rally. The book ends with the campaign barely begun, but it gives a horrifying picture of what even the good guys of the future may be able to do to manipulate the electorate.

SELLING CANDIDATES PSYCHOLOGICALLY

How close is such psychological manipulation of the voter? Certain advertising firms are only too happy to imply that they can already do it with great expertise, for a fee, and certain journalists are only too willing to believe them. One political journalist (Perry, 1968) who toured the country to investigate modern campaign techniques, well before the novel was written, foresaw developments rather similar to those in *The Barons of Behavior:*

162

> The candidate's travels (along with the travels of the candidate for Vice-President and a number of other leading party figures) will be scheduled by a computer. The campaign will be laid out by the critical-path method. Polls will be taken over and over and analyzed and cross-analyzed. Spot commercials will be prepared weeks in advance of the election, and their impact will be almost subliminal. Researchers will read the polls and study the data from a "simulator"; the issues they develop will all be relevant, and they will be aimed like rifle shots at the most receptive audiences.

Although Perry was unwilling to specify the date when this precision campaigning is likely to take place on a large scale, some people seem to have gotten the idea from such accounts as *The Selling of the President 1968* (McGinniss, 1969) that it has already happened, in the successful Nixon campaigns of 1968 and 1972.

The evidence from the McGinniss book and other sources (for example, Nolan, 1972), however, is that the Nixon campaigns owed little or nothing to the behavioral sciences beyond the usual crude use of public-opinion polls. The campaign techniques used by the Nixon organization in 1968 were sophisticated in terms of graphics and video technology rather than in terms of complex psychological analyses of voter motives and potential campaign themes. Most appeals were directed toward the "lowest common denominator" of the American electorate, not to specific motivational subgroups. In spite of this "technically perfect" campaign (as McGinniss described it), Nixon steadily lost ground during the last few weeks to the more old-fashioned campaigner Hubert Humphrey, and came close to losing the election. The major changes in the 1972 Nixon campaign involved the program of political subversion exemplified by Watergate and the withdrawal of Nixon himself behind the façade of "the Presidency." Again, no serious attempt was made to use behavioral-science techniques to sway the masses.

Candidates have so far avoided such techniques not from any excess of moral concern but because the techniques—at least in their present state of development—just don't work very well. One huge practical problem is the psychological diversity of the electorate. A psychologist might be able to tell a candidate, on the basis of public-opinion surveys, that a majority of the public is looking for someone who sounds expert on foreign-policy issues and forthright on domestic issues. But the psychologist would then be very hard put to recommend behaviors that would make the candidate appear expert and forthright to a sufficiently wide range of voters. Attitude change researchers have studied the variables of expertness and trustworthiness for thirty years without arriving at more than a few tentative recommendations, and even those must be modified for any particular communicator and any particular audience (Triandis, 1971; Elms, 1972).

The author of *The Barons of Behavior* acknowledged this problem in inventing a community populated only with oral personalities. A politician's path to office would surely be much smoother if all his constituents responded identically to his campaign appeals. But that dream is fortunately unrealizable in the near or even the semidistant future. Relatively pure oral *or* anal *or* phallic personality types appear to occur rather rarely (Kline, 1972), and they would be much more difficult for psychologists to create than to locate. Furthermore, even if such pure types were plentiful, psychologists know so little about the relationships between personality types and voting behavior that they wouldn't know what to do once they had found them. Almost the only

163

consistent evidence that a personality type might be related to specific political preferences involves the connection between authoritarian personality patterns and the approval of conservative political candidates (Kirscht and Dillehay, 1967; Higgins and Kuhlman, 1967), and even that evidence is not very strong.

COMPUTER SIMULATIONS OF VOTER BEHAVIOR

One group of social-science researchers has instead made use of detailed demographic data to predict and influence voter behavior (Pool, Abelson, and Popkin, 1965). No single demographic variable (other than, to some extent, political party identification itself) relates strongly enough to voting behavior to form the basis for directing appeals in a nationwide political campaign, but a broad array of such variables in combination can be a useful guide. Operating with financial assistance from the Democratic party during the Kennedy campaign of 1960, these researchers carefully categorized American voters into 480 types, based on region of country and size of town lived in, occupational status, sex, religion, and ethnic group—all variables that are tabulated in standard public-opinion surveys. (The 480 categories were the basis for the title of Eugene Burdick's 1964 best-selling novel on a similar campaign, *The 480;* the project may also have helped inspire *The Barons of Behavior.*) They then fed into a computer the survey responses given by representative samples of people in each of the 480 categories, on 52 issues assessed in a variety of public-opinion surveys during the preceding 8 years. The researchers hoped that from such data they could determine the likely responses of voters in each category to whatever John F. Kennedy might say in the campaign on one of the 52 issues. Kennedy could then presumably adjust his statements to strengthen his following in certain categories, while not alienating too many of the voters in other categories. For instance, the data analysis indicated that if Kennedy publicly and emphatically confronted the issue of religious bias in the campaign, he would lose some non-Catholic votes but would gain more than enough Catholic votes to offset them. He could therefore risk antagonizing at least one kind of demographic category by being honest, rather than playing it safe.

164

Kennedy did not make heavy use of the computer experts' advice. His political advisers apparently did not trust computer simulations based on "old" (two years or more) opinion surveys, and wanted to spend scarce campaign money on more traditional means of swaying the voters. But Pool, Abelson, and Popkin themselves concluded after examining the relationships between their recommendations, the path of the campaign, and the actual outcome of the election, that their simulations of voter response may have played a significant role by at least strengthening "sound decisions on a few critical items."

That small beginning may portend elaborate computer-run campaign efforts in the near future. But there is at least one major problem with the 480-category voter-prediction system: it is not psychologically based. We may know that midwestern urban blue-collar white Catholic males have tended to answer poll questions in certain ways in the past; but will they continue to respond in the same ways, given economic changes in the country and given the personal characteristics of a particular candidate who tries to capitalize on their previous concerns? If they realize that the candidate is trying to capitalize on those concerns, will they show a boomerang effect and vote against him, or will they acquiesce meekly? Socioeconomic data cannot answer such questions; and even if the psychologists of the future can, they may not be able to use the information successfully to guide a candidate's campaign behavior in a winning direction. In *The Barons of Behavior*, the main manipulations are directed toward a population group strongly motivated (because of their oral-dependency needs) to avoid recognizing that they are being manipulated. But in the general public there should be enough suspicious anal types, assertive phallic types, and other nongullible personality types never identified by Freud, to make large-scale psychological manipulation of American voters a riskier business than most candidate personality types would want to try.

165

SELLING ISSUES PSYCHOLOGICALLY

At this point a change of focus may be worthwhile. Having found serious problems with the use of personality types and demographic categories in designing political campaigns, we might instead consider the usefulness of the functional approach to political attitudes. Having found personality-based appeals to be rather unuseful in Presidential campaigns, we might look at their value in issue-oriented campaigns. People vary greatly in their reliance on one or another attitude function, and it may be possible to devise appeals that attract the attention only of those people who emphasize a particular function. Because a Presidential candidate must appeal to a wide audience, focusing on a particular functional type among voters will not be a very successful campaign strategy, and attempts to devise different kinds of messages for different types may make the electorate angry, confused, or suspicious. With regard to certain political issues, however, the activist social scientist may wish to influence only a limited portion of the populace anyway, and that portion may be fairly uniform in its functional emphasis. It may then be possible to devise a persuasive campaign on that issue based on a single kind of functional appeal, without much concern about failing to persuade other types or sounding inconsistent from one persuasive campaign to the next.

Hardly any application of the functional approach has been made in political-issue campaigns, although advertisers have done a good deal of fairly unscientific motivational research on what kinds of messages to aim at population subgroups who use certain specialized products. I have come across only two such applications in areas related to politics: one dealing with the reduction of antiminority prejudice and the other with the stimulation of political involvement among minority-group members.

Research on the reduction of racial prejudice through functionally adapted appeals has been done mainly by Daniel Katz and several collaborators (Katz, Sarnoff, and McClintock, 1956; Katz, McClintock, and Sarnoff, 1957; McClintock, 1958; Stotland, Katz, and Patchen, 1959). Many attempts have been made to reduce racial prejudice through information campaigns in the mass media or in the schools, apparently on the assumption that prejudice is based on faulty object appraisal. If a person is prejudiced against blacks because he believes they are usually dirty or stupid, you present evidence that blacks are as clean and intelligent as whites, and the person's prejudice will presumably disappear. But Katz and his colleagues recognized, as have many other social scientists (for example, Allport, 1954; Pettigrew, 1961), that object appraisal is by no means the only basis for racial prejudice and that indeed social adjustment and externalization might be considerably more important. They therefore designed appeals intended for high externalizers and for people whose prejudice came mainly from perceived social pressures, as well as the usual kind of information campaign for those who rely most heavily on object appraisal. (Katz and his associates used other words to describe the attitudinal functions, but the functions were very similar in content to Smith, Bruner, and White's [1956] categories, so I will continue to use the latter labels. Katz did not add a "value-expression" function to his list until later.)

166

Functional bases for racial prejudice were identified mainly through subscales of the California F Scale and the Minnesota Multiphasic Personality Inventory (a widely used screening test for neurotic and psychotic tendencies). Female college students identified as prejudiced externalizers were expected to lower their prejudice most readily in response to a persuasive message that

> consisted of a case study preceded by a general statement of the dynamics of scapegoating, projecting, and compensation as they relate to the development of anti-minority attitudes. The case study described the life story of a college girl to illustrate how these mechanisms supported her ethnic prejudices. The central character was described in favorable and sympathetic terms to maximize identification of the subjects with her problems. The object was to produce some self-understanding on the part of the subjects who were similar to the character described in the development of their prejudices [Katz, McClintock, and Sarnoff, 1957].

The researchers expected only *moderate* externalizers to respond well to this message. They expected high externalizers to show little or no change in prejudice in response to this or any other brief persuasive message, since strong psychological defenses of long standing are not so easily breached.

People strong in social adjustment were expected to show the greatest reduction of prejudice in response to a message stressing that "scientific, religious, and educational leaders were in agreement that where Negroes are given equal opportunities they perform as well as whites" (McClintock, 1958). The assumption was also made, at least initially, that people basing their prejudices mainly on object appraisal would respond most readily to a logical and informational appeal, and that the appeal designed to be most effective for a particular functional category would be substantially less effective for the other categories (Sarnoff, Katz, and McClintock, 1954). 167

Among several different studies based on these general assumptions, conducted over several years, the results are not altogether consistent. However, as predicted, the high externalizers did tend to resist change regardless of type of message, the moderate externalizers tended to respond best to the message designed to reduce externalization, and the social-adjustment-oriented people were most persuaded by the message stressing the opinions of socially prestigious individuals. The low externalizers (who were presumably high in object appraisal, although that function was never directly measured) responded better to the logical-informational message than anyone else, but in several of the studies their prejudice was reduced even more by the message designed to reduce externalization than by the informational message. Stotland, Katz, and Patchen (1959) suggest that the low externalizers who received the externalization-reduction message may have become less prejudiced in response because they felt "that they were not the type of individuals who indulged in scapegoating and that prejudices toward outgroups were not consistent with their usual ways of dealing with people. Thus they wanted to dissociate themselves from the type of person who would use scapegoating because of his own repressed hostility."

This line of research, then, suggests that persuasive campaigns can be successfully designed on the basis of functional analyses to alter the politically related views of certain functional types. But this approach has as big a problem as the previous ones: How do you get the potential audience to pay attention to the messages you have so carefully designed for them? The participants in the Katz group's experiments were a captive audience of college students. Outside the college classroom, high and moderate externalizers tend to be the people *least* likely to pay attention to messages intended to reduce externalization. They don't like to examine their own motives, and they don't want other people to force such an examination on them. So how do you persuade them to listen?

SELLING THE PERSUASIVE CAMPAIGN

168 Harold Mendelsohn (1973) and his colleagues faced this kind of problem not with high externalizers but with Mexican-Americans in Los Angeles, when he was asked to develop a public-television program that would increase Chicano political participation. Los Angeles Chicanos paid little attention to white-oriented television, and seemed particularly unlikely to sit through an educational program on political participation if they had anything else to do. They did often watch a Spanish-language station's presentations of Mexican soap operas, so Mendelsohn and his colleagues decided to develop a "Chicano information-giving soap opera series." But the researchers didn't stop there.

Their first step was to hire Mexican-American personnel to write, direct, produce, and star in the series, titled "Canción de la raza" ("Song of the People"). Their second step was to identify the people they most needed to reach, those who showed the strongest feelings of political powerlessness in the Chicano community, and to emphasize such characters in the series. In this way they hoped to maximize the kind of audience they wanted, on the assumption that people are most likely to watch and to identify with dramatic characters who resemble themselves. Third, the researchers carefully identified the personal and societal symptoms of feelings of political powerlessness in the Chicano community, showed in the programs how these symptoms could be overcome by such things as "constructive communal efforts" and "involvement in legitimate political activism," and stressed how the goals most valued in the community could be achieved through political involvement.

"Canción de la raza" got good local ratings and a regional "Emmy" award. More important, it appears to have been influential in arousing many people to become more active in the community. By combining research on how to get people to pay attention in the first place, on who to appeal to most strongly, and on what to say to them to change their views about politics, the "Canción de la raza" project became an unusually successful example of direct political involvement by social scientists.

Perhaps such popular entertainment programs as "All in the Family" could, in the long run, work similarly to reduce externalization-based prejudice or to effect other changes in the audience's political views. Maybe Archie Bunker needs to be a somewhat sympathetic character in order to keep the bigots watching long enough for the ridicule directed toward his racist views to sink in—although published evidence on these points is unfortunately lacking. Maybe a potential political candidate with certain unpopular characteristics could even, at some future time, quietly commission a well-researched dramatic series with a noble protagonist similar to himself, a person who doesn't push any political message but who does all the things that would cool the hostility of the people most likely to oppose him. I remember a science-fiction story in which Earth authorities, learning of the imminent arrival of a friendly but very ugly alien species, designed a spectacularly popular television puppet show starring two friendly giant snails, who looked just like—surprise!—the aliens who landed to an enthusiastic reception by earthlings a few months later. That's a long way from the rigid mind control of *The Barons of Behavior,* but it's probably a good deal closer to the actual uses that political campaigners will be able to make of research on their audience's personality characteristics in the foreseeable future.

169

screening and monitoring political candidates

The Nixon organization's main campaign innovation in 1972—the systematic use of political subversion on a massive scale—may well have decided the election. But Nixon also got a lot of help from another source: George McGovern.

McGovern's campaign blunders were so numerous that it is hard to identify any one as decisive. But one of the most important was clearly the Eagleton affair. In the first place, McGovern's personally chosen running mate, Thomas Eagleton, turned out to have a history of mental illness. In the second place, McGovern hadn't investigated Eagleton's background thoroughly enough to know of that history, or to know that Eagleton had concealed it. In the third place, McGovern waffled terribly about the whole incident, publicly assuring Eagleton of his support and then dumping him. Finally, having botched his first decision as a Presidential candidate, McGovern botched it all over again, several times in a row, in attempting to replace Eagleton.

Social scientists probably shouldn't even try to help prevent merely inept candidates from running for high office. Ineptness as a candidate does not necessarily guarantee ineptness as a President, and anyway the American people occasionally prefer ineptitude over other qualities. That is how we get passive-negative Presidents. But a number of proposals have been made to screen potential Presidential (and perhaps Vice-Presidential) nominees for character defects or serious personality problems. If Eagleton had been screened, he might actually have passed with flying colors, since he had undergone treatment and was presumably well recovered by the time he ran for the Vice-Presidency. But the screening process at least would have alerted McGovern and other party officials to the potential problems, and would have given the public a fair basis for judging whether they wanted such a person in the nation's second highest office. At most, the screening might have found that Eagleton would be a serious risk in that office and should not run.

170

PSYCHOBIOGRAPHICAL SCREENING

Screening is a vague word, variously interpreted to mean any form of professional prejudgment of political candidates' suitability, up to and including an absolute prohibition on nominating anyone who fails to pass a psychological inquisition by an appropriately qualified panel

Senator Thomas Eagleton prepares for a nationwide television appearance during the 1972 Presidential campaign.

of inquisitors. Such a prohibition would require a Constitutional amendment, so the usual screening proposals fall considerably short of that. Perhaps the mildest of these is the use of psychobiographies as a means of identifying and publicizing the crucial personality variables and probable behaviors in office of leading candidates. Several psychobiographers have already offered their work as a guide to voters with regard to a particular candidate. Would Richard Nixon be likely to suffer a Wilson-style rigidification during his second term? Will Ted Kennedy be more concerned with his public image than with initiating genuine reforms as President? Can psychobiographical analysis be perfected to such a degree that undesirable candidates can be weeded out of the Presidential sweepstakes in advance, either through public pressure or through a more formal screening system?

Eli Chesen argued that books such as his psychobiography of Nixon "can offer an additional check and balance not provided in our Constitution." He did not suggest adding a psychobiographical provision to the Constitution; instead, he was content to increase the voters' information about one candidate, whom Chesen probably preferred not to have been reelected. (In an epilogue added to the paperback edition after Nixon's resignation, Chesen said his greatest regret was that the book had not been published many years earlier.) Nancy Clinch (1973) hoped her book on the Kennedys would help us to "see through and reject the style and blandishments of leaders and candidates who have little else to offer" besides "fashionable glamor"; she was no longer talking about Jack or Bobby.

The most ambitious psychobiographer of all, in this sense, is James David Barber (1972). The first chapter of his book on the Presidency is titled "Presidential Character and How to Foresee It." Barber wanted to "help citizens and those who advise them cut through the confusion and get at some clear criteria for choosing Presidents." Nixon happened to be the candidate most readily at hand for predictive purposes, but Barber feels his fourfold table of Presidential types is ready for use whenever any candidate arrives on the scene. By considering certain aspects of the candidate's earlier development and his first independent political success, we can decide whether he is active or passive, positive or negative, before we decide whether to nominate or to elect him. We know what is wrong with active-negatives and with passives of both types, and that eliminates many candidates right there.

Barber's batting average so far looks pretty good, at least at first glance. Prior to the 1972 election, Barber (1972; see also Barber, 1969, 1971) wrote that Nixon would remain flexible as long as he suffered defeats only on "specific questions of policy." However, if the issue reached "his central concern, the concern of self-management"—in other words, if his "power and sense of virtue" began to be seriously challenged—then "the fat may go into the fire. . . . Only when a crisis gathers around him, one he cannot escape by moving on to some alternative crisis, and he experiences a sense of entrapment is he likely to move toward the classic form of rigidification." And then came Watergate.

Barber (1974) now feels he's batting one for one. On that basis, he has proposed "a new program of research aimed at assessing—*before* the choice is narrowed to a few—the probable course each emerging candidate would follow in the White House. Such a program could draw on the talents of psychologists, historians, journalists, politicians, political scientists, and others. . . ." Barber feels that "a wide diversity

172

of theories and interpretations" would come out of this evaluation, provoking "a feisty intellectual debate, in which the contenders tested alternative theories against the evidence." He clearly has high hopes for his own theory.

DIFFICULTIES IN PSYCHOBIOGRAPHICAL SCREENING

Unfortunately, there are serious problems with Barber's Nixon prediction. The portion of the prediction about Nixon rigidifying under the pressure of attacks on his own character seems to have been confirmed, in terms of the focus of attack. However, Barber predicted not only that Nixon would become rigid under such attack but that he would follow "in the path of his heroes Wilson and Hoover" in going to "a moral commitment, a commitment to follow his private star, to fly off in the face of overwhelming odds." The White House tapes, the only record of the private Nixon, give little sense of any "moral commitment" as a result of the attacks on his Watergate involvement. Nixon was not following nearly as closely in Wilson's path as Barber was in the path of Wilson's psychobiographers, the Georges.

Barber's prediction also seems to me somewhat misplaced in terms of emphasis. Nixon resigned because of the Watergate cover-up, but the cover-up itself was not nearly as important to the fate of our democracy as what Nixon was trying to hide: all those secret manipulations of his opponents that John Mitchell labeled the "White House horrors." Barber does talk about Nixon's "demand for control," his "core need" for power, but the best Barber can do with prediction here is to say, "He has the reins. It is not yet clear where he will drive with them." If Barber could have reliably predicted that Nixon's power need would come to full flower in an attempt to subvert the electoral process itself, *that* would have been a prediction to be proud of!

173

Alexander George (1974) has raised several other important objections not only to Barber's specific attempts at prediction but to psychobiographical prediction in general. Of these objections, two particularly important ones involve the acceptable level of risk and the situation-specific nature of predictions. The risk-level objection is a familiar one to users of psychological screening tests. No screening system is ever completely accurate, so you have to decide in which direction you would like most of your errors to occur. Should you balance the process very heavily in favor of what appears to be the public interest, or rather more in favor of the candidate's interest? If Barber can predict that a candidate has at least a 90 percent chance of effectively serving out his first term as President, should we give the candidate the benefit of the doubt on the other 10 percent, or should we insist on a 99 percent probability? If the candidate has a 60 percent chance of being a great President and a 40 percent chance of killing himself (as might have been predicted of Abraham Lincoln in 1859 on the basis of his previous behavior), is that a good enough gamble?

Even these rather chancy kinds of prediction are better than anyone can do now, and George argues that there's not much hope for improvement. Through psychobiography, we can develop a clearer understanding of why a President responded to a challenge as he did, but we don't know what challenges are likely to face him in the future. Barber acknowledged this problem by specifying, rather broadly, the situation under which Nixon would be likely to crack. But if such a situation had not arisen—if the night watchman at Watergate had not noticed the tape on the lock—Nixon might have finished his second term as an apparently respectable and flexible President. If Abraham Lincoln's wife had died early in his first term, Lincoln might have shot himself and gone down in history as one of our least memorable Presidents. When we begin calculating the odds on whether a President's personality will turn him this way or that, we also have to figure the odds on what else will push him and what will get in his way.

174 Psychobiography is actually the most well-developed means of "screening" Presidential candidates available so far, but several other proposals should be mentioned. Donley and Winter (1970) have developed a technique for quantitatively analyzing the content of inaugural addresses to indicate a President's relative standing on power need and achievement need, and they suggest that the technique could also be applied to the "speeches of political actors while they are seeking office." (Nixon, incidentally, comes out relatively *low* in power need and higher than any other twentieth-century President on achievement need, in Donley and Winter's analysis.) Three decades ago Harold Lasswell (1948) called for the establishment of a National Personnel Assessment Board to give candidates tests to enable "the selection of leaders from among nondestructive, genuinely democratic characters." Nixon's own sometime physician, Arnold Hutschnecker (1969), has proposed administering psychological tests to *everybody* during the school years, in order to detect mental illness and to

weed out "psychopathic personalities before they reached positions of power. . . . A kind of mental-health certificate would be required of all young people as a prerequisite for any job of political responsibility." All these proposals, unfortunately, suffer from the same defects as the Barber prediction system, and most to a greater degree.

PSYCHOLOGICAL MONITORING

Alexander George (1974) has suggested that the psychological monitoring of political leaders once in office is likely to be a good deal easier than the screening of candidates prior to election. But he noted that such monitoring could work only in terms of identifying "major mental illness." The character flaws leading to Wilson's or Nixon's disasters would either go unnoticed until too late, or even if discovered, would not be sufficient Constitutional grounds to remove a President from office.

Monitoring for mental illness is in fact a far bigger can of worms than George suggested. The most careful consideration of the issue published so far, a small volume produced by the Committee on Governmental Agencies of the Group for the Advancement of Psychiatry (1973), uses more space discussing the difficulties inherent in monitoring public officials than the undoubted need to do so or the procedures most likely to be useful. For professional and political reasons, the monitors themselves must be near-perfect: "They should be professionally highly competent, beyond professional and personal reproach, clearly not self-seeking, free of political and administrative involvement, and imbued with the moral courage needed to take and maintain a position." Then they have to get the official to submit to a psychological examination—not an easy task with someone like Richard Nixon, who "hates psychiatrists" and "won't even let one in the same room" (according to one of his associates, quoted by McGinniss, 1969). Having gotten into the same room, perhaps as part of an annual health examination, the examining therapist must be circumspect enough not to get himself either fired (as happened to Louisiana Governor Earl Long's State Director of Hospitals) or killed (as happened to Bavarian King Ludwig II's psychiatrist; Ludwig first attempted to have him skinned alive and then managed to drown him along with the King himself). He must also be careful not to leak any information prematurely about a diagnosis, since anything suggesting even temporary mental illness could have disastrous effects for the

175

official involved and probably for the idea of psychological monitoring thereafter.

The biggest question of all about monitoring is: Once signs of mental illness have been detected in the President, what next? The Twenty-Fifth Amendment provides for temporary or permanent removal from office of a President "unable to discharge the powers and duties of his office." However, the amendment requires that the Vice-President, a majority of the Cabinet, and (if the President objects to his own removal) two-thirds of both Houses of Congress must agree as to what "unable to discharge" means. Recall the House Judiciary Committee hearings on Nixon's impeachment, and imagine what a sanity hearing for the President of the United States would be like.

PSYCHOTHERAPEUTIC TREATMENT IN OFFICE

An alternative to removal from office would be retention of the President in office while he undergoes therapeutic treatment for whatever ails him. The Committee on Governmental Agencies points out that a President would find it difficult to give a psychiatrist an hour a day from his busy schedule. But, more important, the President himself would probably stand to lose more from treatment than he would gain, at least politically. The Eagleton affair indicates only too vividly what a history of psychotherapeutic treatment can do to a politician.

Kenneth B. Clark (1974), a distinguished social psychologist, has advanced a uniquely simple solution to all these difficulties. In his 176 presidential address to the American Psychological Association, Clark proposed that a massive research program be directed toward the development of a "medication" that would eliminate destructive power needs in humans:

> It would seem logical then that a requirement should be imposed upon all power-controlling leaders and those who aspire to such leadership that they accept and use the earliest perfected form of psychotechnological, biochemical intervention which would assure their use of power affirmatively, and reduce or block the possibility of their using power destructively. Such psychotechnological medication would be an internally imposed disarmament.

Clark's intentions are good, and I sympathize with them. But his proposal is a fantasy—one might even say a fantasy of power, if one were suspicious of psychologists. Could we ever develop a drug that would eliminate a Woodrow Wilson's destructive power impulses while retaining his "affirmative" power impulses, in view of the Georges' conclusion that the two kinds of impulses were really one, expressed in different ways as the situation demanded? Could we ever force a Richard Nixon to submit to an "internal disarmament," in view of his apparent concerns about sexual identity?

What else is left? We can go on trusting in the good sense of American voters, and hoping that with a little more information in the form of honest psychobiographies they (and the nominating conventions) will do better than in 1964, 1968, and 1972. Or we can change the system. Arthur Schlesinger, Jr. (1974) argues that even a President whose psyche is inclined to wander can be "tethered to the reality principle" by a rehabilitated and enforced system of accountability to Congress and to the people. Alexander George (1974) suggests that psychobiographical studies, although ill-fitted for the prediction of a particular individual's behavior in office, "may be helpful in efforts to make appropriate adjustments in the structure and management of top-level decision-making processes." We have already learned that we cannot depend on the current political system alone to control the personal vagaries of high officeholders. It is far too much to expect that we can depend on the psychobiographers alone. But in combination, they appeal to my optimism.

personality, politics, and ethics

177

So far in this chapter, we have been considering whether personality researchers *can* intervene successfully in the political process. The next question (and perhaps it should be the first) is, *should* they?

Once upon a time, many social scientists found that an easy question to answer. They saw their sole professional function as studying what *is*, not recommending what *should* be. But it is hard to study political processes in any detail without coming to realize that what *is* often has major implications, many of them negative, for the lives of millions of people. In merely describing and analyzing the current state of affairs, without also drawing conclusions about how it might be improved, a researcher is in effect endorsing the *status quo* and lending support to whatever evils—as well as virtues—it includes. The researcher may conclude that he wants to preserve the *status quo*, because on balance the virtues outweigh the evils or because any other system he can think of would have more evils and fewer virtues than the present one. But he cannot validly insist that his research on politics has no political implications whatsoever.

Researchers on personality in politics have been less criticized than most students of politics for providing aid and comfort to the *status quo*. Beginning with Harold Lasswell's early work and continuing through such landmarks as the authoritarian personality research and the studies of legislative types, a strong theme of political reform, if not of radical change, has been evident in much of the personality-in-politics literature. Ethical issues have therefore been raised in this field much more in terms of "Should researchers intervene politically in this particular way?" than in terms of "Why are they not intervening in any way?"

The philosophical and religious literature on ethical issues is vast, and the social-scientific literature is beginning to approach similar dimensions. I will not try, in this brief concluding section, to summarize even a substantial portion of that literature (see Sjoberg, 1967; Kelman, 1968; Elms, 1972). But I do feel obligated to mention some of the concerns that have been expressed about the kinds of direct intervention discussed earlier in this chapter—contemporary psychobiography, candidate screening, and personality-based campaigning—as well as tentative responses to these concerns.

PSYCHOBIOGRAPHICAL ETHICS

178 Sigmund Freud (Freud and Bullitt, 1967) opposed the publication of psychobiographies of living individuals. He regarded the relationship between psychobiographer and subject as in some ways similar to that of analyst and patient, where "the pledge of professional secrecy" is strictly observed. Freud even suggested the possibility of some "period of post-mortem immunity from biographical study," and indeed the Freud-Bullitt biography of Wilson was not published until after the second Mrs. Wilson's death, out of courtesy to her (and perhaps also out of an effort by Bullitt to avoid her hostility).

Freud's feelings have been shared by some other psychobiographers. Alexander George and Juliette George (1973) have suggested several reasons for avoiding psychobiographies of the living. Such works are not only likely to "constitute an obnoxious invasion of privacy"; they will probably be seriously lacking in the crucial data that public figures prefer to conceal during their active political lives, and the psychobiographer himself "is likely to be caught up in the passions of his time." When Bruce Mazlish began his work on Richard Nixon during the political campaign of 1968, he and several other scholars who at that time planned to collaborate with him agreed not to publish the analysis until after the President's term of office was completed, "in order to prevent misuse of our work for political purposes."

Obviously not all psychobiographers agree with such a position. Mazlish published his psychobiography of Nixon during the election year of 1972—perhaps only coincidentally, but certainly before Nixon's term had ended. Barber's most detailed analysis of Nixon's character came out the same year; Chesen's during the first year of Nixon's second term. Nancy Clinch's psychobiography of the Kennedy family, with considerable attention directed toward Edward Kennedy's political ambitions, was also published in 1973, during a period of intense speculation about his chances for the Presidency. Several hundred psychiatrists, although they were not engaged in writing full-scale psychobiographies, clearly had little concern about the ethics of making public psychiatric diagnoses of an active politician in the case of the *Fact* magazine Goldwater poll. (Many others, however, were concerned enough to criticize the poll or to refuse to participate.)

Writing only about long-dead individuals does solve some of the psychobiographer's ethical and methodological problems. But I don't see how psychobiography can be, or why it need be, limited to the dead. Journalists, candidates' own publicists, and partisans of both sides will continue to write campaign biographies extolling or denouncing the candidate's psychological qualities along with his lineage, his policies, and his physical appearance. Responsible efforts at psychological analysis are needed to offset the irresponsible ones. Unnecessary and abusive invasion of privacy should be denounced, as the Georges (1973) have done with the Clinch book. However, the Supreme Court has severely limited a public figure's right to privacy, and a psychobiography of the Mazlish type does not appear to infringe on that limited right. The psychobiographer will probably find it more difficult to conduct an unbiased study of an active politician than of a deceased one, as the Georges have pointed out, but the same is true of studies of political extremism and most other areas of political psychology. As I have indicated, the wise psychobiographer will choose a subject toward whom he feels considerable ambivalence rather than harsh antagonism or uncritical adulation. But the likeli-

179

hood that it will be harder to write an objective contemporary psycho-biography than an objective historical one should not forbid its being done altogether. The importance of doing such studies may well offset their problems.

THE EVIDENCE BEHIND THE SCREEN

The direct screening and monitoring of political candidates by a panel of psychological examiners has, oddly enough, received rather less attention on ethical grounds than has Barber-style psychobiographical screening. Perhaps it has escaped close ethical inspection because it has not been practiced yet and seems unlikely to be practiced in the near future; perhaps because the screening panel would presumably be selected in as unbiased a fashion as possible rather than self-selected, as are the psychobiographers; perhaps because a dozen psychiatrists and psychologists working together seem more likely to be responsible than one psychobiographer working alone.

Arnold Hutschnecker's (1969) plan to screen all young people for psychopolitical defects and Kenneth B. Clark's (1974) idea for a drug-induced psychological disarmament of political leaders represent such gross abuses of personal rights that even if they were practicable, most people would agree to bar them on ethical grounds. But do we have the right even to ask declared candidates to answer probing questions from our carefully selected panel of experts concerning their private thoughts and hidden impulses?

180 This situation presents different problems from contemporary psycho-biographies, which are based on the public record of a candidate even though the psychobiographer may make inferences about the candidate's private life. A screening panel would probably want to go well beyond the public record in order to draw its conclusions as accurately as possible. In many sensitive nonelective positions, individuals are subjected to personality tests and other forms of psychological probing in order to determine their suitability for the job. One of the conditions of such examinations, however, is the examiner's assurance of the strict confidentiality of the answers. Confidentiality is a basic ethical tenet of professionals who conduct such examinations, just as it is of psychotherapists in their treatment of patients. Public revelation of a candidate's honest responses to a psychological examination could haunt him for the rest of his life, even if he accepts with good grace the panel's decision that he is not an acceptable candidate for

office. Confidentiality in such circumstances therefore appears to be essential on ethical grounds, as well as necessary on practical grounds in order to ensure candidates' cooperation.

But what if the candidate or his devoted followers do not accept the panel's conclusions with good grace? Let us say the panel merely issues a statement asserting that Candidates A, C, and E are psychologically suited for the office, while Candidates B and D are not. Are B and D's supporters likely to let matters rest there? They are probably more likely either to demand strong evidence for the panel's conclusions or to denounce the panel as incompetent. Candidate B may try a bluff, insisting that he is completely normal but that the panel is politically biased. If the panel goes so far as to release its diagnoses of the candidates' shortcomings, still without supportive evidence, Candidate D may argue that, well, yes, he does have depressive tendencies, but no more so than Honest Abe Lincoln, or that psychiatric diagnosis is an inexact science and that the panel misinterpreted the evidence.

Could the panel, at this point, ethically release the interview and test data on which it based its conclusions in order to preserve its credibility and to make certain that an emotionally disturbed or weak candidate never gets to the Oval Office? I don't believe it could; and if it did, I do not see what good that would do in the long run. The first breach of confidentiality would be the last, because no reasonably intelligent candidate would ever again tell the panel anything suspicious about himself. Such a clash of ethical and practical considerations in the panel screening procedure may well mean that psychobiographical "screening" is the only kind of psychological screening for elective office we will ever see.

181

PSYCHOLOGICAL CAMPAIGN ETHICS

Because it is potentially the most powerful and the most covert intervention procedure of all, personality-based political campaigning has aroused the greatest amount of ethical alarm among the general public. The alarm comes in part from imputing to personality researchers far more skill at manipulating voters than they now have or are soon likely to attain. But because some such skills *may* eventually be developed, particularly in terms of influencing segments of the public to change their attitudes toward certain political issues, the ethical implications should be considered seriously.

The ethical issues are usually raised dramatically: Should a bunch of computer experts be allowed to choose the United States President for the entire American populace? Shall we allow ourselves and our children and our children's children to be brainwashed by a pack of heartless technocrats? The answers some people offer are often also dramatic. Herbert Kelman (1965), for instance, has argued that "any manipulation of the behavior of others constitutes a violation of their essential humanity." Kelman has considerable doubts about the propriety of a psychologist using his professional skills to influence others even in a serious scientific experiment, let alone a political campaign. Others have no doubts at all: they would ban the use of psychological data in election campaigns, pure and simple.

The conscientious personality researcher can easily find himself in a dilemma at this point. He may indeed be reluctant to take advantage of others' needs and weaknesses to advance a particular political cause or candidate, but he recognizes that the opposition candidate's supporters are likely to use all the influence they can get to advance their own cause. Even if they refrain from hiring another personality expert, they will probably use their practical experience in observing voter behavior, as well as their natural and acquired persuasive skills, to mold the opinions of as large an audience as possible. If the personality researcher truly believes his cause will benefit mankind and that the other side will harm it, why should he refrain from using the skills at his disposal?

182 That's the kind of argument the hero of Purdom's (1972) science-fiction novel *The Barons of Behavior* keeps telling himself and other people throughout the book, before and after every manipulation of the voters. When his political candidate tells him the psychological manipulations are "the most revolting thing I've ever seriously considered doing," he responds:

> It revolts me just as much as it revolts you. . . . [Our opponents are] taking some of the most valuable knowledge men have ever possessed and they're using it to destroy everything that makes human society valuable. We aren't going to do one thing that will cause anybody any serious harm, however. Nothing we're going to do will have any permanent effect on any voter in this country. The only long-term effect we'll have on their lives will be the effect we'll have if we win. We'll be getting them out of the hands of a sadistic little bastard who's using them like private toys he can play with any time he feels like making somebody miserable.

B. F. Skinner, the well-known behaviorist, offers a rather similar argument in defending the use of operant-conditioning procedures to establish what he sees as an ideal society. In his Utopian novel, *Walden Two* (1948), Skinner has his protagonist, Frazier, ask a critic, *"What would you do if you found yourself in possession of an effective science of behavior?* Suppose you suddenly found it possible to control the behavior of men as you wished. What would you do?" When the critic says, "I think I would dump your science of behavior in the ocean," Frazier responds: "But you would only be leaving the control in other hands. . . . The charlatan, the demagogue, the salesman, the ward leader, the bully, the cheat, the educator, the priest—all who are now in possession of the techniques of behavioral engineering."

That kind of argument makes a good deal of sense to me, although I don't buy Skinner's ideas of what constitutes a perfect society. Influence per se is not the major moral issue that Kelman and others would make it. People have been trying to influence each other through rational arguments, emotional appeals, threats, and other means since the beginning of human history. Political campaign messages made more persuasive by social-scientific research are in principle no more moral or immoral than the parables of Jesus or Charles Darwin's arguments for evolution.

The crucial ethical issue is: What are those messages doing to the people who receive them? Do the messages delude people, lead them to vote against their own and the nation's (or the world's) interests, encourage them to discharge their stored-up hostilities on innocent victims? Or do the messages lead people to consider the basic campaign issues more clearly, to look at the candidate with less bias, to rely on object appraisal rather than on externalization in their treatment of other people? The research by Katz and his colleagues on reducing racial prejudice illustrates my point: Was Katz acting unethically because he tried to alter people's racial opinions on the basis of information he had collected about their personalities, or was he acting ethically because he was working to give them insight into their own faulty reasons for hating people of another color?

Social scientists who offer their services to political campaigns do have ethical choices to make. But the choices do not simply involve whether or not to help influence others; the influencing will continue, even if they give no help at all. The important choices are what kinds of candidates they wish to help, what political causes they wish to advance, and what personality bases for political action—rational or ir-

183

rational, self-aware or unconscious—they wish to encourage. These are all value-laden choices, and in the first two the values may have little to do with the researcher's scientific knowledge. But in the third, the basic scientific commitment to increasing the fund of objective knowledge seems to me directly relevant to the promotion of political awareness rather than political obfuscation.

The primary goal of research on personality in politics is to increase scientific knowledge of an essential aspect of the political process. But I think most researchers in the field would be rightly disappointed if their research only increased scientific knowledge and did not somehow change for the better the role of personality in politics.

bibliography

Abramson, Paul R. Political efficacy and political trust among black school-children: Two explanations. *Journal of Politics*, 1972, *34*, 1243–1269.

Adelson, Joseph. The political imagination of the young adolescent. *Daedalus*, 1971, *100*, 1013–1050.

Adorno, Theodor W.; Frenkel-Brunswik, Else; Levinson, Daniel J.; and Sanford, R. Nevitt. *The authoritarian personality*. New York: Harper & Row, 1950.

Allport, Gordon W. *The nature of prejudice*. Cambridge, Mass.: Addison-Wesley, 1954.

Almond, Gabriel A. *The appeals of communism*. Princeton: Princeton University Press, 1954.

Arterton, F. Christopher. The impact of Watergate on children's attitudes toward political authority. *Political Science Quarterly*, 1974, *89*, 269–288.

Ashmore, Richard D. The authoritarian personality in the key of C. *Contemporary Psychology*, 1975, *20*, 499–500.

Bales, R. F., and Slater, P. E. Role differentiation in small decision-making groups. In T. Parsons, R. F. Bales et al. (eds.), *Family, socialization and interaction process*. Glencoe, Ill.: Free Press, 1955.

Barber, James David. *The lawmakers*. New Haven: Yale University Press, 1965.

Barber, James David. Will there be a "Tragedy of Richard Nixon"? Unpublished paper, 1969.

Barber, James David. The interplay of presidential character and style: A paradigm and five illustrations. In F. I. Greenstein and M. Lerner (eds.), *A source book for the study of personality and politics*. Chicago: Markham, 1971.

Barber, James David. *The presidential character*. Englewood Cliffs, N.J.: Prentice-Hall, 1972.

Barber, James David. President Nixon and Richard Nixon: Character trap. *Psychology Today*, 1974, *8* (5), 113–118.

Barzun, Jacques. *Clio and the doctors*. Chicago: University of Chicago Press, 1974.

Beck, Paul Allen. A socialization theory of partisan realignment. In R. G. Niemi and associates (eds.), *The politics of future citizens*. San Francisco: Jossey-Bass, 1974.

Beck, Paul Allen, and Jennings, M. Kent. Parents as "middle-persons" in political socialization. *Journal of Politics*, 1975, *37*, 83–107.

Bell, Daniel (ed.). *The radical right*. New York: Doubleday, 1963.

Bettelheim, Bruno, and Janowitz, Morris. *Social change and prejudice*. Glencoe, Ill.: Free Press, 1964.

Block, Jeanne H. Rebellion re-examined: The role of identification and alienation. Paper presented at the Foundations' Fund for Research in Psychiatry conference on Adaptation to Change, Puerto Rico, June 1968.

Blumenfeld, Ralph. *Henry Kissinger: The private and public story*. New York: New American Library, 1974.

Boshier, Roger. To rotate or not to rotate: The question of the Conservatism Scale. *British Journal of Social and Clinical Psychology*, 1972, *11*, 313–323.

185

Boyd, Richard W. Electoral trends in postwar politics. In J. D. Barber (ed.), *Choosing the president*. Englewood Cliffs, N. J.: Prentice-Hall, 1974.

Bronfenbrenner, Urie. The mirror image in Soviet-American relations. *Journal of Social Issues*, 1961, *17* (3), 45–56.

Brown, Sam. The politics of peace. *Washington Monthly*, August 1970, 24–46.

Browning, Rufus P., and Jacob, Herbert. Power motivation and the political personality. *Public Opinion Quarterly*, 1964, *28*, 75–90.

Burdick, Eugene. *The 480*. New York: McGraw-Hill, 1964.

Burke, Peter J. Leadership role differentiation. In C. McClintock (ed.), *Experimental social psychology*. New York: Holt, Rinehart and Winston, 1972.

Campbell, Angus; Gurin, Gerald; and Miller, Warren E. *The voter decides*. Evanston, Ill.: Row, Peterson, 1954.

Chesen, Eli S. *President Nixon's psychiatric profile*. New York: Peter Weyden, 1973.

Chesler, Mark, and Schmuck, Richard. Social psychological characteristics of super-patriots. In R. A. Schoenberger (ed.), *The American right wing*. New York: Holt, Rinehart and Winston, 1969.

Christiansen, Bjorn. Attitudes towards foreign affairs as a function of personality. In H. Proshansky and B. Seidenberg (eds.), *Basic studies in social psychology*. New York: Holt, Rinehart and Winston, 1965.

Christie, Richard. Eysenck's treatment of the personality of communists. *Psychological Bulletin*, 1956, *53*, 411–430.

Christie, Richard, and Geis, Florence. Some consequences of taking Machiavelli seriously. In E. F. Borgatta and W. W. Lambert (eds.), *Handbook of personality theory and research*. Chicago: Rand McNally, 1968.

Christie, Richard, and Geis, Florence. *Studies in Machiavellianism*. New York: Academic Press, 1970.

Citrin, Jack. Comment: The political relevance of trust in government. *American Political Science Review*, 1974, *68*, 973–988.

Citrin, Jack; McClosky, Herbert; Shanks, J. Merrill; and Sniderman, Paul M. Personal and political sources of political alienation. *British Journal of Political Science*, 1975, *5*, 1–31.

Clark, Kenneth B. *Pathos of power*. New York: Harper & Row, 1974.

Clinch, Nancy Gager. *The Kennedy neurosis*. New York: Grosset and Dunlap, 1973.

Coffin, William Sloane. Interview. *Playboy*, August 1968.

Coles, Robert. Shrinking history, Part one. *New York Review of Books*, February 22, 1973, 15–30.

Coles, Robert. The politics of middle class children. *New York Review of Books*, March 6, 1975, 13–16.

Committee on Governmental Agencies of the Group for the Advancement of Psychiatry. *The VIP with psychiatric impairment*. New York: Charles Scribner's Sons, 1973.

Congressional Quarterly. Weekly Report. 1975, *33* (January 18), 120.

Costantini, Edmond, and Craik, Kenneth H. Women as politicians: The social background, personality, and political careers of female party leaders. *Journal of Social Issues*, 1972, *28* (2), 217–236.

Czudnowski, Moshe M. Political recruitment. In F. Greenstein and N. W. Polsby (eds.), *Handbook of political science*, vol. 2. Reading, Mass.: Addison-Wesley, 1975.

de Rivera, Joseph. *The psychological dimension of foreign policy*. Columbus, Ohio: Charles E. Merrill, 1968.

Donley, Richard E., and Winter, David G. Measuring the motives of public officials at a distance: An exploratory study of American Presidents. *Behavioral Science*, 1970, *15*, 227–236.

Donovan, J., and Shaevitz, M. Student political activists: A typology. *Youth and Society*, 1973, *4*, 379–411.

Dulles, Allen W. The real Woodrow Wilson. *Look*, 1966, *30* (25), 50.

Easton, David, and Dennis, Jack. *Children in the political system*. New York: McGraw-Hill, 1969.

Edelman, Murray. *Politics as symbolic action*. Chicago: Markham, 1971.

Elms, Alan C. Psychological factors in right-wing extremism. In R. A. Schoenberger (ed.), *The American right wing*. New York: Holt, Rinehart and Winston, 1969.

Elms, Alan C. *Social psychology and social relevance*. Boston: Little, Brown, 1972.

Elms, Alan C., and Milgram, Stanley. Personality characteristics associated with obedience and defiance toward authoritative command. *Journal of Experimental Research in Personality*, 1966, *2*, 282–289.

Erikson, Erik H. *Childhood and society*. New York: Norton, 1951.

Erikson, Erik H. *Young man Luther*. New York: Norton, 1958.

Erikson, Erik H. The strange case of Freud, Bullitt and Woodrow Wilson: I. A dubious collaboration. *New York Review of Books*, February 9, 1967, 3–8.

Erikson, Erik H. *Gandhi's truth*. New York: Norton, 1969.

Erikson, Erik H. *Dimensions of a new identity: The 1973 Jefferson lectures in the humanities*. New York: Norton, 1974.

Etheridge, Lloyd S. Personality and foreign policy. *Psychology Today*, 1975, *8* (10), 37–42.

Eysenck, Hans J. *The psychology of politics*. London: Routledge and Kegan Paul, 1954.

Eysenck, Hans J. Social attitudes and social class. *British Journal of Social and Clinical Psychology*, 1971, *10*, 201–212.

Fact magazine. The unconscious of a conservative. Entire issue of *Fact*, 1964, *1* (5), 1–64.

Fallaci, Oriana. An interview with Oriana Fallaci: Kissinger. *New Republic*, December 16, 1972, 17–22.

Feuer, Lewis S. *The conflict of generations*. New York: Basic Books, 1969.

Fiedler, Fred E. The contingency model: A theory of leadership effectiveness. In H. Proshansky and B. Siedenberg (ed.), *Basic studies in social psychology*. New York: Holt, Rinehart and Winston, 1965.

Finer, Herman. *Dulles over Suez: The theory and practice of his diplomacy*. Chicago: Quadrangle Books, 1964.

Finifter, Ada W. Dimensions of political alienation. *American Political Science Review*, 1970, *64*, 389–410.

Flanigan, William H. *Political behavior of the American electorate*, Second edition. Boston: Allyn and Bacon, 1972.

Flavell, John H. Concept development. In P. H. Mussen (ed.), *Carmichael's manual of child psychology*, Third edition, vol. 1. New York: Wiley, 1970.

Freud, Sigmund. Leonardo da Vinci and a memory of his childhood. In J. Strachey (ed.), *The standard edition of the complete psychological works of Sigmund Freud*, vol. 11. London: Hogarth Press, 1957 (original German publication, 1910).

Freud, Sigmund. *New introductory lectures in psycho-analysis*. In J. Strachey (ed.), *The standard edition of the complete psychological works of Sigmund*

187

Freud, vol. 22. London: Hogarth Press, 1964 (original German publication, 1933).

Freud, Sigmund, and Bullitt, William C. *Thomas Woodrow Wilson: A psychological study.* Boston: Houghton Mifflin, 1967.

Fulbright, J. William. *The arrogance of power.* New York: Random House, 1966.

Gamson, William A., and Modigliani, Andre. *Untangling the cold war.* Boston: Little, Brown, 1971.

Garcia, F. Chris. *Political socialization of Chicano children.* New York: Praeger, 1973.

George, Alexander L. Assessing presidential character. *World Politics*, 1974, *26*, 234–282.

George, Alexander L., and George, Juliette L. *Woodrow Wilson and Colonel House.* New York: John Day, 1956.

George, Alexander L., and George, Juliette L. Preface to Dover Edition, *Woodrow Wilson and Colonel House.* New York: Dover, 1964.

George, Alexander L., and George, Juliette L. Psycho-McCarthyism. *Psychology Today*, 1973, 7 (1), 94–98.

Gibb, Cecil A. Leadership. In G. Lindzey and E. Aronson (eds.), *The handbook of social psychology*, Second edition, vol. 4. Reading, Mass.: Addison-Wesley, 1969.

Glad, Betty. *Charles Evans Hughes and the illusions of innocence.* Urbana, Ill.: University of Illinois Press, 1966.

Glad, Betty. Contributions of psychobiography. In J. N. Knutson (ed.), *Handbook of political psychology.* San Francisco: Jossey-Bass, 1973.

Greenstein, Fred I. *Children and politics*, Revised edition. New Haven: Yale University Press, 1965.

Greenstein, Fred I. *Personality and politics: Problems of evidence, inference and conceptualization.* Chicago: Markham, 1969.

Greenstein, Fred I. The study of personality and politics: Overall considerations. In F. I. Greenstein and M. Lerner (eds.), *A source book for the study of personality and politics.* Chicago: Markham, 1971.

Greenstein, Fred I. Political psychology: A pluralistic universe. In J. N. Knutson (ed.), *Handbook of political psychology.* San Francisco: Jossey-Bass, 1973.

Greenstein, Fred I. What the President means to Americans: Presidential "choice" between elections. In J. D. Barber (ed.), *Choosing the president.* Englewood Cliffs, N.J.: Prentice-Hall, 1974.

Greenstein, Fred I. Personality and politics. In F. I. Greenstein and N. W. Polsby, (eds.), *Handbook of political science*, vol. 2. Reading, Mass.: Addison-Wesley, 1975.

Greenstein, Fred I. The benevolent leader revisited: Children's images of political leaders in three democracies. *American Political Science Review*, in press.

Guhin, Michael A. *John Foster Dulles: A statesman and his times.* New York: Columbia University Press, 1972.

Gusfield, Joseph R. *Symbolic crusade.* Urbana, Ill.: University of Illinois Press, 1963.

Guterman, Stanley S. *The Machiavellians.* Lincoln, Nebr.: University of Nebraska Press, 1970.

Haan, Norma; Smith, M. Brewster; and Block, Jeanne. The moral reasoning of young adults: Political-social behavior, family background and personality correlates. *Journal of Personality and Social Psychology*, 1968, *10*, 183–201.

Halberstam, David. *The best and the brightest.* New York: Random House, 1972.

Hess, Robert D., and Easton, David. The child's changing image of the President. *Public Opinion Quarterly*, 1960, *14*, 632–642.

Hess, Robert D., and Torney, Judith V. *The development of political attitudes in children.* Chicago: Aldine, 1967.

Higgins, Jerry, and Kuhlman, David M. Authoritarianism and candidate preference: II. *Psychological Reports*, 1967, *20*, 572.

Hikel, Gerald Kent. *Beyond the polls: Political ideology and its correlates.* Lexington, Mass.: D. C. Heath, 1973.

Hobson, Laura Z. As I listened to Archie say "Hebe" . . . *New York Times*, September 12, 1971, D1.

Hofstadter, Richard. *The paranoid style in American politics.* New York: Knopf, 1965.

Hofstadter, Richard. A disservice to history. *New York Review of Books, 8,* February 9, 1967, 6–8.

Hollander, E. P., and Julian, J. P. Studies in leader legitimacy, influence and innovations. In L. Berkowitz (ed.), *Advances in experimental social psychology,* vol. 5. New York: Academic Press, 1970.

Holsti, Ole R. Cognitive dynamics and images of the enemy. *Journal of International Affairs*, 1967, *21*, 16–39.

Hoopes, Townsend. *The devil and John Foster Dulles.* Boston: Little, Brown, 1973.

Horn, John L., and Knott, Paul D. Activist youth of the 1960's: Summary and prognosis. *Science*, 1971, *171*, 977–985.

Hutschnecker, Arnold A. The mental health of our leaders. *Look,* 1969, *33* (14), 51–54.

Hyman, Herbert H., and Sheatsley, Paul B. The authoritarian personality: A methodological critique. In R. Christie and M. Jahoda (eds.), *Studies in the scope and method of "The authoritarian personality."* Glencoe, Ill.: Free Press, 1954.

Janis, Irving L. Motivational factors in the resolution of decisional conflicts. In M. R. Jones (ed.), *Nebraska symposium on motivation, 1959.* Lincoln, Nebr.: University of Nebraska Press, 1959.

Janis, Irving L. *Victims of groupthink.* Boston: Houghton Mifflin, 1972.

Jaros, Dean; Hirsch, Herbert; and Fleron, Frederic J., Jr. The malevolent leader: Political socialization in an American subculture. *American Political Science Review*, 1968, *62*, 64–75.

Jennings, M. Kent, and Niemi, Richard G. *The political character of adolescence.* Princeton: Princeton University Press, 1974.

Kael, Pauline. The current cinema: Poetry and politics. *New Yorker,* January 20, 1973, 80–86.

Kalb, Marvin, and Kalb, Bernard. *Kissinger.* Boston: Little, Brown, 1974.

Katz, Daniel. The functional approach to the study of attitudes. *Public Opinion Quarterly*, 1960, *24*, 163–204.

Katz, Daniel. Patterns of leadership. In J. N. Knutson (ed.), *Handbook of political psychology.* San Francisco: Jossey-Bass, 1973.

Katz, Daniel; McClintock, Charles; and Sarnoff, Irving. The measurement of ego defense as related to attitude change. *Journal of Personality*, 1957, *25*, 465–474.

Katz, Daniel; Sarnoff, Irving; and McClintock, Charles. Ego-defense and attitude change. *Human Relations*, 1956, *9*, 27–46.

Kelman, Herbert. Manipulation of human behavior: An ethical dilemma for the social scientist. *Journal of Social Issues*, 1965, *21* (2), 31–46.

189

Kelman, Herbert. *A time to speak: On human values and social research.* San Francisco: Jossey-Bass, 1968.
Keniston, Kenneth. *The uncommitted.* New York: Harcourt Brace Jovanovich, 1965.
Keniston, Kenneth. *Young radicals.* New York: Harcourt Brace Jovanovich, 1968.
Keniston, Kenneth. Notes on young radicals. *Change,* 1969, *1* (6), 25–33.
Keniston, Kenneth, *Radicals and militants.* Lexington, Mass.: D. C. Heath, 1973.
Kerpelman, Larry C. *Activists and nonactivists: A psychological study of American college students.* New York: Behavioral Publications, 1972.
Kirkpatrick, Jeane J. *Political woman.* New York: Basic Books, 1974.
Kirscht, John P., and Dillehay, Ronald C. *Dimensions of authoritarianism: A review of research and theory.* Lexington, Ky.: University of Kentucky Press, 1967.
Kish, G. B., and Donnenwerth, G. V. Sex differences in the correlates of stimulus-seeking. *Journal of Consulting and Clinical Psychology,* 1972, *38,* 42–49.
Kissinger, Henry A. The white revolutionary: Reflections on Bismarck. *Daedalus,* 1968, 97, 888–924.
Kline, Paul. *Fact and fantasy in Freudian theory.* London: Methuen, 1972.
Knutson, Jeanne N. Prepolitical ideologies: The basis of political learning. In R. G. Niemi and associates (eds.), *The politics of future citizens.* San Francisco: Jossey-Bass, 1974a.
Knutson, Jeanne N. *Psychological variables in political recruitment: An analysis of party activists.* Berkeley, Calif.: The Wright Institute, 1974b.
Kohlberg, Lawrence. Moral and religious education and the public schools: A developmental view. In T. Siger (ed.), *Religion and public education.* Boston: Houghton Mifflin, 1967.
Kohlberg, Lawrence. Stage and sequence: The cognitive-developmental approach to socialization. In D. A. Goslin (ed.), *Handbook of socialization theory and research.* Chicago: Rand McNally, 1969.
Kornitzer, Bela. *The real Nixon: An intimate biography.* Chicago: Rand McNally, 1960.
Kraft, Joseph. In search of Kissinger. *Harper's,* January 1971.
Kraut, Robert E., and Lewis, Steven H. Alternate models of family influence on student political ideology. *Journal of Personality and Social Psychology,* 1975, *31,* 791–800.

Lamare, James W. Language environment and political socialization of Mexican-American children. In R. G. Niemi and associates (eds.), *The politics of future citizens.* San Francisco: Jossey-Bass, 1974.
Lamb, Karl A. *As Orange goes.* New York: Norton, 1974.
Lane, Robert E. *Political ideology.* Glencoe, Ill.: Free Press, 1962.
Lane, Robert E. *Political thinking and consciousness.* Chicago: Markham, 1969.
Langton, Kenneth P., and Jennings, M. Kent. Political socialization and the high school civics curriculum in the United States. *American Political Science Review,* 1968, *62,* 852–867.
Lasswell, Harold D. *Psychopathology and politics.* Chicago: University of Chicago Press, 1930.
Lasswell, Harold D. *Power and personality.* New York: Norton, 1948.
Lasswell, Harold D. *The political writings of Harold D. Lasswell.* Glencoe, Ill.: Free Press, 1951.
Lasswell, Harold D. The selective effect of personality on political participation. In R. Christie and M. Jahoda (eds.), *Studies in the scope and method of "The authoritarian personality."* Glencoe, Ill.: Free Press, 1954.
Levine, Mark H., and Denisoff, R. Serge. Draft susceptibility and Vietnam war attitudes: A research note. *Youth and Society,* 1972, *4,* 169–176.

Liebert, Robert. *Radical and militant youth.* New York: Praeger, 1971.
Liebschutz, Sarah F., and Niemi, Richard G. Political attitudes among black children. In R. G. Niemi and associates (eds.), *The politics of future citizens.* San Francisco: Jossey-Bass, 1974.
Lifton, Robert Jay. *Revolutionary immortality.* New York: Vintage Books, 1968.
Lifton, Robert Jay. *History and human survival.* New York: Random House, 1970.
Link, Arthur. *Wilson: The road to the White House.* Princeton: Princeton University Press, 1947.
Lipset, Seymour M. *Rebellion in the university.* Boston: Little, Brown, 1972.
Lipset, Seymour M., and Raab, Earl. *The politics of unreason.* New York: Harper & Row, 1970.
Lupfer, Michael, and Kenny, Charles. "Watergate is just a bunch of honky jive": The impact of Watergate on black and white youths' view of the Presidency. *Proceedings of the Division of Personality and Social Psychology,* 1974, 163–165.

McClintock, Charles. Personality syndromes and attitude change. *Journal of Personality,* 1958, *26,* 479–493.
McClosky, Herbert. Conservatism and personality. *American Political Science Review,* 1958, *52,* 27–45.
McClosky, Herbert, and Scharr, John H. Psychological dimensions of anomy. *American Sociological Review,* 1965, *30,* 14–40.
McConaughy, J. B. Certain personality factors of state legislators in South Carolina. *American Political Science Review,* 1950, *44,* 897–903.
McEvoy, James III. *Radicals or conservatives?* Chicago: Rand McNally, 1971.
McEvoy, James III. Review of *The psychology of conservatism. Contemporary Sociology,* in press.
McGinniss, Joe. *The selling of the President 1968.* New York: Trident Press, 1969.
McGrory, Mary. The corruption of high office. *Sacramento Bee,* November 26, 1973.
Marcus, George E. Psychopathology and political recruitment. *Journal of Politics,* 1969, *31,* 913–931.
Matthews, Donald R. *U.S. Senators and their world.* Chapel Hill, N.C.: University of North Carolina Press, 1960.
Mazlish, Bruce. *In search of Nixon.* Baltimore: Penguin Books, 1973.
Mendelsohn, Harold. Some reasons why information campaigns can succeed. *Public Opinion Quarterly,* 1973, *37,* 50–61.
Milbrath, Lester W. *Political participation.* Chicago: Rand McNally, 1965.
Miller, Arthur H. Political issues and trust in government: 1964–1970. *American Political Science Review,* 1974a, *68,* 951–972.
Miller, Arthur H. Rejoinder to "Comment" by Jack Citrin: Political discontent or ritualism? *American Political Science Review,* 1974b, *68,* 989–1001.
Moore, Henry T. Innate factors in radicalism and conservatism. *Journal of Abnormal and Social Psychology,* 1925–26, *20,* 234–244.
Mosher, Donald L., and Mosher, Joan B. Relationships between authoritarian attitudes in delinquent girls and the authoritarian attitudes and authoritarian rearing practices of their mothers. *Psychological Reports,* 1965, *16,* 23–30.

Neustadt, Richard E. *Presidential power: The politics of leadership.* New York: Wiley, 1960.
Newcomb, Theodore M. Attitude development as a function of reference groups: The Bennington study. In G. E. Swanson; T. M. Newcomb; and E. L. Hartley (eds.), *Readings in social psychology,* Revised edition. New York: Holt, Rinehart and Winston, 1952.
New York Times. T. V. Mailbag. *New York Times,* October 3, 1971, D17.

Nie, Norman H., and Verba, Sidney. Political participation. In F. I. Greenstein and N. W. Polsby (eds.), *Handbook of political science*, vol. 4. Reading, Mass.: Addison-Wesley, 1975.

Niemi, Richard G. *How family members perceive each other*. New Haven: Yale University Press, 1974.

Nimmo, Dan. *The political persuaders*. Englewood Cliffs, N.J.: Prentice-Hall, 1970.

Nixon, Richard M. *Six crises*. New York: Pyramid, 1968.

Nixon, Richard M. *White House transcripts*. New York: Bantam Books, 1973.

Nolan, Martin F. The re-selling of the president. *Harper's*, November 1972, 79–81.

O'Connor, Robert E. Political activism and moral reasoning: Political and apolitical students in Great Britain and France. *British Journal of Political Science*, 1974, 4, 53–78.

O'Kelly, Victoria, and Solar, Diana. Machiavellianism in parents and children. *Psychological Reports*, 1971, 29, 265–266.

Perry, James M. *The new politics*. New York: Clarkson N. Potter, 1968.

Pettigrew, Thomas F. Social psychology and desegregation research. *American Psychologist*, 1961, 16, 105–112.

Pomper, Gerald M. *Voters' choice*. New York: Dodd, Mead, 1975.

Pool, Ithiel de Sola; Abelson, Robert P.; and Popkin, Samuel L. *Candidates, issues and strategies*. Cambridge, Mass.: M.I.T. Press, 1965.

Prewitt, Kenneth. Political efficacy. In D. L. Sills (ed.), *International encyclopedia of the social sciences*, vol. 12. New York: Macmillan, 1968.

Pruitt, Dean G. Definition of the situation as a determinant of international action. In H. C. Kelman (ed.), *International behavior*. New York: Holt, Rinehart and Winston, 1965.

Purdom, Tom. *The barons of behavior*. New York: Ace Books, 1972.

Raven, Bertram H. The Nixon group. *Journal of Social Issues*, 1974, 30 (4), 297–320.

Ray, J. J. Are conservatism scales irreversible? *British Journal of Social and Clinical Psychology*, 1972, 11, 346–352.

Renshon, Stanley Allen. *Psychological needs and political behavior*. New York: Free Press, 1974.

Renshon, Stanley Allen. Psychological analysis and Presidential personality: The case of Richard Nixon. *History of Childhood Quarterly*, 1975, 2, 415–450.

Rogow, A. A. *James Forrestal: A study of personality, politics, and policy*. New York: Macmillan, 1963.

Rogow, A. A. *The psychiatrists*. New York: Putnam, 1970.

Rohter, Ira S. Some personal needs met by becoming a radical rightist. Paper presented at American Psychological Association Convention, Chicago, 1965.

Rokeach, Milton. *The open and closed mind*. New York: Basic Books, 1960.

Rutherford, Brent. Psychopathology, decision-making and political involvement. *Journal of Conflict Resolution*, 1966, 10, 387–407.

Sampson, Edward E. (ed.). *Stirrings out of apathy: Student activism and the decade of protest*. Entire issue of *Journal of Social Issues*, 1967, 23 (3).

Sanford, Nevitt. Authoritarian personality in contemporary perspective. In J. N. Knutson (ed.), *Handbook of political psychology*. San Francisco: Jossey-Bass, 1973.

Sarnoff, Irving; Katz, Daniel; and McClintock, Charles. Attitude-change procedures and motivating patterns. In D. Katz; A. M. Lee; S. Eldersveld; and D.

Cartwright (eds.), *Public opinion and propaganda.* New York: Holt, Rinehart and Winston, 1954.

Schlesinger, Arthur M., Jr. *A thousand days.* Boston: Houghton Mifflin, 1965.

Schlesinger, Arthur M., Jr. Can psychiatry save the Republic? *Saturday Review/World,* 1974, *1* (26), 10–16.

Schwartz, David C. *Political alienation and political behavior.* Chicago: Aldine, 1973.

Sears, David O. Political socialization. In F. I. Greenstein and N. W. Polsby (eds.), *Handbook of political science,* vol. 2. Reading, Mass.: Addison-Wesley, 1975.

Sears, David O., and McConahay, John B. *The politics of violence.* Boston: Houghton Mifflin, 1973.

Sjoberg, Gideon (ed.). *Ethics, politics and social research.* Cambridge, Mass.: Schenkman, 1967.

Skinner, B. F. *Walden Two.* New York: Macmillan, 1948.

Smith, M. Brewster. Political attitudes. In J. N. Knutson (ed.), *Handbook of political psychology.* San Francisco: Jossey-Bass, 1973.

Smith, M. Brewster; Bruner, Jerome; and White, Robert W. *Opinions and personality.* New York: Wiley, 1956.

Smith, M. Brewster; Haan, Norma; and Block, Jeanne. Social-psychological aspects of student activism. *Youth and Society,* 1970, *1,* 261–288.

Sniderman, Paul. *Personality and democratic politics.* Berkeley, Calif.: University of California Press, 1975.

Sorensen, Theodore. *Kennedy.* New York: Harper & Row, 1965.

Srole, Leo J. Social integration and certain corollaries: An exploratory study. *American Sociological Review,* 1956, *21,* 709–716.

Stogdill, Ralph M. *Handbook of leadership.* Glencoe, Ill.: Free Press, 1974.

Stotland, Ezra; Katz, Daniel; and Patchen, Martin. The reduction of prejudice through the arousal of self-insight. *Journal of Personality,* 1959, *27,* 507–531.

Strickland, Donald A. The non-vivus psychoanalysis of political figures: A review. *Journal of Conflict Resolution,* 1967, *11,* 375–381.

Thomson, J. G., Jr. How could Vietnam happen? An autopsy. *Atlantic Monthly,* April 1968.

Tolley, Howard, Jr. *Children and war.* New York: Teachers College Press, 1973.

Tomkins, Silvan S. Left and right: A basic dimension of ideology and personality. In R. W. White (ed.), *The study of lives.* New York: Atherton, 1963.

Triandis, Harry C. *Attitude and attitude change.* New York: Wiley, 1971.

Tuchman, Barbara W. Can history use Freud? *Atlantic Monthly, 219,* February 1967, 39.

Verba, Sidney. *Small groups and political behavior.* Princeton: Princeton University Press, 1961.

Verba, Sidney, and Nie, Norman H. *Participation in America.* New York: Harper & Row, 1972.

Vidmar, Neil, and Rokeach, Milton. Archie Bunker's bigotry: A study in selective perception and exposure. *Journal of Communication,* 1974, *24,* 36–47.

Ward, Dana. Kissinger: A psychohistory. *History of Childhood Quarterly,* 1975, *2,* 287–348.

Weber, Max. Politics as a vocation. In H. H. Gerth and C. Wright Mills (eds. and trans.), *From Max Weber.* New York: Oxford University Press, 1946 (original German publication, 1918).

White, Ralph K. *Nobody wanted war.* New York: Anchor Books, 1970.

Wilson, Glenn D. (ed.). *The psychology of conservatism.* New York: Academic Press, 1973.

Wolfinger, Raymond E.; Wolfinger, B. K.; Prewitt, K.; and Rosenhack, S. America's radical right: Politics and ideology. In D. E. Apter (ed.), *Ideology and discontent.* Glencoe, Ill.: Free Press, 1964.

Wood, James L. *The sources of American student activism.* Lexington, Mass.: D. C. Heath, 1974.

index

195

197

PICTURE CREDITS

200

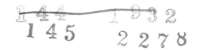

A
B   6
C   7
D   8
E   9
F   0
G   1
H   2
I   3
J   4